MW00533332

The Sherman Tour Journals of Colonel Richard Irving Dodge

William T. Sherman

Richard Irving Dodge

The Sherman Tour Journals of Colonel Richard Irving Dodge

Edited by Wayne R. Kime

University of Oklahoma Press : Norman

Other Works Written or Edited by Wayne R. Kime

Pierre M. Irving and Washington Irving: A Collaboration in Life and Letters (Waterloo, Canada, 1978)

(ed.) *Raising the Wind: The Legend of Lapland and Finland Wizards in Literature* (Newark, Del., 1981)

(ed.) *Miscellaneous Writings, 1803–1859,* by Washington Irving (Boston, 1981)

(ed. with Andrew B. Myers) *Journals and Notebooks, Volume IV, 1826–1829,* by Washington Irving (Boston, 1984)

Donald G. Mitchell (Boston, 1985)

(ed.) *The Plains of North America and Their Inhabitants: A Critical Edition,* by Richard Irving Dodge (Newark, Del., and London, 1989)

(ed.) *The Black Hills Journals of Colonel Richard Irving Dodge* (Norman, 1996)

(ed.) *The Powder River Expedition Journals of Colonel Richard Irving Dodge* (Norman, 1997)

(ed.) *The Indian Territory Journals of Colonel Richard Irving Dodge* (Norman, 2000)

Library of Congress Cataloging-in-Publication Data

Dodge, Richard Irving, 1827–1895.
The Sherman tour journals of Colonel Richard Irving Dodge / edited by Wayne R. Kime.
p. cm.
Includes bibliographical references and index.
ISBN 0-8061-3425-9 (alk. paper)
1. West (U.S.)—Description and travel. 2. Dodge, Richard Irving, 1827–1895—Diaries. 3. Dodge, Richard Irving, 1827–1895—Journeys—West (U.S.) 4. Sherman, William T. (William Tecumseh), 1820–1891—Journeys—West (U.S.) 5. United States. Army—Biography. 6. United States. Army—Military life—History—19th century. 7. Fortification—West (U.S.)—Evaluation—History—19th century. 8. Frontier and pioneer life—West (U.S.) 9. Indians of North America—West (U.S.)—History—19th century. I. Kime, Wayne R. II. Title.

E595 .D635 2002
917.804'2—dc21

2002020550

The paper in this book meets the guidelines for permanence and durability of the Committee on Production Guidelines for Book Longevity of the Council on Library Resources, Inc. ∞

Copyright © 2002 by the University of Oklahoma Press, Norman, Publishing Division of the University. All rights reserved. Manufactured in the U.S.A.

1 2 3 4 5 6 7 8 9 10

In memory of my great-grandparents,
Thorpe and Phillis Hall Waddingham
immigrants from England who joined the procession westward

Contents

Illustrations

Maps

Preface

THE TWO JOURNALS PUBLISHED IN THIS VOLUME, WITH entries dated between June 23 and September 28, 1883, record Colonel Richard Irving Dodge's activities during a period he considered the high point of his career thus far as an officer of the United States Army: his participation in the valedictory inspection tour of military forts, cities, and settlements in the western states and territories by William T. Sherman, the General of the Army. Of the twenty journals compiled by Dodge and now housed in the Everett D. Graff Collection of Western Americana at the Newberry Library, Chicago, Illinois, these are chronologically the nineteenth and twentieth. The first six, written between May and October 1875, comprise a record of Dodge's experiences as commander of an eight-company army escort to a geological surveying expedition in the Black Hills of Dakota Territory. My edition of these journals was issued by the University of Oklahoma Press in 1996 as *The Black Hills Journals of Colonel Richard Irving Dodge.* The next four, written between October 1876 and January 1877, detail Dodge's activities as commander of the infantry and artillery battalions in the Powder River Expedition, under Brigadier General George Crook, against the Sioux and Northern Cheyenne Indians. Also edited by me, these were published in 1997 as *The Powder River Expedition Journals of Colonel Richard Irving Dodge*. The next eight, written at intervals between September 1878 and December 1880, record a period of varied service chiefly in Indian Territory, the expanse of land that later became the state of Oklahoma. My edition of these documents, *The Indian Territory Journals of Colonel Richard Irving Dodge*, appeared in 2000. The present volume thus completes publication by the University of Oklahoma Press of all Dodge's journals known to exist.

Taken as a group, these personal records encompass a period of eight years, but they do not comprise a continuous chronological account, nor do they portray a common set of circumstances. The unifying feature is their authorship by Dodge, an articulate career officer whose rank gave him some access to top-level commanders like Generals Crook, John Pope, John M. Schofield, Alfred H. Terry, Philip H. Sheridan, and Sherman and whose duty with infantry regiments kept him in regular contact with junior officers, enlisted men, civilians, and the Plains Indians whose cultures had interested him for many years. A soldier-author, Dodge published three books during this period: *The Black Hills* (1876), *The Plains of North America and Their Inhabitants* (1877), and *Our Wild Indians* (1882). His private journals also merit publication, for they deal with matters of permanent historical interest and do so lucidly, suggestively, sometimes memorably.

The 1883 journals are the centerpiece of Dodge's years of contact with General Sherman, who was then rounding out his fourteen-year leadership of the nation's peacetime army. The opportunity to join the summer tour was a direct outgrowth of Dodge's service during 1881 and 1882 as an aide-de-camp at army headquarters in Washington, D.C. During that period of almost daily contact, he and Sherman had formed a relationship both professional and, though qualified by their difference in rank, also personal. Their broad agreement on issues of federal policy regarding the Native American tribes led Sherman to give his official sanction to *Our Wild Indians* through an introductory letter in which he commended the work to the American reading public.

The sketch presented here of Dodge's tour of duty as a member of the general's personal staff thus affords some insight into the personalities of the two men, the interests and concerns that actuated them both, and the tone and character of activity at army headquarters. A related group of impressions derives from review of the interim period between the end of Dodge's assignment as aide and the beginning of Sherman's summer tour. Dodge's experiences as commander of an army regiment in the field and Sherman's as he attempted to set the army on a steady course for the years after his retirement both shed light on the procedures, internal problems, and initiatives of the army of that period and, more generally, on the American society it served.

Dodge's day-to-day record of the 1883 tour adds significantly to the information contained in previously published accounts of that long journey. Because his motives for compiling the journals were private and personal rather than official, he characterized his companions and their interactions with freedom, capturing in unique fashion the day-to-day flavor of the experience. At the same time, he recorded his impressions of the scenes he encountered in the course of the expedition. Most of these places he had never visited, and those he knew from past travels appeared transformed from what he remembered of them from only a few years before.

For Dodge and his companions the tour constituted a panoramic series of views that together exemplified the nation's consolidation of its development westward since the close of the Civil War. Significantly, much of the journey was accomplished by railroad travel, a convenience made possible by the rapidly approaching completion of two new transcontinental railroads. Like others who recorded their experiences on this tour, Dodge portrayed in his journals a nation confident in its prosperity and energetically placing the imprint of its ownership on the western wilderness. Sherman's chief purpose on the tour was to identify a system of forts, especially along the northwestern frontier, that would guarantee to the United States a permanent network of protection sufficient to meet any military emergency, even though virtually no prospect of such a demand for defense then existed.

Following the annotated texts of Dodge's journals, this volume concludes with a survey of the continuing relationship between Dodge and Sherman in the years after the inspection tour. In a series of letters, the two veteran officers reviewed events in recent decades and sought to trace out some of the patterns of historical development that had informed them. Thereafter they remained aware of each other's activities through various means, most prominently through articles in the weekly *Army and Navy Journal,* a semi-official newspaper that did much to maintain the morale of the small, underfunded, widely dispersed army of that period. Despite the geographical separation and differences in age and personal circumstances, Sherman and Dodge remained army comrades and friends, manifesting the esprit de corps Sherman had sought to foster during his last years of army service.

The final occasion in which the two men appeared together in public was at once symbolic of their personal relationship, the status of the peacetime army, and the mood of the United States in 1889. Astride his mount near the head of a great parade in New York City, Dodge led a brigade of regular army troops past the reviewing stand where Sherman sat among a group of dignitaries behind the recently elected president, Benjamin Harrison. In tribute to the commander in chief, and it may be imagined also out of respect for his former commander, at the prescribed point Dodge directed his gaze to where the president stood and, on behalf of the men marching behind him, lifted his sabre in formal salute.

Except in its coverage of the relationship between Dodge and Sherman, this volume contains little new information about the latter figure, about whom a large body of published information has already accumulated, much of it of high quality. However, since the preponderance of attention to Sherman has always inclined toward his Civil War career rather than the nineteen years of eventful military activity that followed it, an account of his relationship with a senior subaltern like Dodge during the later period may serve a useful supplementary function. Similarly, the description of army affairs given here is selective, emphasizing events and issues that touched on the Dodge-Sherman relationship and the circumstances immediately surrounding it. However, through this coverage the commentary sets forth particular instances of concerns, conflicts, and programs that have been identified in earlier studies as characterizing Sherman's last years in command of the army. Finally, like Dodge's journal account of the 1883 inspection tour, this volume provides glimpses of the United States in the 1880s, an exuberant nation assured of its place in the world, given to colorful demonstrations of patriotic display, and profoundly at peace.

For courtesies and assistance extended to me as I prepared this work, I am indebted to many persons, not all of whom are mentioned here. Financial support came from Fairmont State College, the Fairmont State College Foundation, the West Virginia Humanities Council, the National Endowment for the Humanities, and the Newberry Library, to all of which I express sincere thanks. For their support of my applications for research aid, I am grateful to Professors Ralph M. Aderman and Richard D. Rust and to Robert G. Masters, former library director at Fairmont State College. Wallace and Sue Jungers, Kathleen Moyne, Eleanore Hofstetter, Jude Olsen, Gene and Kay Rosselot, and Peggy Wolivar were gracious hosts during my expeditions in search of information. Once again, Robert L. Heffner, Jr., provided expert assistance with the maps, and John Piscitelli with photographs. These two colleagues have assisted me throughout the publication of the Dodge journals, and I thank them for work well done. Alicia Kime, my wife, recreated a newspaper illustration using a computer program, improving on the original without altering its essential character. I owe thanks to two anonymous readers of this book when it was still in manuscript for their careful study and their suggestions for improving it. Among the supportive—and stoic—listeners during certain one-sided conversations while the work was taking shape, I mention my son Evan, my wife Alicia, my friends Ron and Susan Hamilton and their son Nicholas, and especially my friend and running companion David Bohnke.

Institutions whose facilities and personnel have assisted me in my research include Newberry Library, Chicago; National Archives, Washington, D.C.; U.S. Army Military History Institute, Carlisle Barracks, Pennsylvania; the U.S. Military Academy, West Point, New York; the Manuscript Division, Library of Congress, Washington, D.C.; Oklahoma Historical Society, Oklahoma City; Western History Collection, University of Oklahoma, Norman; Kansas Historical Society, Topeka; Beinecke Rare Book and Manuscript Library, Yale University, New Haven, Connecticut; New York Public Library, New York City; New-York Historical Society, New York City; Columbia University Library,

New York City; Rutgers University Library, New Brunswick, New Jersey; University of Pennsylvania Library, Philadelphia; University of Delaware Library, Newark; Towson State University Library, Baltimore, Maryland; Johns Hopkins University Library, Baltimore, Maryland; History Library, Museum of New Mexico, Santa Fe; Northwestern University Library, Evanston, Illinois; West Virginia University Library, Morgantown; Vermont Historical Society, Montpelier; and Fairmont State College Library, Fairmont, West Virginia. I am especially grateful to the staff of the Fairmont State College Library for their friendly and efficient services. Once again, Sharon Mazure, in charge of interlibrary loans, obtained for me source material that proved of considerable value.

For permission to quote from unpublished or copyrighted material and to reproduce photographs I thank the following: Newberry Library, Chicago; U.S. Army Military History Institute, Carlisle, Pennsylvania; U.S. Military Academy Library, West Point, New York; the Manuscript Division, Library of Congress; the Beinecke Rare Book and Manuscript Library, Yale University.

Finally, I extend grateful thanks to Patricia Heinicke, Jr., the able copy editor of this volume, to Alice Stanton, who supervised the editing and production of the work, and, for their cooperation throughout the publication of Dodge's journals, to the able staff of the University of Oklahoma Press.

WAYNE R. KIME

Fairmont, West Virginia

Note on Editorial Policy

THE GENERAL AIM IN PRESENTING THE TEXTS OF Dodge's journals written during the summer of 1883 is to coordinate the realization of two not always compatible goals: fidelity to what the author wrote and utility for the reader. Dodge compiled his journals under a variety of circumstances: indoors and outdoors, at leisure and in haste, in comfortable circumstances and in awkward or trying ones. Not surprisingly, the character of his entries varies widely, from considered, relatively finished discourses to disjointed "telegraphic" notes. Yet despite the variations in their style, the manuscript texts all exhibit Dodge's tendency as a journal writer to take liberties with the standard practices of written expression. For example, he freely abbreviated words and names, and at some points he almost dispensed with punctuation. At times he seems to have regarded the shift of his pencil from one line to the next as a sufficient substitute for whatever terminal punctuation one might ordinarily expect.

Presenting Dodge's manuscript journals in printed form clearly necessitates certain adjustments in order to render them accessible to a modern reader. The procedures I have followed in editing these texts are identical to those detailed in editorial notes to three volumes previously issued by the University of Oklahoma Press, *The Black Hills Journals of Colonel Richard Irving Dodge* (1996), *The Powder River Expedition Journals of Colonel Richard Irving Dodge* (1997), and *The Indian Territory Journals of Colonel Richard Irving Dodge*

(2000). For fuller discussion of the matters summarized here, the interested reader is referred to either of the first two volumes.

Except to correct spelling errors that are so serious that they might baffle or so odd that they might distract, I have allowed Dodge's variant spellings and even misspellings to stand. Where confusion seems possible, it is obviated by an editorial interpolation within square brackets or else by a footnote. For proper names that Dodge spells in more than one way, the correct spelling is indicated in an identifying note at the point where the name is first mentioned.

Abbreviations employed by Dodge appear here, with few exceptions, just as he wrote them. Abbreviations that may be problematical are filled out within square brackets or explained in notes at the points where they appear. Superscript letters written in connection with abbreviations are brought down to the line except in datelines, for which a standard format is used. Ampersands and "&c" (for *et cetera*) are allowed to stand.

Dodge's habits of capitalization, generally conventional though far from consistent, are respected. He did adopt quite often the traditional practice of capitalizing for emphasis, but his intention in doing so is clear and presents no difficulty. No effort is made to regularize his capitalization, except that the first letters in proper names and in daily entries are always capitalized.

The inconsistent punctuation and formatting of Dodge's journal entries requires some editorial regularization, for to present it unchanged would result in frequent ambiguity and pervasive distraction. Thus, for example, the sometimes irregular spacing between his paragraphs and entries is made uniform unless it seems to carry a special significance, such as to mark a place to insert information he expected to obtain in the future, or to signify text written at a new sitting.

A few rules of thumb are adopted to govern the representation of Dodge's terminal punctuation. If a sentence at the end of a paragraph or a day's entry concludes without a punctuation mark, none is supplied. If, within paragraphs, a sentence concludes without punctuation and the one that follows it begins with a capital letter, no punctuation is supplied. If, as occasionally occurs, a sentence concludes with a comma, semicolon, or colon, the error is corrected and the change noted. Question marks and exclamation marks are supplied as called for when Dodge concluded sentences without punctuation, but otherwise his terminal pointing is left essentially as he wrote it.

Dodge liked to record colorful and characteristic dialogue, but in doing so he often failed to complete pairs of quotation marks or to insert them at all. Thus, when necessary, omitted quotation marks are supplied within brackets. Parentheses and dashes, whether single or in pairs, are treated similarly.

Within sentences, distinguishing between what Dodge may have regarded as commas, hyphens, or something else can be quite difficult. Fortunately, once one recognizes the effective interchangeability within sentences of Dodge's commas and his dashes, or as I call them, "extended dots," problems of interpreting his meaning become rare. In transcribing the journals, I have recorded as dashes only those marks that clearly justify the identification; they appear in the edited text with a space between them and what precedes them. In more doubtful situations I have interpreted the marks as commas.

Cancellations are relatively infrequent in Dodge's journals, and on the whole they are not especially significant. Most often he deleted matter, not to censor himself, but to correct errors, insert afterthoughts, and revise for style. However, in the interest of completeness all canceled matter is included here, except that deleted words and phrases that he immediately rewrote are ignored. Mere slips of the pencil and canceled fragments of illegible letters are also ignored.

Dodge often employed the caret (‸) to indicate placement of inserted matter. Here the caret is used to denote interlineated material, which is shown in a free space above the printed line (see the list of editorial symbols and abbreviations below).

Dodge assigned no page numbers in any of his journals. Ordinarily he wrote his entries straightforwardly—more or less filling each page, writing first on the front and then on the back of each leaf, and passing from front to back in a journal. No systematic numbering of pages is supplied here, but in order to facilitate the location of blank pages, reversed text, and other variations from the norm, page numbers are shown within square brackets at the points where that information is called for. The page numbers given are designated *R* for *recto*, the first or front side of a sheet on which Dodge ordinarily wrote before turning it over, or else *V* for *verso*, the reverse side. Thus [*38V*] means the reverse side of the thirty-eighth manuscript page. Page numbers given without *R* or *V* denote both sides of a sheet.

Dodge began almost all his entries with a dateline, but in doing so he adopted several formats and provided varying amounts of information. Some consistency is imposed here on these diverse practices. Making use of all the information Dodge included in any particular dateline but presenting at a minimum the month and date, the information is given in the following format:

> *Designation of day (e.g., Thanksgiving), day of the week, month, date, year. Place, camp number*

Any ordinals appearing in the manuscript dateline, as in *July 23rd*, are presented as cardinal numbers, so that in this case the date would appear as *July 23*.

Editorial Symbols and Abbreviations

[roman]	Editorial additions.
[*italic*]	Editorial explanations.
< >	Restorations of canceled matter. Cancellations immediately written over are shown next to the letters or numerals written over them, without intervening space.
? ? or [?]	Doubtful readings. The paired question marks are used within square or angle brackets. A single doubtful word is followed immediately by a question mark within square brackets, without an intervening space.
unrecovered	Unrecovered word.
^	Interlinear insertion.

Editorial situations not covered by these symbols are explained at the points where they occur.

The
Sherman Tour Journals
of
Colonel Richard Irving Dodge

Abbreviations

The following abbreviations are employed in citations throughout the volume:

ACP	Appointment, Commission, and Personal File
AG	Adjutant General
AGO	Adjutant General's Office
ANJ	*Army and Navy Journal*
BHJ	*The Black Hills Journals of Colonel Richard Irving Dodge*
GCMO	General Court-Martial Order
G.O.	General Order
Graff	Everett D. Graff Collection of Western Americana, Newberry Library, Chicago, Illinois
HQA	Headquarters of the Army
ITJ	*The Indian Territory Journals of Colonel Richard Irving Dodge*
JMSI	*Journal of the Military Service Institution of the United States*
LC	Library of Congress, Washington, D.C.
LR	Letters Received
LS	Letters Sent
NARA	National Archives and Records Administration
OWI	Dodge, *Our Wild Indians*
PNA	Dodge, *The Plains of North America and Their Inhabitants*
PREJ	*The Powder River Expedition Journals of Colonel Richard Irving Dodge*
Reg	Register
RID	Richard Irving Dodge
S.O.	Special Order
SW	Secretary of War
USMA	United States Military Academy, West Point, New York
WTS	William Tecumseh Sherman
Yale	Yale Collection of Western Americana, Beinecke Library, Yale University, New Haven, Connecticut

Introduction

At Army Headquarters

The appointment in December 1880 of Lieutenant Colonel Richard Irving Dodge, Twenty-third Infantry, as an aide-de-camp to William T. Sherman, the General of the Army, marked the high point of Dodge's career as a United States Army officer thus far. In the thirty-two years since his graduation from West Point, he had done much solid service, winning the respect of his colleagues as what one later termed "a duty officer second to none."[1] However, until recent years his accomplishments had rarely won widespread attention. Receiving his commission shortly after the War with Mexico, in which other young officers had already won fame, in the next decade he served chiefly at remote posts on the Texas frontier. During the greater part of the Civil War, he performed essential but inglorious staff duties behind the lines. His contributions during the conflict were later recognized by the award of brevet commissions through the rank of colonel,[2] but he was not among those whose conspicuous field service entitled them at once to high place in the postwar army.

1. *ANJ*, May 16, 1891, p. 649.

2. On March 30, 1865, Major Dodge was awarded the brevet rank of lieutenant colonel "for faithful and meritorious service in the recruitment of the armies of the United States." On the same day he was breveted colonel "for faithful and meritorious service connected with the organization of the volunteer armies of the United States" (Heitman, *Historical Register*, 1:376). Dodge took the oaths necessary to accept these commissions on April 8, 1865, and August 22, 1867, respectively (RID ACP File, AGO).

Dodge's rise to prominence began in 1867 when, at the lineal rank of major, he joined his regiment in Nebraska and began more than a decade of additional duty on the western frontier. Here his youthful experience as a plains campaigner combined with a strong constitution, sound judgment, and administrative ability to render him an exceptionally valuable officer. In 1875, when relations between the federal government and the Sioux Indians were at a flash point, Dodge commanded an eight-company military escort to a group of scientists who were exploring the Black Hills of Dakota Territory, especially with regard to deposits of gold and other valuable minerals reputed to exist there.[3] Remarkably, the unlawful intrusion of this large body of men onto the Sioux reservation for five months yielded not a single incident of violence. In 1876, near the end of the Great Sioux War that broke out in that year, Dodge commanded fifteen companies of infantry and artillery troops in the Powder River Expedition, under Brigadier General George Crook, which broke the strength of the Northern Cheyenne Indians and helped bring the conflict to a close.[4] Less than two years afterward, following an outbreak of the displaced Northern Cheyenne from their reservation in Indian Territory, Brigadier General John Pope assigned him to help restore peace to that troubled region. Despite the sometimes desperate conditions that prevailed among reservation Indians and the interference he encountered from representatives of the Office of Indian Affairs (the "Indian Bureau") who bore responsibility for their welfare, Dodge performed this task with conspicuous success.[5]

Though not the stuff of colorful story, accomplishments like these would have entitled Dodge to consideration for promotion if that form

3. For the circumstances surrounding this assignment, see *BHJ*, pp. 3–12, 23–25. See also Parker, *Gold in the Black Hills*.

4. Dodge's record of his participation in the campaign, with an analysis of Crook's character and military abilities, can be found in *PREJ*. Another first-person narrative of the Powder River Expedition, by an enlisted man, forms part of Smith, *Sagebrush Soldier*. A recent volume recounting events in the Great Sioux War is Robinson, *A Good Year to Die*. For a brief description of the military operations during the conflict, see Greene, "The Great Sioux War: A Military Perspective," in *Battles and Skirmishes*, pp. xv–xxvi.

5. See *ITJ*, pp. 158–350, 404–34. See also Berthrong, *The Cheyenne and Arapaho Ordeal*, pp. 62–74; Hoig, *Fort Reno and the Indian Territory Frontier*, pp. 77–96.

of recognition were available in the small United States Army of the era, but it was not. The promotion of field officers, ranking from major to colonel, was with rare exceptions governed solely by length of service at a particular rank.[6] In December 1880 Dodge stood eighth in seniority among lieutenant colonels of infantry,[7] and he could realistically expect promotion to full colonel before many more years. But with competition for the few brigadier generalships extremely keen, the likelihood of his ever winning nomination to that rank was small. The selection of Dodge by General Sherman as a member of his personal staff was therefore all the more gratifying. The appointment brought with it the interim rank of colonel and a consequent increase in salary, but more importantly it constituted official recognition of his merit as a professional soldier. As the son and grandson of men who had fought for their country in the War of 1812,[8] Dodge was proud of his profession. On December 18, encamped along a trail through Indian Territory to the village in southern Kansas where he would begin a railroad journey to army headquarters in Washington, D.C., he recorded in a journal entry his response to the recent events that had culminated in his new assignment. "All has happened admirably," he wrote, "& I am a truly fortunate man."[9]

Dodge's new commander, General Sherman, had at this time served as the nation's highest ranking army officer for eleven years.[10] The

6. See Coffman, *The Old Army*, pp. 222-34. Promotions through the rank of captain were made on the basis of an officer's seniority within his regiment rather than within the entire arm of the service.

7. *Official Army Register*, 1881, p. 160.

8. Brigadier General Richard Dodge (1772-1832), a surveyor and trader in northern New York, commanded U.S. forces at Sackett's Harbor, New York, during the war. His son James Richard Dodge (1795-1880) served him as an aide-de-camp (Williams, *The Life of Washington Irving*, 1:380; Aderman, *A Genealogy of the Irvings of New York*, pp. 2, 7; Wheeler, *Reminiscences and Memoirs of North Carolina*, p. 394).

9. *ITJ*, p. 436.

10. A considerable body of literature exists relating to the career and character of William T. Sherman (1820-1891). Especially useful for their account of Sherman's military service after the Civil War are a biography (Marszalek, *Sherman*) and a specialized study (Athearn, *William Tecumseh Sherman and the Settlement of the West*). Other recent biographies include Hirshson, *The White Tecumseh* and Fellman, *Citizen Sherman*.

worst of the conflicts and frustrations that had troubled his tenure as General of the Army—niggardly appropriations from Congress, subjection to the intrusive whims of civilian secretaries of war, the imperious wills of junior officers who commanded staff departments outside his control—were behind him now, accommodated as fully as he thought possible. His reputation as the fierce combatant whose march from Atlanta, Georgia, to the Atlantic coast in the winter of 1864–1865 had helped shatter the morale of the Confederacy was firmly established, but in the years since the conflict the public's perception of him had mellowed. By many persons he was regarded with affection as the "old warrior," a grizzled, graying leader whose still-erect bearing, keen glance, and tart tongue evinced soldierly qualities that were somehow comfortable, a source of national pride. The postwar mandate of the army—to mediate between the advancing western tide of settlers and the native Indian inhabitants whose ancestral lands they appropriated—was not yet fulfilled, especially on the nation's southwest and northwest frontiers. Yet events were clearly verging toward a state of affairs wherein, as Sherman declared in his annual report three years later, the Indians were "substantially eliminated from the problem of the Army."[11]

At sixty years of age, Sherman looked ahead to a few more years of active service in which, taking advantage of the generally peaceful times, he would set the army on a course to ensure the nation's security in the foreseeable future. Even though he deplored involvement in politics as potentially the ruin of soldiers like himself, he had developed skill in dealing with persons of influence and was active in the public sphere, serving on various advisory boards, commissions, and planning committees. He attended receptions, dinners, and social gatherings of all kinds, often traveling hundreds of miles to preside at the annual reunions of military fraternities. Observers noted that the wiry general kept a schedule that would overwhelm most younger men. On occasion he admitted a wish to break free of the hurry and pomp of official life, but in some respects he had come to savor it. Amidst all his activities, the chief focus of Sherman's attention as a public servant

11. *Report of the Secretary of War* (1883), p. 45.

remained the army he led. As he often said, he hoped to be remembered first for his work as a soldier.

By law, the General of the Army was entitled to the full-time service of six aides-de-camp, and in recent years Sherman had availed himself of this privilege to the full. These officers were his executive assistants, senior subalterns who attended to routine office matters and performed such other duties as might be assigned them. All accompanied him to official functions in the national capital, and on his frequent trips outside Washington he was also joined by one or more who made the necessary arrangements for baggage, transportation, and lodging and kept track of expenses. The general and his staff were together regularly and developed a bond of official familiarity which, though modified by the differences in rank, verged in some instances toward personal friendship. Several of Sherman's aides had served him for years and now assisted him in capacities that suited their individual backgrounds and abilities. Captain John M. Bacon, Ninth Cavalry, an aide-de-camp since 1871, helped conduct Sherman's semi-official correspondence and attended to some of his personal business affairs. Major Orlando M. Poe, of the Engineers, had been an aide since 1873 and took responsibility for keeping abreast of developments in that elite department. Captain John E. Tourtelotte, Seventh Cavalry, had been a member of the headquarters staff since 1871. A widely traveled man of independent means, he often accompanied the general to social or diplomatic functions where his gentlemanly bearing would be an asset. From time to time Tourtelotte was called upon to provide a legal opinion on some vexed question of policy not dealt with in the army *Regulations*.[12]

During 1880 the three other positions on Sherman's staff became vacant,[13] and after considerable delay, on December 15 he announced

12. "On General Sherman's Staff as Aide-de-Camp," pp. 65–67, John C. Tidball Papers, USMA; *ANJ*, January 4, 1873, p. 323; May 31, 1873, p. 663; Heitman, *Historical Register*, 1:179, 795, 966; *ITJ*, p. 202n.

13. Captain Joseph C. Audenried, Sixth Cavalry, an aide-de-camp to Sherman since 1866, died on June 3, 1880. Lieutenant Colonel Alexander McD. McCook, Tenth Infantry, an aide since 1875, was promoted to the colonelcy of the Sixth Infantry on December 14. Lieutenant Colonel William D. Whipple, an aide since 1873, resigned as of January 1, 1881, to become assistant adjutant general for the Division of the Missouri (*ANJ*, January 4, 1873, p. 323; December 18, 1880, p. 394; Heitman, *Historical* Register, 1:175, 659, 1026).

the new incumbents. He had selected one officer from each of the three arms of the field service under his authority—infantry, cavalry, and artillery. The infantry was represented by Lieutenant Colonel Dodge, who became at once the senior aide-de-camp in lineal rank. The successful candidate from the cavalry regiments was Major Albert P. Morrow, Ninth Cavalry, who had recently distinguished himself in operations against the Apache Indians. Major John C. Tidball, Second Artillery, represented that branch of the service. He had just completed *A Manual for Heavy Artillery Service*, which was to become a standard textbook at his former duty station, the Artillery School at Fortress Monroe, Virginia, and also at West Point. Two of the three new aides, Dodge and Tidball, were West Point graduates; Morrow had begun his military career during the Civil War as a volunteer enlisted man.[14] Sherman thus demonstrated by his selections that preferment in the officer corps lay within reach of men from all walks of life. All three officers satisfied the general's chief criterion for selection: long periods of duty in the field.

Standing together in dress uniform, their dark blue jackets shining with brass buttons and epaulettes and hung with looped aiguillettes of gold braid, the general's staff formed a handsome group of men. Early in 1881 an observer remarked that Sherman "seems determined to keep up the reputation of his staff in all respects, good looks not excepted."[15] Dodge, who stood over six feet tall and weighed more than two hundred pounds, emanated what one of his former students at West Point termed a "magnificent presence"[16] and so contributed to the favorable impression. Though not inclined to vain personal display, he was well acquainted with the social requirements of military

14. Dodge and Tidball both graduated from West Point in 1848, the former rated nineteenth, the latter eleventh in a class of thirty-eight (Cullum, *Biographical Register*, 2:212–14, 217–18). During the Civil War, Morrow served chiefly with volunteer cavalry regiments from Pennsylvania. He was commissioned a captain in the regular Army and assigned to the Seventh Cavalry on July 28, 1866 (Hamersley, *Records of Living Officers*, p. 159).

15. *ANJ*, January 15, 1881, p. 477.

16. James H. Wilson to George W. McCrary, September 23, 1877 (RID ACP File, AGO). From May 1858 to November 1860 Dodge was assistant instructor of infantry tactics at the U.S. Military Academy.

service in state capitals and major cities. And as General Sherman once remarked, in times of peace the duties of an aide-de-camp were more social than military.[17]

The properly military portion of headquarters staff duty was transacted on weekdays at a not yet completed building on Pennsylvania Avenue that housed offices of the State Department, the army, and the navy. Dodge worked at a large, pigeonholed desk in one of two rooms that flanked the general's office, at the end of the entry corridor on the main floor. The streams of visitors who presented themselves to an attendant outside Sherman's door were freely admitted. Sherman's large, shadowy office was furnished with spare simplicity, evidently dedicated to official business. Its furniture included a large roller desk, a revolving bookcase, a pine map case, and two converging rows of cane-bottomed chairs that together formed a V. A large window, equipped with a cloth shade on rollers but without curtains or draperies, afforded a view of the president's mansion across a wide expanse of lawn. The only articles of decoration were engravings and paintings ranged along the walls, mainly the gifts of Sherman's war comrades but also including a few acquisitions of his own. Floor-to-ceiling panels in one corner concealed a clattering elevator, but the general read, wrote, and thought to himself as if oblivious to the racket. Smoking or chomping on an ever-present cigar, he sat at his desk against the wall, usually with his back to visitors. To those who announced themselves, he turned and offered a hearty welcome; but many citizens simply sat for a few moments on the cane-bottomed chairs, content to be witnessing the General of the Army at work.[18]

Each weekday morning Sherman would arrive at headquarters at about nine o'clock, brimming with nervous energy and ready for the day's tasks. During the morning he would summon one member of his staff or another by a shouted surname—his invariable mode of address to them—or with short, quick steps would enter one of the side offices to declare his wants and perhaps pass a few moments in conversation.

17. See WTS to RID, September 2, 1882 (HQA LS); below, p. 51.

18. "On General Sherman's Staff as Aide-de-Camp," pp. 12–19, John C. Tidball Papers, USMA.

The atmosphere was businesslike but not formal, seemingly pleasant to all concerned. At one or two o'clock in the afternoon he took lunch, with sometimes a glass of neat whisky, at an eating place nearby. He returned to headquarters only on afternoons when some unusual matter required his attention. Otherwise, he devoted the later hours of the day to other commitments, and if possible to a few hours at home.[19]

Sherman possessed a retentive memory and prided himself on his ability to recall incidents in the careers of other officers, especially those with whom he had been associated over the years. He was aware of Dodge's claims to recognition long before the opportunity arose to appoint him an aide-de-camp. In 1867, then commander of the Division of the Missouri, he had met and conferred with Major Dodge during an inspection tour of army posts along the Union Pacific Railroad, then beginning construction westward from Omaha, Nebraska.[20] In the years that followed, Dodge's frontier service brought him to Sherman's attention on other occasions, and by 1879 the general had formed a settled opinion of the younger man as a "judicious" and "active good officer."[21] "Dickie" Dodge—his nickname since West Point days—had a wide circle of friends in the army and was known for good fellowship and good sense.[22] Hearty recommendations of him from General Pope and perhaps others of his former commanders, including Brigadier General Randolph B. Marcy, Sherman's trusted inspector general, made the selection as aide a natural one.[23]

19. *ANJ*, May 20, 1882, p. 956; March 31, 1883, p. 799; "On General Sherman's Staff as Aide-de-Camp," pp. 12–19, 21–22, 34–36, 50, 79–81, John C. Tidball Papers, USMA.

20. *New York Times*, June 15, 1867, p. 1; June 22, 1867, p. 1; June 24, 1867, p. 1; *Cincinnati Gazette*, June 24, 1867, p. 3; *ANJ*, June 29, 1867, p. 709; July 6, 1867, p. 725.

21. WTS to General Philip H. Sheridan [telegram], May 2, 1879; WTS to Sheridan [letter], May 2, 1879 (Military Division of the Missouri, Indian Territory Operations Special File).

22. For the nickname, see "On General Sherman's Staff as Aide-de-Camp," p. 73, John C. Tidball Papers, USMA; *ANJ*, August 8, 1885, p. 34.

23. In 1871–1872 General Marcy presided over a board of officers, one of whom was Dodge, which prepared a draft revision of the regulations governing the army. The board's report was published in 1873 as *Revised Army Regulations*, but owing to the press of other business the House of Representatives never enacted it as law. Marcy and Dodge were both avid outdoorsmen and published authors. See *PNA*, pp. 33, 41, 274 n, 374, 377. After a forty-four-year career, Marcy retired from active duty on January 2, 1881. See *ANJ*, January 8, 1881, p. 449.

In Dodge's initial weeks at army headquarters, he and Sherman began to form a friendship based on shared values and interests and broad similarities of character. Both, for example, were masters of conversation who relished anecdotage, debate, and give-and-take on all topics, and who were aware of their talent in this area. Sherman considered himself "the best talker in seven states,"[24] but Dodge was a lively competitor. A newspaper correspondent who accompanied the Black Hills Expedition described him as "a fine conversationalist, [who] of course loves to talk; but, when a man can talk well, he is pardonable in any little display of vanity."[25] The two men stimulated each other to feats of verbal performance, sometimes to the discomfiture of more taciturn types.[26] Both were wide readers, with more than casual knowledge

24. *ANJ*, June 30, 1883, p. 1082, in an article reprinted from the *Washington Republican*.

25. *Chicago Tribune*, August 21, 1875, p. 2; quoted in *BHJ*, p. 19 n.

26. In his memoirs, Tidball mentioned the verbal fluency of both Sherman and Dodge, but whereas he praised the general's habits of speech and noted his enjoyment of "sprightly conversation and amusing anecdotes," the similar qualities of his fellow aide evidently irritated him. He wrote a generally unflattering sketch of Dodge that focused on him as a tiresome talker:

> His proclivity for talking and laughing, possessed by him as a cadet, seems to have increased as time advanced, making him one of the greatest talkers in the army, and he indulged this propensity on all occasions and at all times. It was simply talk not conversation; a sort of monologue, a constant clatter in which those around could take but little part. He was not given to long stories, but rattled along relating trifling incidents, generally of his own experience, and of but little importance or interest to his listeners, keeping up all the while a constant laughing by way of accompanym[en]ts. Having a rapid utterance he covered much ground in a short space of time, in fact so much that at the end of any given period no one was able to make head or tail of what he had been saying, except only when now and then he let drop some remark that could be jotted down as a kind of oasis in the great desert of his remarks. His long service upon the plains and among the mountains of the West had educated him in the ways of that kind of life. To this was added an enthusiastic fondness for hunting and fishing in both of which he had uncommon skill. Upon these subjects, as upon some others of a kindred nature his talk, when restrained within bounds, was interesting and instructive. I never knew why the general was persuaded to make him an aid, but he evidently did fancy him, although I thought he did weary a little of his clattering talk. ("On General Sherman's Staff as Aide-de-Camp," pp. 51, 73–77, John C. Tidball Papers, USMA)

Eugene C. Tidball speculates that his namesake, "who had a reputation for taciturnity, was amused, frustrated, or bored" when in continued contact with Dodge and Sherman ("General Sherman's Last March," p. 8).

on a range of subjects. Dodge was the more literary in his tastes, perhaps inheriting that inclination through membership in the Irving family, which gave him his middle name.[27] The texts of Shakespeare's plays were at his fingers' ends, while Sherman's enthusiasm for the drama ran more to performances than to reading. But here, fortuitously, another source of common interest presented itself. Dodge's only son, Frederick, had recently begun a career as an actor on the legitimate stage. In 1879 and 1880, billed as "the New Hamlet," he performed with a repertory company in New York City and on tour as far west as Kansas. Under the stage name Frederick Paulding, he had become known as "the Army actor," his relationship to Dodge frequently being noticed by newspapers like the semiofficial weekly, the *Army and Navy Journal*.[28] Sherman, an inveterate playgoer, may have attended performances by Fred's company during its annual appearances in Washington. At any rate, as a lover of the theater he knew of the younger Dodge's accomplishments, if not at first hand then certainly through conversation with the proud father.

Themes rich with potential for elaboration by these two discussants were army stories and tales of life on the plains. Both men were drawn to the western wilderness, Dodge from long habitude, Sherman as a respite from the constraints of life in eastern cities. Another officer, Colonel James F. Rusling, recalled the latter's satisfaction when, on a visit to Fort Garland, Colorado, he immersed himself in mountain life just as he found it. "He threw off all reserve," Rusling wrote, and "entered fully into the life of the pioneer and Indian. He asked a thousand questions of everybody and was never at a loss for a story or a joke, and added to the effect of these by the twinkle of his eye, the toss of his head, and the serio-comic twitch of his many-wrinkled features,

27. Dodge's paternal grandmother, Ann Sarah Irving (1770–1808), was the eldest sister of Washington Irving, the American author, and the Dodge and Irving families were otherwise related by marriage. Dodge's aunt, Eliza Dodge (1801–1887), married Oscar Irving in 1844, and in 1836 another aunt, Helen Dodge (1802–1885), married Pierre M. Irving, later the authorized biographer of Washington Irving (Williams, *The Life of Washington Irving*, 2:254; Aderman, *A Genealogy of the Irvings of New York*, pp. 6, 8).

28. See *ANJ*, January 10, 1880, p. 452; April 9, 1881, p. 745; April 16, 1881, p. 766.

in a way indescribable."[29] Since assuming command of the army, Sherman had on several occasions made extended tours of inspection in the West. His desire to keep current about events and conditions in that vast region continued unabated, and in this respect Dodge, more than any other of his aides, was able to satisfy him.

The first major event in Washington wherein the general and his new aides-de-camp appeared together in public was a peaceful one, the inauguration of James A. Garfield as president on March 4, 1881. Sherman was grand marshal of the processions that preceded and followed the inaugural ceremony, and his staff naturally helped make the preliminary arrangements. Colonel Tidball was assigned chief responsibility for coordinating the two marches, first from the White House to the Capitol for the swearing in, and then back to the executive mansion, where the new chief executive would review the units as they moved past. Finding temporary shelters for the state militia organizations that would reach the city the night before, ensuring that all participants understood where and in what order they were to join the parade, and satisfying the requirements of imperious state governors and commanders of militia as those needs multiplied from day to day were together a daunting task for the new aide. Years afterward Tidball recalled that he had never before been obliged to cope with so many self-important cranks. The state officials were determined to array their attendants in colorful costumes, with feathers, sashes, and extravagances of all sorts.[30] Their republican exuberance demanded expression, but Sherman, who enjoyed parades but was wary of unsoldierly display,[31] stipulated that the regular army and navy units, and also the naval cadets from Annapolis, Maryland, should march in traditional fashion, in dress uniform.

29. Rusling, *Men and Things I Saw in Civil War Days*, pp. 139–40. Sherman's visit to Fort Garland occurred in September 1866, in the course of an inspection tour.

30. Tidball feared the event would degenerate into "a mere harlequinade . . . instead of the dignified parade it . . . should be" ("On General Sherman's Staff as Aide-de-Camp," p. 124, John C. Tidball Papers, USMA).

31. Tidball wrote that while Sherman "had great fondness for parades, reviews, etc., he looked upon them only as a means for the creation and maint[en]ance of a good soldiery, and not merely as a show [of] gaily dressed men with flaunting banners and blaring trumpets" (Ibid., p. 51e).

John C. Tidball (Massachusetts Commandery, Military Order of the Loyal Legion; U.S. Army Military History Institute)

A storm on the night of March 3 dropped slushy snow on the city, soaking the drapes and bunting that had been hung along the parade route. At daylight, workers hurried to sweep the temporary bleachers and reviewing stands and then Pennsylvania Avenue, but the prospect was for a bedraggled procession at best when, in mid-morning, wintry sunlight broke through the clouds and improved conditions somewhat. The national capital was crowded with visitors, many of whom soon lined the route of march and overflowed the galleries outside the Capitol building. At approximately 10:30 A.M. the parade began, led by the president, the president-elect, and their military escort. General Sherman appeared next, on a spirited gray horse, followed by his aides, also mounted, and then a division of regular troops. After these came the president-elect's party, in carriages, and then four more divisions of state troops and civic societies.

Arrived at the Capitol, Sherman and his staff sat astride their mounts in front of the inaugural stand, their teeth chattering in the frigid wind. The inauguration ceremony took place, President Garfield addressed the crowd at some length, and at last the one-mile return march began. The sequence of marching units was the same as before, but additional participants now joined the rear of the procession and lent it a carnival air. Amidst the music of brass bands, the parade passed underneath thirty-three iron arches, draped with flags, that spanned the avenue. Several military brigades, among them the Pennsylvania State Militia, the naval cadets, and the six-company contingent of marines, received special praise for their bearing during this part of the day's observances. As the latter units moved crisply past Willard's Hotel, a country visitor was heard to allow, "Well, now, them fellers are doin' purty good walkin.'"[32] Other groups won applause for their resplendent appearance. The Cleveland Troop, which escorted the president-elect, wore dark blue chasseur uniforms with gold lacing across the front, and gold plumes on their helmets. The Citizen's Corps of Utica, New York, also wore uniforms of dark blue, bordered and faced with light blue, and bearskin shakos. The five hundred members of the Central Republican Club of New York City wore handsome badges of

32. *ANJ*, March 19, 1881, p. 688.

light blue silk and satin. A streamer bearing the club's name in silver gilt hung loosely from the center design, a Maltese cross within a ring of corded silk. In front of the White House, General Sherman stood on a reviewing stand alongside the new president as the colorful procession made its way past, while his aides-de-camp remained behind the grandstand for another cold, tedious hour.[33]

Despite its inauspicious beginning and continuing discomforts, the day of the Garfield inauguration was a great success. The throng of spectators was unprecedented, and the procession of military and civic organizations was the largest ever to complement a presidential inauguration. It was agreed that Washington had not seen so fine a military display since the Grand Review of returning Union troops in May 1865.[34] A few days afterward, Sherman and his staff took part in another ceremony, stiff with protocol—the president's annual reception for army and navy officers then in the city.

It now became possible to direct attention more specifically to army affairs. In addition to routine duties, each of the new aides was assigned responsibility for some project or sphere of activity within the service that related to his special competence. Morrow would assist Tourtelotte in reviewing court-martial proceedings so as to inform the general of cases or legal issues that required his attention. Tidball was to preside over a board of officers who would investigate possible changes in the light artillery equipment to be supplied the army.[35] Dodge would head up a similar board, to study the practicability of adopting a single magazine gun design for use by troops in all branches of the army.

33. *ANJ*, March 5, 1881, p. 638; *New York Times*, March 4, 1881, p. 1; March 5, 1881, pp. 1–2; *Washington Herald* (Army and Navy Edition), March 6, 1881, p. 1; "On General Sherman's Staff as Aide-de-Camp," pp. 121–38, John C. Tidball Papers, USMA.

34. *New York Times*, March 4, 1881, p. 4; *ANJ*, March 19, 1881, p. 688. The *Times* printed excerpts from comments on the inauguration first published in newspapers of Augusta, Georgia; Providence, Rhode Island; Charleston, South Carolina; Boston, Massachusetts; Hartford, Connecticut; and Springfield, Massachusetts (March 5, p. 2).

35. The Light Artillery Board submitted a report of its findings in September 1881. General Sherman and Brigadier General Stephen V. Benet, the chief of ordnance, approved the proceedings of the board and suggested that the guns it recommended be given a series of tests (*ANJ*, August 6, 1881, p. 12; WTS to SW, September 19, 1881, AGO Reg LR).

The two latter assignments reflected Sherman's determination that, despite its chronic underfunding and the small likelihood of a serious conflict in the near future, the army should change with the times, moving beyond its dependence on outmoded arms and tactics that in some instances dated back to the Civil War era. The idea of equipping soldiers with a reliable rifle that was capable of firing in rapid succession bullets stored in a reserve compartment, or magazine, was of great interest to Dodge. He knew at first hand the shortcomings of the differently styled breech-loading rifles then in use by cavalry and infantry troops. In combat against Indians neither the cavalry carbine, with its short range, nor the infantry rifle, with its size and heft, was sufficiently versatile to perform adequately in all circumstances.[36] Meeting at various points in the eastern states including Troy, New York, Springfield, Massachusetts, and Governor's Island, New York Harbor, the Magazine Gun Board would conduct studies of weaponry submitted for its inspection by manufacturers in the United States and abroad. Should the board be able to recommend a design for general adoption by the army, it would contribute significantly to the effectiveness of the nation's military force. The armies of France and Germany had already adopted magazine weapons, and to protect its credibility as a developing international power the United States should follow their example.

Sherman and Dodge had discussed ideas like these by March 21, when an order was issued from army headquarters designating the membership of the Magazine Gun Board and directing it to assemble in New York City on July 5 to begin its work.[37] However, a few weeks

36. See *ITJ*, p. 27; see also *ANJ*, November 13, 1876, p. 229, and a reprinted statement by Charles King, "Arms or Tactics?" *ANJ*, March 27, 1880, p. 685.

37. The officers detailed for the Magazine Gun Board were Dodge; Captain F. W. Benteen, Seventh Cavalry; Captain George Shorkley, Fifteenth Infantry; Captain H. G. Litchfield, Second Artillery; Captain John E. Greer, Ordnance Department; and Captain George L. Browning, Seventh Infantry, recorder (G.O. 31, HQA, March 21, 1881, reprinted in *ANJ*, March 26, 1881, p. 697). Before the board submitted its report, in September 1882, its activities attracted much attention in the United States and abroad. The report was published, without supporting documents, in *ANJ*, October 7, 1882, p. 219. It was published in full as Appendix 30 in the report of the chief of ordnance, *Report of the Secretary of War* (1882), pp. 329–33. A consolidated file comprising correspondence related to the work of the Magazine Gun Board is 1699 AGO 1881, available in NARA microfilm publication M689, Roll 18.

later the general released Dodge from this important assignment and designated another senior officer, Colonel John R. Brooke, Third Infantry, to serve in his stead.[38] Sherman had known beforehand that Dodge was already involved with a quite different project, one that also promised to advance the interests of the army. Releasing him from membership on the Magazine Gun Board would enable Dodge to continue work on that important undertaking.

Our Wild Indians

At the time he learned of his appointment as an aide-de-camp, Dodge had just completed the manuscript of a book that had engaged his attention at intervals for several years. In fact, he was about to begin a month's leave of absence in which he hoped to find a publisher in New York City and make arrangements necessary for the book's production.[39] His plans had necessarily been delayed by the assignment in Washington, but he remained eager to bring his as yet untitled work before the American reading public. The book was a wide-ranging discussion of American Indians, especially the Plains Indians with whom he had come into contact during much of his career. Based on research among printed authorities as well as on personal experience, Dodge's manuscript approached its subject from two separate but related points of view.

First, by describing distinctive beliefs and customs of the aboriginal peoples, Dodge's work opened to view what he termed "the social or inner life of the wild Indian of the present day."[40] Second, it portrayed the Indians in terms of the impact on them of American culture, especially federal authority. Here he expressed views characteristic of army officers of the era who were called upon to enforce what they regarded

38. S.O. 98, HQA, April 29, 1881 (Dodge Papers, Graff). The two orders pertaining to Dodge were reprinted in *Report of the Secretary of War* (1882), pp. 331–32.

39. See *ITJ*, pp. 434–36. By S.O. 257, Department of the Missouri, November 22, 1880, Dodge was granted a month's leave of absence, with permission to apply for an extension of three months (*ANJ*, December 4, 1880, p. 349). The date on which the period of leave would begin was left to his discretion.

40. "Author's Preface," *OWI*, p. vi.

as a futile and ill-conceived Indian policy.[41] Enumerating the results of effectively imprisoning Indian tribes on reservations, sometimes far from their ancestral homes, and placing them under the authority of corrupt or incompetent agents of the Indian Bureau, he expressed pity for the Indians and dismay at the system that was so mistreating them. The federal government had effectively denied Indian tribes the ability to continue in their traditional nomadic way of life, but despite solemn promises to support them in an alternative mode of existence while they mastered new means of support such as farming, it had failed to do so. Indian reservations were sinks of lawlessness, privation, disease, and resentful apathy. In vigorous terms Dodge called attention to these conditions and urged that means be adopted to correct them.

Writing as a patriot and also a friend to the Indian, he proposed radical revisions of United States Indian policy. He compared Indians to the African American slaves, who had been denied basic rights as citizens before the Civil War but had later vindicated the faith of those who favored granting them freedom. He expressed confidence in the Native Americans' latent capacity for growth. These primitive people had the potential to contribute significantly to the national welfare, once they had been made ready to assume the rights and responsibilities of citizenship. For the present, however, Dodge argued that responsibility for the Indians should rest with the army, whose officers—unlike many Indian Bureau employees—were disinterested, honest, and sensitive to the tribes' needs. In his view, only the military was capable of wielding the day-to-day authority that ensured the force of law and could foster healthy cultural change.[42]

Dodge's proposition that responsibility for Indian tribes should be wrested from the Indian Bureau and returned to the army was hardly new. It had been hotly contested for more than a decade, with entrenched adherents ranged on both sides of the question. What

41. A study of army officer's attitudes toward Indians during this period is Smith, *The View from Officers' Row*. See also Coffman, *The Old Army*, pp. 254–261; Tate, *The Frontier Army in the Settlement of the West*, p. 237; and Utley, *Frontier Regulars*, pp. 45, 188–89.

42. *OWI*, pp. 639–53. Compare this with Dodge's earlier recommendations in *PNA*, pp. 359–66.

gave Dodge's manuscript unique power, and potential effectiveness in the continuing debate, was the connection it established between actual conditions he had witnessed and the ideas he advanced to root out their causes. His work was an authoritative report and recommendation from the field. The project was thus more than an attempt to supplement current anthropological knowledge; it was also the product of Dodge's determination to speak out on behalf of the Indians, many of whom he had come to know, respect, and pity. Shortly after his arrival in Washington, he lent the manuscript to a Professor Angel, who recognized its value and communicated his judgment to Henry L. Dawes, chairman of the Senate Committee on Indian Affairs. Presently Dawes also borrowed the work, and upon returning it he assured Dodge that he had borrowed a good many "nuggets" for use as a legislator. Gratifyingly, the senator predicted that when published, the work would be a "valuable contribution to Indian literature."[43]

Discussions of the "Indian question" were being issued frequently at just this time. George W. Manypenny's *Our Indian Wards*, a lengthy treatment by an influential apologist for the Indian Bureau, had appeared in 1880. Helen Hunt Jackson's bitter indictment of the federal government, *A Century of Dishonor*, was issued in January 1881. The Military Service Institution, a semiofficial body, was offering a prize that year for the best essay on Indian affairs submitted to its review board.[44] The future of Indian policy was undergoing spirited discussion, and a contribution by Dodge, already an acknowledged authority, would be timely.

43. H. L. Dawes to RID, March 27 and April 4, 1881 (Dodge Papers, Graff). The intermediary between Dodge and Dawes may have been William P. Angel (d. 1889), a New York politician who in earlier years had been actively interested in study of the American Indian.

44. Twelve essays were submitted for review by the three judges, former Secretary of War George W. McCrary, former Brigadier General (and Confederate General) Joseph E. Johnston, and Brigadier General Alfred H. Terry. The winning entrant was Colonel John Gibbon, Seventh Infantry. Two other essays, by First Lieutenant C. E. S. Wood, Twenty-first Infantry, and Captain Edmond Butler, Fifth Infantry, were also judged especially able (*ANJ*, January 1, 1881, p. 430; June 25, 1881, p. 986). The contents of the three discussions were summarized in *ANJ*, July 9, 1881, p. 1019.

In Sherman's view, publication of Dodge's book manuscript would both advance the political interests of the army and also add to the work of other army officers as a contribution to knowledge. Lieutenant General Philip H. Sheridan, commander of the Division of the Missouri, was officially sponsoring cultural studies of Indian tribes by two talented young officers, First Lieutenant John G. Bourke, Third Cavalry, and Captain William Philo Clark, Second Cavalry.[45] Like Dodge, these men had already contributed to the anthropological record by collecting specimens of Indian material culture, many of which they donated to the Smithsonian Institution and other repositories. Dodge's earlier volume, *The Plains of North America and Their Inhabitants* (1877), had devoted about one-half its length to chapters on Indian customs and beliefs. That section of the work had won praise from reviewers on both sides of the Atlantic as the finest discussion of its kind then available.[46] Sherman had purchased a copy of *Plains* and so was familiar with Dodge's writing talent and political views.[47] The new book, he understood, was an expanded and updated version of the Indian chapters in *Plains*, together with much new material.

Dodge intended to publish this latest volume as a private venture, as he had *Plains* and an earlier book, *The Black Hills* (1876). However, since the new work meshed neatly with activities already initiated under army auspices, Sherman gave his aide-de-camp the opportunity to move ahead on the book project as part of his regular duties. In the months that followed, he would assist Dodge in equally substantial ways that greatly enhanced the book's reputation and sales success.

45. Hutton, *Phil Sheridan and His Army*, pp. 341–42. See also *ANJ*, September 27, 1881, p. 147; December 31, 1881, p. 472.

46. For a summary of the reviews, see PNA, pp. 26–30. Dodge's work has been issued under three titles. The earliest, assigned it by Dodge's English editor, William Blackmore, was the English edition, *The Hunting Grounds of the Great West* (London: Chatto & Windus, 1876). The second, more in accordance with the author's wishes, was the American edition, *The Plains of the Great West and Their Inhabitants* (New York: G. P. Putnam's Sons, 1877). A recent edition, based on the author's manuscript and with the title Dodge intended, is *The Plains of North America and Their Inhabitants* (Newark: University of Delaware Press, 1989), cited here as *PNA*.

47. WTS to RID, September 16, 1884 (Sherman Papers, LC).

Dodge had been delighted at the favorable reception of *Plains*, which the *Atlantic Monthly* had recommended as an "excellent book" that "must long serve as the most trustworthy compendium of an evanescent phase of our nation's history."[48] Still, sales of the work had been disappointing. Issued by G. P. Putnam's Sons of New York at the steep price of four dollars, copies sold slowly. In 1881, four years after publication, eighty-three copies from the modest first edition were still in stock.[49] The Putnams had brought out the volume in a creditable fashion, granting Dodge a generous royalty of 20 percent on the price of copies sold at retail, but in his view the firm's conservative marketing methods had failed to realize the book's sales potential. He planned to find a new publisher who would bring its successor before a wider audience.

To achieve this aim, Dodge selected A. D. Worthington of Hartford, Connecticut, a former bank employee and traveling salesman whose firm marketed its publications through subscriptions and canvassing by agents.[50] Unlike the Putnams, Worthington felt little concern to accumulate a list of titles whose solid merit would reflect credit on his house. So long as the books that appeared under his imprint gave no offense to reviewers or in any other way discouraged potential purchasers, he was relatively indifferent to their content. His publications were commodities, to be distributed to the widest possible audience.

To achieve that goal, Worthington was not shy of proclaiming the merits of his products and extolling his methods of marketing them. In a pamphlet sent to persons who had expressed interest in enlisting as his agents, he boasted that his firm formed a segment of the book

48. *Atlantic Monthly* 39 (June 1877): 756.

49. On October 1, 1885, two copies were still on hand. Since 1881, sixty-one copies had been sold through normal trade channels, twenty more at auction (Statement of Account, G. P. Putnam's Sons with RID, October 22, 1885—Dodge Papers, Graff).

50. So far as is known, A. D. Worthington was not related to Thomas Worthington, of Ohio, against whom Sherman had filed charges of insubordination in 1862. (See Hirshson, *The White Tecumseh*, pp. 131–32.) The publisher was related to R. Worthington, a New York publisher and bookseller with a large, miscellaneous, and not very profitable range of products. See *Publisher's Weekly*, February 25, 1882, p. 195; August 26, 1882, p. 226; September 16, 1882, p. 269; September 23, 1882, p. 437; October 14, 1882, p. 521.

trade that had grown "at a rate little dreamed of by the plodding publishers of fifteen years ago." Through his initiatives, he continued, "the subscription-book business has been raised to the order and dignity of a science."[51] The principles of this science he expounded in a booklet, forwarded to agents, entitled *The Art of Canvassing, or What to Do and What Not to Do, to Achieve Success.*[52] Dodge's would be the sixth book Worthington had offered for sale, and the first dealing with the American Indian.[53]

The agreement between author and publisher specified that Dodge would supply an acceptable manuscript, cooperate in securing illustrations, and assist in marketing. In return, Worthington was to bear all costs of production, advertising, and distribution and was to pay the author a royalty of ten cents on each copy sold. In the summer of 1881 Dodge therefore busied himself with final revisions of his text and with arranging for the illustrations. James E. Taylor of New York City, a well-known illustrator for *Frank Leslie's Illustrated Weekly Magazine,* drew eleven sketches that, engraved by another artist, became part of the published work. The Matthew Brady studio in Washington, D.C., produced a handsome three-quarter length portrait of Dodge in his dress uniform; engraved on steel, it served as the frontispiece.

51. A. D. Worthington & Co., *Illustrated Descriptive Catalog of Popular and Standard Books*, pp. [1–2] (Trade Catalogs, Special Collections, University of Delaware Library).

52. No copy of *The Art of Canvassing* has been located. Worthington described it as "an invaluable guide, replete with counsels, suggestions, and practical instructions, which are worth their weight in gold" (*Illustrated Descriptive Catalog of Popular and Standard Books*, p. [2]).

53. As itemized in the *Illustrated Descriptive Catalog of Popular and Standard Books*, the five earlier publications were Thomas M. Knox, *The Oriental World. A Record of Recent Travel, Adventure, and Exploration in Turkey, Egypt, Asia Minor, Syria, and the Holy Land* (1875); Mrs. T. B. H. Stenhouse, *"Tell It All": The Story of a Life's Experience in Mormonism* (1874); C. C. Bombaugh, *Gleanings for the Curious, from the Harvest-Fields of Literature* (1875); Mary Clemmer, *Ten Years in Washington: or, Life and Scenes in the National Capital as a Woman Sees Them* (1873); Franklin Chamberlin, *Chamberlin's Legal Counsellor. A Business Law-Book* (1873) (pp. [5–31]). All five volumes were issued with lengthy subtitles not recorded here (Trade Catalogs, Special Collections, University of Delaware Library). The dates of publication are supplied from *The National Union Catalog of Pre-1956 Imprints*, which, however, does not contain an entry that lists A. D. Worthington as publisher of the work by Chamberlin.

At the Smithsonian Institution, Dodge secured an engraved facsimile of a curiosity in his possession, a chronological chart in hieroglyphics, which he believed the only calendar ever produced by Plains Indians.[54] He secured recent photographs of four military men, Brigadier General George Crook, Brigadier General Nelson A. Miles, Colonel Ranald S. Mackenzie, Fourth Cavalry, and the late Lieutenant Colonel George A. Custer, Seventh Cavalry, for engraving and publication together as a full-page illustration, entitled "Famous Indian Fighters."

General Sherman may have provided advice and assistance as Dodge assembled this diverse material. Sherman was himself in correspondence with James E. Taylor about watercolor depictions of Civil War scenes then being prepared by the artist for display at army headquarters.[55] Moreover, as a long-time regent of the Smithsonian Institution, he wielded considerable influence there. A request for cooperation from a member of his staff would have received thoughtful attention.

In fact, Dodge was himself already well known at the Smithsonian, having corresponded with its employees and associates on several subjects, including the threatened extinction of the American bison, little-known flora of the Rocky Mountain region, specimens required by the institution for its exhibits of native fauna, and the sign language in use by Plains Indians.[56] In the summer of 1881 he donated to the institution several items from his personal collection of Indian artifacts and secured its cooperation in preparing illustrations of these

54. For the provenance of this item, originally obtained by Captain Garrick Mallery, First Infantry, see *ANJ*, April 21, 1877, p. 593. Dodge's account of the copy in his possession is in *OWI*, pp. 399–401; the facsimile illustration appears on p. 403. Dodge had intended to include a discussion of the chart by William Blackmore in *The Plains of North America and Their Inhabitants*, but the Englishman did not get around to writing it; see *PNA*, pp. 20, 46, 388. Pictorial calendars were later discussed by James Mooney in his authoritative "Calendar History of the Kiowa Indians," *Seventeenth Annual Report of the Bureau of Ethnology*, pp. 131–468.

55. For example, see *ANJ*, August 28, 1880, p. 62, and WTS to Taylor, June 23, 1881, both concerning the artist's watercolor representation of the Grand Review in Washington, D.C.; WTS to Taylor, July 29, 1881, concerning another painting in progress, of Union troops crossing the Big Black River in May 1863 (HQA LS).

56. J. A. Allen to RID, October 30, 1877 (on the bison); Spencer Baird to RID, October 25, 1880 (on Rocky Mountain flora); Spencer Baird to RID, March 22, 1880 (on specimens required); Garrick Mallery to RID, December 1, 1879; April 10, July 3, July 6, and November 18, 1880 (on sign language) (Dodge Papers, Graff).

and other objects for publication in the forthcoming book.[57] Spencer Baird, the director, made available for his use a room wherein the designs for six full-page plates, each in fifteen colors, were meticulously etched onto stone tablets. Preparing these color plates was a laborious undertaking. First, each group of objects to be represented together was photographed. A photographic print was then supplied to an artist, who, with the original objects set before him as models, etched the stone chromo-lithographic tablets, with special attention to coloring and detail. To print each of the six plates that were prepared in this manner, fifteen separate printings of the same sheets would be required.[58] The process would increase the publisher's production cost, but if the results were as striking as hoped, the six plates should greatly enhance the book's sales appeal.

At the time when Worthington or another member of his firm first read through Dodge's manuscript text, it had undergone only minor revisions since being completed and copied the previous December. The publisher was troubled by some of the more polemic passages, which in his judgment posed a serious threat to sales. To some persons, any book on Indians by a soldier like Dodge would be suspect. However cogent his rationale might be for the policy changes he recommended, his undisguised contempt for the Indian Bureau and the "professional humanitarians" who supported it would surely offend many clergymen, for the Indian Bureau was a darling of the religious press.[59] These concerns led Worthington to insist that Dodge delete from the forthcoming book its first twelve chapters, a detailed discussion of the Indian question, as "too argumentative, and not within the scope of a work designed to furnish to the vast reading public of the United States a popular account of the daily life of our Indians."[60]

Dodge complied, but only in part. He felt strongly about the issues treated in the passages that had given concern to the publisher, and

57. Spencer Baird to RID, August 31, 1881 (Dodge Papers, Graff).

58. [A. D. Worthington & Co.], "Thirty-Three Years' Personal Experience Among Our Wild Indians," p. [1] (Dodge Papers, Graff).

59. *OWI*, p. 653. See also *PNA*, pp. 364–66.

60. RID, "Explanatory," *A Living Issue*, p. [1]. The words quoted here are Dodge's, not the publisher's.

he was unwilling to deprive the book of its political thrust. He did prune a few passages dealing chiefly with legislative history, but the greater part of the argument he simply moved to the conclusion of the manuscript text. If Worthington ever noticed the maneuver, he made no objection. He had already determined to market the book without any reference to the debate over federal Indian policy.

General Sherman was in Washington during almost the entire summer of 1881, and he was therefore in regular contact with Dodge as these arrangements were being made. Ordinarily the general passed a few weeks each summer away from the capital, at some out-of-the-way resort with his family or else on an official errand that combined duty with pleasure. However, this year the summer months passed under a cloud of apprehension. On July 2, while standing in a Washington railroad station, President Garfield was shot and seriously wounded by a disappointed office-seeker, Charles J. Guiteau. In the weeks that followed, Garfield lingered and then rallied, arousing hopes of his eventual recovery, but he remained unable to perform official duties. In the Cabinet and elsewhere the question was debated whether the vice president, Chester A. Arthur, should assume *pro tem* the executive functions of the presidency. Meanwhile, fears were expressed that an angry mob might attempt to wrest Guiteau from custody. Sherman declined an offer of troops to help preserve the peace from the militia of the District of Columbia, assuring Colonel Amos Webster that less inflammatory methods of maintaining civil order should suffice.[61] Nevertheless, federal troops in the vicinity were made aware that duty in the city at short notice remained a possibility.

Learning that General Sheridan proposed to undertake a tour to Yellowstone National Park with his family and a group of dignitaries, on July 15 Sherman approved at once, wishing him a good spell of "rest and recreation." He noted only that certain of Sheridan's immediate subordinates ought to remain within easy reach in case of need. For himself, he continued, he planned to remain "pretty close" to the capital all year "to give me a good excuse for a trip to Texas, Arizona, and Cali-

61. WTS to Webster, August 27, 1881 (HQA LS). See also *ANJ*, September 3, 1881, p. 95.

fornia early next spring."[62] Fluctuations in Garfield's condition forced Sherman to cancel commitments made months before to attend various civic gatherings. Late in August he warned Governor Hobart B. Bigelow of Connecticut that, since Garfield was then "in extreme danger," as commanding general, he "of all officials" must remain in Washington. Further, he might not be able to attend two upcoming events, the Groton Heights Centennial celebration at New London on September 6, and the New England Fair at Worcester, Massachusetts the next day.[63]

However, the daily bulletins describing the condition of the president took on a more hopeful tone, and on September 1 Sherman left the city, accompanied by Dodge. The two officers took rooms at the Fifth Avenue Hotel in New York City, the general's preferred place of residence there, and made visits and short excursions before continuing on to Groton and Worcester.[64] Sherman delivered a short address at the Worcester grave of a Revolutionary hero, General Artemas Ward. On the return trip he conferred at Governor's Island, New York Harbor, with Major General Winfield S. Hancock, commander of the Military Division of the Atlantic, before arriving back in Washington on September 15. Four days later President Garfield, lying in great pain at Elberon, New Jersey, sank into unconsciousness and died.

Contrary to the fears of some, the public mood at news of this dire event was not vindictive. On the afternoon of September 21 all officers of the army and navy on duty in the capital escorted the remains of the late president from the Baltimore and Potomac depot to the Capitol building, where he was to lie in state. Sherman and Rear Admiral E. T. Nichols led the procession, followed by approximately two hundred officers, in ranks of two on either side of the hearse, army on the right, navy on the left. Bands sounded a funeral march as the streets of Washington again filled with militia corps, marine and artillery brigades, and civic societies. Two days later a yet longer procession including Cabinet members, the Supreme Court, members of Congress,

62. WTS to Sheridan, July 15, 1881 (HQA LS).

63. WTS to Bigelow, August 26, 1881. See also the letter from WTS to George F. Hoar, of Worcester, Massachusetts, dated the same day (HQA LS).

64. *ANJ*, September 3, 1881, p. 95; September 17, 1881, p. 147; WTS to John E. Tourtelotte, September 11, 1881 (HQA LS).

and diplomatic representatives escorted the body back to the depot, whence it was transported to Cleveland, Ohio, for interment. Officers of the army received orders to wear badges of mourning on their left arms and on their swords for six months.[65]

The resumption of routine that followed these anxious weeks coincided with a familiar ritual at army headquarters: preparation of the annual report, in which Sherman forwarded to the secretary of war with his own remarks the detailed accounts he had received from commanders of the several military departments and divisions. Sherman always confined himself in the introductory statement to topics that concerned the army at large, shifting his emphasis as circumstances changed from year to year. In the report for 1881 he announced that serious war conditions no longer existed between the army and tribes of Indians. True, another Apache outbreak in Arizona Territory had not yet been brought under control, but the troubles with more northerly tribes, such as the unruly Utes of Colorado and the recalcitrant Sioux under Sitting Bull, seemed largely past. Good progress had been made in locating formerly hostile Indians on their proper reservations. Sherman thus devoted his primary attention to other matters of concern, chiefly the deployment, efficiency, and morale of the army as the period of Indian wars drew nearer its close.

By statute, at this period the enlisted force of the regular army was limited to twenty-five thousand men, a number that in Sherman's view was far too low. He asserted with pride that "in physique, in intelligence, in patriotic devotion to the honor and glory of the country," the fighting men of the army "will compare favorably with any similar establishment on earth." Still, the effectiveness of this body as a deterrent force was inhibited by the inadequate numerical strength of the individual companies that comprised it, the dispersion of its fighting units, and the abject conditions under which some of these units were obliged to perform their duties. Sherman argued "most earnestly" that, in view of the army's acknowledged contributions to the current national prosperity, increased attention should be paid to fostering its continued well-being. He called on Congress to pass a law authorizing

65. *ANJ*, September 24, 1881, p. 160.

each of the 430 companies in the regular forces to enroll at least fifty privates, a measure that would strengthen current artillery and infantry units by 25 percent.

Second, he described difficulties encountered by the army in its effort to reduce the number of its 190 posts. Communities threatened with closure of facilities in their vicinities were so clamorous to their political representatives that the status quo often prevailed, even though the presence of troops there was no longer necessary to protect life and property. To enable the army to commit its limited manpower more effectively, Sherman proposed the formation of an impartial board, with authority to study "the whole problem of internal defense" and to dispose of forts and installations that did not require permanent occupancy. By "permanent" Sherman of course meant the indefinite future, in which he could foresee no utilization of army forces that was materially different from what was being required of them at present. With this long-term perspective in view, he recommended that a statute still in force forbidding the construction of permanent army buildings except by special approval of Congress should be repealed. "The time for temporary structures has passed away," he declared. Construction of substantial stone or brick "would be true economy," for it would benefit the health and morale of soldiers and would ultimately cost less than the frequent repair and replacement required by wooden structures.[66]

Not mentioned in the annual report were other problems that concerned Sherman from year to year because of their negative impact on the morale of the army. One was the slow rate of promotion through the officers' ranks, particularly at the lower levels. In time of war, performance in the field might properly earn rapid elevation in rank that would provoke little objection from those who were thus passed over—in technical phrase, "overslaughed." However, during peacetime, promotion came almost invariably from seniority in rank alone. Whatever its shortcomings, this was the system Sherman thought most equitable. If it dampened some youthful ambitions, it need not do so unduly since forms of recognition other than promotion—special

66. *Report of the Secretary of War* (1881), pp. 32-36.

assignments, regimental staff details, desirable postings, commendations, mention in reports and general orders—were available to reward demonstrated merit. Besides, simply earning the good opinion of one's fellow officers ought to remain a powerful incitement; Sherman wished to instill a code of thought and conduct that joined all commissioned officers in dedication to patriotic duty and personal honor.[67]

But maintaining that esprit de corps was made difficult by a second demoralizing influence, the favoritism and political machination that so often led to the award of plum assignments and made possible the avoidance of hard or disagreeable service. For himself, the general shunned even the appearance of seeking preferment for friends and family members,[68] but others were less scrupulous. For example, Major David G. Swaim was a mid-level officer in the judge-advocate general's department at the time his boyhood friend James A. Garfield was elected president. Within a few weeks he was nominated for promotion to brigadier general, with authority over the entire Bureau of Military Justice.[69] The action was in Sherman's view a blow to the professional spirit of the whole army. Concerns like these had dictated his opposition several years before to the elevation of Lieutenant Colonel George Crook to a brigadier generalship. No matter how admirable Crook's recent successes in the far West might have been, promoting him would overslaugh four lieutenant colonels and twenty-five colonels of infantry, not a few of whom could boast service records years longer

67. For example, see Sherman's reprimand of Captain Philip L. Lee, Tenth Cavalry, who in November 1879 was found guilty of conduct unbecoming an officer and gentleman; *ITJ*, p. 67.

68. Probably the best-known instance of Sherman's unwillingness to exert his influence to advance the careers of those close to him occurred amidst the efforts of a relation by marriage, Colonel Nelson A. Miles, Fifth Infantry, to win a brigadier generalship. Sherman recognized the military ability of Miles but refused to offer support for his promotion. See Johnson, *The Unregimented General*, pp. 214–15. But Miles enlisted the aid of other influential persons and eventually won his brigadiership on December 15, 1880. See Coffman, *The Old Army*, p. 269; Fellman, *Citizen Sherman*, p. 281. A survey of Sherman's troubled relationship with Miles is given by Peter R. DeMontravel in *A Hero to His Fighting Men*, pp. 137–54.

69. *ANJ*, January 29, 1881, p. 519; February 26, 1881, p. 610; April 2, 1881, p. 721; March 14, 1885, p. 645; December 26, 1885, p. 435; Hamersley, *Records of Living Officers*, pp. 14–15.

and hardly less distinguished than his.[70] However, Sherman had no real power in the matter. Even nominating a man to fill one of the rare vacancies in the list of general officers was not a privilege he enjoyed.

Armed conflict between the army and the Indians might be almost a thing of the past, but within the service itself conflicts raged between senior officers, giving the commanding general a full measure of concern. Some antipathies expressed themselves through legal proceedings, such as the costly and time-consuming court-martial that pitted two infantry colonels, David S. Stanley and William B. Hazen, against each other in 1880. Others grew from events during the Civil War that had led to protracted campaigns for vindication or revenge. For example, the dismissal during the war of two officers, Granville O. Haller and Fitz-John Porter, resulted in long and ultimately successful efforts by both to win reinstatement.[71] Sherman himself was embroiled in controversy, the publication of his *Memoirs* in 1875 having spawned a progeny of counterstatements and verbal assaults.[72] But the form of competition most distressing to him in 1881 was the one among deserving senior colonels and brigadier generals for promotion to the ranks immediately below his.

Many officers still on the active list had served temporarily during the Civil War as general officers of regular army units or of volunteers.

70. *Official Army Register* (1873), pp. 184–85. On October 24, 1881, Sherman wrote to General Pope of the continuing frustration this act, authorized by President Ulysses S. Grant, had caused him:

> General Grant more than any other President before or since ignored the rule of promoting the senior. In Crook's case he passed the whole list of Colonels, and promoted a Lieutenant Colonel, so that subsequent Presidents find in his action a full warrant for the utter disregard of the rule itself. Both Terry and Mackenzie had almost a positive promise of promotion [from former President Hayes and the late President Garfield], and both of these officers believe I have defeated their hopes. If President Arthur will consult me I shall advise him to adhere to the old rule to promote the senior when he is worthy, and thereby avoid the necessary heart-burnings which will attend the practice of picking out favorites; but if he simply ask if Terry and Mackenzie are qualified, I must answer in the affirmative. (HQA LS)

71. For the Hazen-Stanley controversy, see Kroeker, *Great Plains Command*, pp. 154–63. For Haller, see Hamersley, *Records of Living Officers*, pp. 389–90; *ANJ*, March 30, 1878, p. 537; *ITJ*, pp. 322–23. For Porter, see Eisenschiml, *The Celebrated Case of Fitz-John Porter*, and Schofield, *Forty-Six Years in the Army*, pp. 460–66.

72. Marszalek, *Sherman*, pp. 461–67; Fellman, *Citizen Sherman*, pp. 316–40.

Through that field service they had developed military abilities that in too many cases had not been adequately utilized in the years since. Brigadier General John Pope, commander of the Department of the Missouri, had served with distinction in his assignment since 1870, and he craved promotion to major general and command over one of the three geographical divisions—the Military Divisions of the Pacific, of the Missouri, and of the Atlantic. Major General John M. Schofield had occupied his rank since 1869 and richly merited a new assignment commensurate with it—namely, one of the divisions. But none was vacant. Schofield had agreed to make a visit to Europe in order to give Sherman time to find him a suitable position, but this would be a daunting task.[73] The current commander of the Division of the Pacific, Major General Irvin McDowell, had assumed that position when Schofield vacated it, at the urgent request of Generals Sherman and Grant, to become commandant of cadets at West Point. But McDowell now showed no inclination to retire and so permit Schofield to reoccupy his old post.[74] Meanwhile other generals, including brigadiers George Crook, O. O. Howard, Nelson A. Miles, and Christopher C. Augur, all had their ambitions, their adherents, and their entitlements to consideration. Talented younger officers such as Colonel Ranald S. Mackenzie, Fourth Cavalry, clamored for a general's star and deserved it.

The army was top-heavy with military talent and experience, with too small a command organization to employ it fully. As one means of correcting the problem, Sherman supported a measure that had been considered but not enacted by Congress in its most recent session: to require the retirement of army officers at the age of sixty-two. As another solution, more limited in its effect, he was considering the possibility of vacating his own command.[75] Such an action would enable him to continue performing whatever special duties the president might delegate to him, and it would also permit his heir-apparent,

73. Schofield, *Forty-Six Years in the Army*, pp. 446–51; WTS to General W. S. Hancock, June 13, 1881 (HQA LS); *ANJ*, December 25, 1880, p. 418.

74. "McDowell has held on with a selfishness and tenacity that seemed to me at times almost indecent," Sherman wrote to Schofield on September 29, 1882 (HQA LS).

75. WTS to General W. S. Hancock, June 13, 1881 (HQA LS).

Sheridan, to vacate his Chicago command and each of the three major generals—Hancock, McDowell, and Schofield—to command a military division.

Sherman was an efficient administrator with a detailed knowledge of the units under his authority and a keen sense of priorities that enabled him to marshal his limited forces effectively. But the sort of problems posed by cronyism, political influence, and the conflicting claims of other generals he found more frustrating, for they admitted no easy solution. To officers who wrote him complaining of their slow promotion or soliciting his advice as to the best strategy for obtaining nomination to a higher rank, he could offer little encouragement or assistance. To Pope, whom he admired, he counseled finding some friend to make his case, preferably an influential senator. He wrote frankly to Mackenzie that, when he had last recommended him for promotion, he was "overruled with almost an admonition" not to meddle. To Colonel Henry J. Hunt, a veteran artillery officer, he explained that only mandatory retirement for age would break the logjam of officers who ranked him on the lineal list. As to himself, he added, "I am in favor of compulsory retirement . . . at 62 or 65, don't care which."[76]

In view of his frustration at the lack of authority to correct problems within the army that he recognized so clearly, Sherman must have welcomed the opportunity to assist deserving officers under his command, when it arose. For example, in April 1881 he wrote Sheridan pointing out the personal difficulties then being faced by Colonel Alexander McD. McCook, Sixth Infantry, his former aide-de-camp. McCook's wife was seriously ill, and since his regiment had a just claim for transfer to a more desirable station, such a move might well prove helpful to him at a critical time. A few months later Sheridan acted on this tacit suggestion, and a suitable exchange of regimental stations occurred.[77]

76. WTS to General John Pope, October 24, 1881; WTS to Colonel Ranald S. Mackenzie, September 28, 1882; WTS to Hunt, April 20, 1881 (all in HQA LS).

77. WTS to General Philip H. Sheridan, May 10, 1881 (HQA LS); *ANJ*, March 16, 1881, p. 698; September 10, 1881, p. 114.

Though in a sense less personal, Sherman's action to promote the forthcoming book by Dodge was no less effective. By December 1881 the work had been assigned a title, *Our Wild Indians*,[78] and Dodge had received proofsheets for review. Sherman now read through the proofs himself and addressed Dodge a fifteen hundred-word letter, obviously intended for publication, in which he praised the book and commended it heartily to the American reading public. Whether he volunteered this favor or acceded to a request is not known, but Dodge was deeply grateful for his commander's willingness to associate his name with *Our Wild Indians*. The published work was "Dedicated (by permission) to William Tecumseh Sherman, General of the Army of the United States."[79]

In his commendatory letter, Sherman addressed both aims of *Our Wild Indians*—to present factual data about its subject in a readable yet authoritative manner and also to advocate reform. Emphasizing the author's years of contact with Indians, he characterized the book as "the record of your personal observations, with dates, facts and figures, which constitute the very best testimony available on the subject-matter treated of." In the greater part of his letter he discussed Dodge's criticism of United States Indian policy. He began in statesmanlike fashion by observing that he could not agree with Dodge "and the world generally in accusing our ancestors and the General Government with a deliberate purpose to be unjust to, and to defraud these people." Dodge's blanket condemnation of Indian agents as incompetent or dishonest was also an exaggeration, he thought,[80] but he did register

78. Except for a few unpublished fragments, the manuscript of Dodge's book has not survived, and the title he originally intended to give it is not known. The work was published with a sesquipedalian title whose length and colorful language were characteristic of volumes issued by A. D. Worthington: *Our Wild Indians: Thirty-Three Years' Personal Experience Among the Red Men of the Great West. A Popular Account of Their Social Life, Religion, Habits, Traits, Customs, Exploits, etc. With Thrilling Adventures and Experiences on the Great Plains and in the Mountains of Our Wide Frontier*. The Worthington publication that followed *Our Wild Indians* was *Our Famous Women*, also with a lengthy subtitle (1883).

79. *OWI*, p. [iii]. The dedication was printed on six lines, in two different fonts and four type sizes.

80. Actually Dodge did not make this claim in *Our Wild Indians,* as an anonymous correspondent of the *Army and Navy Journal* later pointed out. That individual also expressed agreement with Dodge in his general condemnation of Indian agents (April 22, 1882, p. 870).

agreement with the book's criticism of the reservation system as it was then administered. The cause of the Indian Bureau's failure lay "elsewhere, in the nature of things, rather than in a systematic desire to do wrong."

Sherman went on to point out an essential connection between certain Indian beliefs and customs described by Dodge and the reforms to Indian policy he was advocating. In the general's view, the absence in the Indian of "a moral sense as connected with religion"—a principle developed at some length by Dodge[81]—demonstrated the folly of efforts by the Indian Bureau to induce changes in behavior through religious instruction. He was convinced, he wrote, that "the military authorities of the United States are better qualified to guide the steps of the Indian towards that conclusion which we all desire, self-support and peaceful relations with his neighbors, than the civilian agents, most of whom are members of some one of our Christian churches." Congress, of course, exercised jurisdiction over Indian policy. Sherman expressed confidence that its members would welcome *Our Wild Indians,* since it would afford them new comprehension of the issues surrounding the government's relationship with Native Americans, a subject "which has always been involved in honest doubt." Concluding his statement, Sherman commended the book to all thinking Americans:

> The subject-matter of your volume has dramatic interest to a large class of the American people, is fair and just in its reasoning, and liberal in its tone; and I therefore take great pleasure in recommending it to the military student and to the general reading public, as by far the best description extant of the habits, manners, customs, usages, ceremonies, etc., of the American Indian as he now is.
>
> You are hereby authorized to use my name as authority for its publication and circulation; and I invite all persons interested in the subject of the North American Indian to read this book carefully, to the end that public opinion may aid the national authorities to deal justly and liberally with the remnants of that race which preceded us on this continent.[82]

81. See *OWI*, pp. 101–15; see also *PNA*, pp. 247–48.
82. *OWI*, pp. xxxv–xxxix.

Dating the letter at Washington, D.C., January 1, 1882, the general appended his signature in his flowing hand. Reproduced in facsimile, that signature concluded the letter as published in *Our Wild Indians*, where it served as the introduction.

When printed, bound, and ready for distribution, *Our Wild Indians* was a strikingly attractive book. Its binding was of deep red cloth, richly illuminated with designs in black ink and gold foil. On the front cover, between pressed patterns at top and bottom, appeared an engraving in gold of an Indian war shield, with a tomahawk and war club arranged crosswise behind it. To the right was the book's short title, with below it the facsimile signatures of the author and the general. The spine was decorated in gilt from top to bottom, with the names of Dodge and Sherman printed in letters of equal size. At the bottom of the spine, just above an engraving that showed a mounted Indian about to thrust his lance at a fleeing buffalo, appeared in conspicuous capital letters the word "illustrated," announcing a major feature of the work's sales appeal. The twenty-five pages of illustrations, listed immediately after a brief preface by Dodge, included two engravings on steel, seventeen on wood, and the six chromo-lithograph plates. In a note preceding a list of the plates' contents, the publisher described the processes involved in their preparation. He emphasized the minute accuracy of the impressions, "no expense or pains having been spared."[83] The text, crisply printed and generally free of compositional errors, appeared on 653 pages following the front matter.

A. D. Worthington's boastful characterization of the volume as "the most artistic and sumptuous book ever issued from the American press" was of course transparent advertiser's hyperbole.[84] Still, *Our Wild Indians* was a creditable production and a good value at the prices offered. The extra cloth edition described here, printed on tinted paper with sprinkled edges, was for sale at $3.50. A leather-bound "library" edition was priced at $4.00, and a plain cloth edition, printed on white

83. "List of Chromo-Lithograph Plates, with Descriptions and Explanations," *OWI*, p. ix. The engravers and printers of the plates were identified here as Bingham, Dodd & Co., Hartford, Connecticut.

84. "Thirty-Three Years' Personal Experience Among Our Wild Indians," p. [1] (Dodge Papers, Graff).

paper and without the steel engravings and fifteen-color plates, cost $2.75. The book was not for sale in bookstores; it could be purchased only directly by mail from the publisher or else through one of his agents. The initial print run was an optimistic twenty thousand copies.

Worthington now launched an ambitious marketing campaign. To create public awareness of the book, he sent 150 copies of the library edition to major newspapers from New England to Virginia and as far west as Illinois, soliciting reviews. This gambit proved successful, for in the early months of 1882 the book was widely and favorably noticed in the public press. The *New York Herald* praised Dodge's "bright, fresh, and frank" writing style and "painstaking labor" in compiling so thorough a treatment. The *Chicago Inter-Ocean* assured its readers that *Our Wild Indians* "will be considered the standard authority on its subject, as it deserves to be." Chaplain George G. Mullins, in charge of education in the army, suggested in the *Army and Navy Register* that copies of the book be placed in the reading rooms of military posts. Within the army an awareness of the book's merits was made certain by an extended review in the *Army and Navy Journal*, the lead article in its issue for February 18, 1882. According to the anonymous reviewer, *Our Wild Indians* "is one of the most valuable contributions ever made to the study of Indian life and character."[85]

The next stage in Worthington's sales program was to canvass in the national capital for subscriptions from well-known persons to purchase the book. His agent for this purpose, a Rev. Wilson, applied himself energetically to the task. Early in March the *Army and Navy Journal* remarked, perhaps archly, that the clergyman's subscription list "bids fair to be a most valuable autograph album."[86] The Rev. Wilson obtained signatures of the president, members of his Cabinet, General

85. "Thirty-Three Years' Personal Experience Among Our Wild Indians," p. [2] (Dodge Papers, Graff); *ANJ*, February 18, 1882, pp. 640–41. See also *New York Times*, May 21, 1882, p. 11; *JMSI* 3 (1882): 287.

86. "Washington is an excellent missionary field for Gen. Dodge to work in," the writer continued. "If the public business could be suspended for a day, and the time devoted by the members of Congress and other public officials to reading his book we might save time and money in the end by promoting a peaceful end of our Indian problem" (*ANJ*, March 4, 1882, p. 681). As in this instance, Dodge was often erroneously referred to as "General," even occasionally by Sherman.

Sherman and various other high-ranking army officers, former president Ulysses S. Grant, and many other persons of special note. Worthington had now enlisted the support of major newspapers and public personages whose approval of the work would likely stimulate sales. By late June eight thousand copies of *Our Wild Indians* had been spoken for, and new orders were pouring in.[87]

Little is known about what parts, if any, Dodge and Sherman played in this stage of the publisher's sales campaign. A widely attended reception at the home of the general on January 17 afforded opportunity for conversation about the forthcoming book, whose issue within a few more weeks was common knowledge. By writing his introductory letter, Sherman had lent *Our Wild Indians* a character that was, if not quite official, then at least ratified by official recognition and support. But beyond that point he could hardly pass if he were to preserve the dignity of his office. For his own part, as author of the work Dodge kept in mind possible outlets for distribution, especially to army officers and men. He called on Brigadier General Rufus Ingalls, the quartermaster general, to discuss the possibility of copies being purchased by the government for distribution to army posts.[88] Confident that he had produced a work of real usefulness, he made no secret of his desire for it to achieve a wide circulation.

Dodge was well pleased with the physical product of Worthington's bookmaking, but the publisher's emphasis in advertisements on the book's design, illustrations, and generally exciting contents did not fully satisfy him. He had conceived *Our Wild Indians* as also a tract for the times, a passionate call for change. Some reviewers had recognized this aim, but as the marketing of the work continued Dodge was troubled at representations of it as in effect an attractive acquisition for placement on a parlor table. For this reason, he drafted a separate discussion of the Indian question as he viewed it, issuing the result as a pamphlet, *A Living Issue*.

87. Statement of Account, A. D. Worthington & Co. with RID, January 1, 1883 (Dodge Papers, Graff).

88. Alexander J. Perry, Deputy Quartermaster General, to RID, November 18, 1882 (Dodge Papers, Graff). General Ingalls had subscribed for a personal copy of *Our Wild Indians*.

In the preface to that work, dated May 20, 1882, Dodge described Worthington's early objections to the political views expressed in the manuscript that became *Our Wild Indians*. However, he wrote, "[t]he facts and arguments set forth in that MSS. are (in my opinion) of too much importance to the honor of the Country to be lost; and I am in too much earnest to remain silent under all the wrongs and outrages heaped upon the Indian."[89] Dodge thus sought to turn the temporary fame of *Our Wild Indians* to some positive legislative effect. He signed the pamphlet's prefatory statement not as an army officer but as a plain citizen, Richard I. Dodge. Issued early in June, *A Living Issue* bore on its title-page a quoted statement by Senator George F. Edmunds, chairman of the Judiciary Committee, affirming the value to civilized society of "the courage of sincere, individual opinion" expressed in matters of public affairs.[90]

Inspection Tours, South and North

During the early months of 1882 General Sherman brought into sharper focus his views on the proper deployment of U.S. troops along the southern and northern national borders in the western states and territories. Three great railroad routes now spanned the region: the Southern Pacific, along the border with Mexico, and two branches of the Union Pacific, across the central plains. Two more railroads were nearing completion: the Atlantic and Pacific across central New Mexico

89. "Explanatory," *A Living Issue*, p. [2]. Dodge noted that the wording in some portions of the pamphlet "is identical with that in 'Our Wild Indians.' That book, designed to be a minute and careful study of the interior life of the Wild Indians, gives only general conclusions as to their management and ultimate destination. This pamphlet gives the facts and arguments on which those conclusions are based."

The precise impact of *Our Wild Indians* and *A Living Issue* on sentiment that led to the reform of federal Indian policy cannot be gauged. However, Dodge's efforts warranted discussion by Loring Benson Priest in his classic survey of the public debates that ended in enactment of the Dawes Severalty Act of 1887; see Priest, *Uncle Sam's Stepchildren*, pp. 39, 119, 196.

90. In full, the quoted statement by Edmunds was as follows: "There is, perhaps, no one thing so valuable to the right progress of civilized society as the courage of sincere, individual opinion; and, as regards public affairs, the man who tries honestly to form an accurate conclusion, and bravely to maintain and advance it, without counting the number of his adversaries, will fulfill the best mission of a citizen."

and Arizona and the Northern Pacific, passing west from Duluth, Minnesota, to Portland, Oregon, and Puget Sound in Washington Territory. All these projects were powerful facilitators of national development. "No person," Sherman had written recently, "who has not been across the continent by the several routes, can possibly comprehend the changes there."[91]

In earlier years small army detachments had protected settlements along the great wagon routes against lawlessness and depredation, but those routes had now been supplanted by railroads. Sherman thus intended to refine a plan for the housing and transportation of army units near railroads along the nation's southwestern and northwestern borders. As the general had suggested in his annual report for 1881, only forts already existing at points of strategic importance—as, for example, at the junction of several rail routes—should be made permanent, all others being disposed of at once or else maintained for a few more years and then abandoned. Eventually, with a cordon of permanent posts within easy each of the Southern Pacific and Northern Pacific lines, the small United States Army could guarantee the nation's security along its two continental borders.

Sherman had last traversed these approximate routes only a few years before. In 1879 he had passed over the southern road as one of a party accompanying President Rutherford B. Hayes, but that hurried journey had not afforded him opportunity to perform the careful onsite inspections necessary to warrant recommendations. The northern route he had not seen since 1877, when the Northern Pacific had been constructed only as far west as Bismarck, Dakota Territory.[92] In

91. *Report of the Secretary of War* (1882), p. 5. Sherman had made virtually the same statement in a report from the Pacific Northwest in 1877; see *Travel Accounts*, p. 69. Sherman's perception of railroad construction as a crucial contributor to development of the western states and territories is a major theme of Athearn, *William Tecumseh Sherman and the Settlement of the West*. A more general account of the army's role in promoting this process is Tate's *The Frontier Army in the Settlement of the West*. For an early discussion of the army's impact, see *ANJ*, August 20, 1881, p. 54.

92. Sherman's record of this journey, in a series of letters to the secretary of war, was published the following year in *Reports of Inspection Made in the Summer of 1877 by Generals P. H. Sheridan and W. T. Sherman of Country North of the Union Pacific Railroad*. It has been reprinted in *Travel Accounts*, pp. 41-83, to which further citations of *Reports of Inspection* refer.

the coming year he hoped to pass over both the railroads, so as to consider the military requirements there for a last time in his career. As a preliminary to the southern tour, early in 1881 he dispatched Colonel Poe, his specialist in engineering, to study several of the posts in Texas and New Mexico that he proposed to visit. Poe's report, with recommendations, appeared in the public press shortly after his return from the assignment,[93] provoking outcries of alarm from communities identified as no longer in need of a military presence nearby.

In February 1882 preparations for the general's initial inspection tour began in earnest. Post and departmental commanders along the proposed itinerary received due notice, and railroad officials were asked what accommodations they could supply in regard to equipment and scheduling. Some of the latter correspondence Sherman conducted himself, asking for no special arrangements other than the use of a single car that could be left at railroad sidings at a convenient distance from posts he would need to reach by wagon transport.[94] He pointed out to the businessmen that the projected journey should benefit their corporations, both for the publicity the tour would receive and also for the enhanced security the roads would eventually gain from the army policy he had in mind. He volunteered to pay regular train fare for himself and his party, which would consist of Colonel Morrow, Colonel Poe, Poe's daughter Winifred, and his own daughter Lizzie.[95] He noted, however, that the government reimbursed army officers' travel expenses at the miserly rate of eight cents per mile. Most of his correspondents responded generously to this tacit request, extending the privilege of their roads without charge.[96] Sherman

93. *ANJ*, February 26, 1881, p. 619; April 2, 1881, p. 728; April 9, 1881, p. 749. As a consequence of the Poe report, General Augur, commander of the Department of Texas, directed expeditions in the southwestern section of Texas in search of suitable post sites (*ANJ*, June 18, 1881, p. 963).

94. For example, see WTS to H. M. Hoxie, January 20, 1882; WTS to C. P. Huntington, January 20, 1882 (HQA LS).

95. WTS to General Irvin McDowell, February 1, 1882 (HQA LS). Lizzie was Mary Elizabeth Sherman, Sherman's younger daughter, then twenty-nine years of age.

96. Collis P. Huntington, president of the Southern Pacific Railroad, was not so generous. In a letter to Huntington of May 19, 1882, Sherman enclosed payment of $210.00 and with pointed politeness affirmed the likelihood that "I will never have occasion to tax your time or patience again" (HQA LS).

planned to devote the month of March to Texas, April to New Mexico and Arizona Territories, and a few days in May to California, returning east via the Atlantic and Pacific route and arriving back in Washington in mid-May.

Almost from its inception, the borderlands tour took on a public character. Demonstrations of good feeling greeted the celebrity general repeatedly as he passed through these remote regions. In Texas he was feted at Forts Clark, Ellis, and Bliss and welcomed exuberantly by the local citizenry. In speeches before the city fathers of San Antonio and El Paso he expressed gratified wonder at the growth in those places since his last visit, in 1871. From the latter city he and his party made an excursion 125 miles into Mexico on the Mexico Central Railroad, then under construction. Earlier, near Fort Clark, they had watched a Southern Pacific construction crew laying track toward New Orleans, Louisiana, at the rate of two miles per day.[97] Truly, settlements along the seventeen hundred-mile border with Mexico were being linked together at railroad speed.

Residents of the towns west of El Paso greeted the Sherman train with sometimes alarming enthusiasm. On the party's arrival by wagon at Tombstone, Arizona Territory, a "cowboyish-looking individual" rode up and asked whether the general was present. Assured that he was, he raised his pistol and fired two shots in rapid succession, the signal for a cacophonous welcome that included fireworks, ringing anvils, and discharge of guns of all types. That evening the celebration continued with a bonfire in the main street, an outdoors dinner, and a brief speech by Sherman.[98] At Tucson, military and civil authorities vied in their efforts to please the distinguished guest, who enjoyed himself immensely. The tour reached its end point in San Francisco, California, on April 23. At the Presidio, headquarters of the Division of the Pacific, Sherman conferred with General McDowell, attended a recep-

97. WTS to Robert T. Lincoln, March 18, 1882; March 26, 1882; *ANJ*, April 8, 1882, pp. 803, 809, 815. A consolidated file that includes Sherman's inspection reports and recommendations for posts along the Rio Grande frontier is 1513 AGO 1882, available in NARA microfilm publication M989, Roll 91.

98. *ANJ*, April 22, 1882, p. 860; April 29, 1882, p. 880. The quotation is from the latter article.

tion, reviewed the troops, and visited army colleagues before running a gamut of social engagements in the city proper. One of these, at the Poodle Dog Restaurant, was convened in his honor by fifteen old friends, companions during his residence in San Francisco more than three decades earlier, first as a military officer and later as a banker.[99]

Clearly for Sherman the ten-week tour, which concluded in Washington, D.C., on May 14, combined the official with the personal. During its progress he addressed to Secretary of War Robert T. Lincoln a series of letters that exhibited this same double quality, conjoining general description of travel and sightseeing with other matter, the result of his official inquiries. In the latter passages he set forth in plain terms and in considerable detail his analysis of military needs, together with recommendations for action by the secretary. Along the Texas frontier Sherman identified six key posts: on the lower Rio Grande River, Forts Duncan, McIntosh, and Sam Houston; on the more northerly western section, Fort Davis, Camp Rice (later redesignated Fort Hancock), and Fort Bliss. He urged a Congressional appropriation of two hundred thousand dollars for further construction at these six locations, recommending the abandonment of all intervening forts and other facilities. In New Mexico and Arizona, he saw need for only four posts along the southern frontier: Forts Grant, Huachuca, Apache, and Thomas. To preserve and strengthen these, he recommended the expenditure of another two hundred thousand dollars, noting, however, that once General Crook had subdued the Apaches, the two latter forts could likely also be abandoned.[100]

Sherman thus achieved his aim of identifying a line of posts within easy reach of the Southern Pacific Railroad that, without inordinate expense, would "put that whole frontier in a good and permanent condition of defense."[101] Naturally, in his view the costs to the govern-

99. *ANJ*, May 13, 1882, p. 932.

100. WTS to Robert T. Lincoln, March 18, 1882; March 26, 1882; March 30, 1882; April 14, 1882 (HQA LS).

101. WTS to Robert T. Lincoln, October 16, 1882 (HQA LS). This letter was published in *Report of the Secretary of War* (1882), pp. 10–17. It contained the general's recommendations to that date for the army's posts to be made permanent along the nation's five "frontiers," which he identified as the Atlantic and Gulf, the northern, the southern or Mexican, the Pacific, and the interior.

ment of a journey such as he had made were more than compensated by the benefits of his thoughtful presence in the districts he inspected. The objections of critics like Senator James B. Beck of Kentucky, who accused him early in 1882 of traveling at public expense in luxurious state, nominally on official errands but actually for pleasure, incensed him. In a letter to his brother John, a senator from Ohio, he vented angry frustration at Beck. The upcoming tour would cost him at least one thousand dollars out of his own pocket, he wrote, and to be criticized as greedily helping himself to government funds while doing his duty was absurd.[102]

Not long after his return to army headquarters, Sherman traveled to Detroit, Michigan, to attend a reunion of the Society of the Army of the Potomac. Then, on his arrival back in the capital, he expressed a resolve to stay put. "Got enough travelling," he brusquely informed a reporter; "got to stay at home and get to work."[103] Not mentioned in this statement was his eager anticipation of the second reconnaissance tour, which he expected would begin early in the fall. Though not yet made public, plans for the northwestern excursion were already well advanced. Its official purpose was identical with that of the recently completed journey—to inspect military posts along the Northern Pacific Railroad so as to identify the locations that would remain essential to the nation's permanent defense. The rapidly approaching completion of the Northern Pacific would make the examination far more convenient than it had been five years before. The road was now in service past Bozeman, Montana Territory, adjacent to Fort Ellis, and

102. WTS to John Sherman, February 28, 1882 (HQA LS). Three days earlier Sherman had addressed Beck directly, referring to comments by the senator in the *Congressional Record* for that day: "I don't know whether to be more amused than surprised," he began, "at your reference to the fact that I travel in Palace cars at public expense on the plea of inspecting military posts. When General Sherman travels under orders he draws eight cents a mile, just as any second Lieutenant. If he has a Palace car he pays for it out of his own pocket for the quartermaster will not. Never in my life did I hire at public expense a Palace or sleeping car, and when I have had such a luxury, it has been as the guest of some more wealthy gentleman" (HQA LS). Beck was not yet satisfied, however. He continued to complain of travel funds being wasted by army officers on journeys of no real value. See *ANJ*, May 6, 1882, p. 916.

103. *ANJ*, June 24, 1882, p. 1080. The interview was acknowledged as from the New York *World*.

was under construction through difficult terrain toward Missoula, not far from another post.

The late-summer tour would follow the railroad as far as Fort Ellis, but from that point it would involve travel by wagon, on horseback, and perhaps even afoot through the region where the construction crews had not yet penetrated. Sherman planned to retrace a part of the route he had followed in his 1877 reconnaissance expedition. From Fort Ellis he would proceed south, to renew acquaintance with Yellowstone National Park, then west across the continental divide to the Bitterroot Valley. Returning northward along that valley to Missoula, he would follow the old Mullan wagon road further west to Fort Coeur d'Alene, in Idaho Territory.[104] The cross-country portion of the tour would be too rugged for ladies, but for himself Sherman relished the prospect of travel through the semi-wilderness. Three official acquaintances, Morrison R. Waite, chief justice of the Supreme Court, and associate justices John Marshall Harlan and Horace Gray, had expressed interest in accompanying him. He promised himself some satisfaction in introducing these distinguished easterners to the rigors of army-style travel.

Sherman's plans for the second inspection tour were suddenly overset when, in conversation with Robert T. Lincoln on June 5, he learned that the secretary had accepted an invitation from Sheridan to join another expedition of his own to the Yellowstone National Park and points in its vicinity. That the nation's two highest-ranking army officers should both be absent from their posts for weeks at a time was not to be thought of. Sherman at once decided to postpone his northwestern journey until the following summer. After all, he had done his full share of traveling in the months just past, and Sheridan's idea of introducing Lincoln to some of the undeveloped territory under his authority seemed prudent in view of the close working relationship the two men would need to maintain in future years.

104. WTS to General Irvin McDowell, February 21, 1882; WTS to General Alfred H. Terry, March 7 and May 20, 1883; WTS to General Philip H. Sheridan, May 20, 1883 (HQA LS). During his 1877 tour of the northwest, Sherman had recommended establishment of a post on Lake Coeur d'Alene (*Travel Accounts*, pp. 69, 83). Accordingly, on April 16, 1878, Fort Coeur d'Alene was established on the north shore of the lake where the Spokane River debouches from it (Frazer, *Forts of the West*, p. 46).

Following an exchange of letters with Judge Waite to confirm the postponement of their journey until the summer of 1883, just after the adjournment of the Supreme Court's spring term, on June 19 Sherman telegraphed Sheridan wishing him a good trip. He concluded this message with a statement that, while not unanticipated, was of considerable significance to both men. He had begun shaping his private affairs, he wrote, "so as to enable you to take my place" as General of the Army before the convening of Congress in December 1883.[105] From the date of this telegram, Sherman's inspection tour of the northwestern forts formed part of a planned sequence of events that would culminate in his retirement from the army on his sixty-fourth birthday, February 8, 1884.

Assignment's End

By June it was clear that, when approved by Congress, the annual army appropriation bill would likely include a clause mandating the retirement from active service of commissioned officers upon their reaching the age of sixty-four. Sherman welcomed the development for several reasons, not least because the first general officer to be retired under the law would be Major General McDowell, the dog-in-the-manger commander of the Division of the Pacific. His departure would enable Schofield to reoccupy his old command, placing an officer of appropriate rank in charge of all three military divisions.[106] That arrangement should last out Sherman's tenure in office, after which time the vacancy created by Sheridan's departure from the Division of the Missouri would initiate another round of competition between the present brigadiers. As he wrote a departmental commander in late June, he hoped to "gracefully retire" with the military mosaic all in place, the divisions under major generals and the departments within them under brigadier generals or senior colonels.[107]

105. WTS to Morrison R. Waite, June 6 and June 15, 1882; WTS to General Philip H. Sheridan, June 15 and June 19, 1882 (HQA LS).

106. WTS to Colonel Orlando B. Willcox, June 27, 1882; WTS to General John M. Schofield, September 29, 1882 (HQA LS).

107. WTS to Colonel Orlando B. Willcox, June 27, 1882 (HQA LS).

It had been known for several months that Sherman would soon lose a member of his personal staff, Colonel Dodge, who was in line for promotion to a regular colonelcy and the command of a regiment. At the beginning of 1882 Dodge had stood sixth in seniority among lieutenant colonels of infantry.[108] By June several resignations had resulted in his imminent advancement, even without operation of the anticipated compulsory retirement law. The retirement on June 22 of Colonel Daniel Huston, Fifth Infantry, promoted Lieutenant Colonel John D. Wilkins to command of that crack regiment, which had distinguished itself under its former colonel, now Brigadier General Nelson A. Miles. It was widely assumed that Wilkins would retire almost immediately, leaving Dodge to command the Fifth.[109] However, the resignation on June 26 of another officer, Colonel William H. Wood, Eleventh Infantry, made Dodge eligible for promotion to that command instead.[110] The president forwarded his nomination for the position to Congress without delay, but since confirmation of such appointments was ordinarily done in leisurely fashion, several more weeks would likely elapse before Dodge could be ordered to join his new regiment.[111] Until then, he remained officially a member of the general's personal staff.

Sherman had received recommendations, and even some direct applications, to fill the anticipated vacancy among his aides-de-camp, when in mid-July he received a letter from General Pope, who named as a worthy candidate Dodge's junior colleague and friend Captain George M. Randall, Twenty-third Infantry.[112] Responding to Pope, Sherman agreed that Randall's good standing was well deserved, he having "rendered a large share of that very kind of frontier service which ought to be rewarded, and which I have endeavored to do during my term of office." Still, he wrote, he had decided some time before that

108. *Official Army Register* (1882), p. 343.

109. *ANJ*, June 24, 1882, p. 1081. Wilkins, a graduate of West Point in the class of 1842, had completed forty years of active service.

110. *ANJ*, July 1, 1882, pp. 1104, 1109.

111. *ANJ*, July 1, 1882, p. 1110; July 8, 1882, p. 1133.

112. For Dodge's earlier contacts with Randall, see *PREJ*, pp. 129–30, 167, 169–70; *ITJ*, index. In 1889 Randall was selected as an aide-de-camp to Major General George Crook (*ANJ*, July 20, 1889, p. 959; July 27, 1889, p. 986).

in times of peace the General of the Army required no more than three or perhaps four aides. He had let it be known that, barring unforeseen conditions, he would no longer fill the vacancies that occurred on his staff. Colonels Tidball, Morrow, and Dodge would be his last appointments.[113]

Once Dodge joined his regiment in Dakota Territory, he was likely to remain on the north-central plains for some time. Accordingly, in the interim before his confirmation, Sherman granted him permission to visit his family, all of whom resided in the eastern states. He traveled first to his childhood home in rural North Carolina, where he saw his sisters and ailing mother, and then to the residence he maintained for his wife and son in New York City.[114] On August 11 a telegram reached him at the latter place, containing the first order he received at his new rank. He was designated a member of a blue-ribbon court martial that was to begin meeting ten days hence at Newport Barracks, Kentucky, headquarters of the Department of the South.[115] The case was one of particular concern to Sherman, who remained determined to combat political influence and favoritism in the issuance of army appointments and assignments to duty.

The accused officer, Major Joseph H. Taylor, was a respected West Point graduate with a solid record, but he would appear before the court to answer charges of conduct prejudicial to good order and military discipline. At the time of the alleged offense, Taylor occupied a responsible position as assistant adjutant general for the Department of the South. On July 29 an order was issued by the Adjutant General's Office at Washington, directing his transfer to the Department of the Platte, with headquarters at Omaha, Nebraska, to serve there in the same capacity. But having brought his family with him to Newport Barracks and made arrangements to remain in that location,

113. WTS to General John Pope, July 15, 1882 (HQA LS).

114. Dodge's wife, Julia Rhinelander Paulding Dodge, resided with Frederick, their only child, at 110 West 125th Street. Dodge and she had not shared a home since 1876, in part owing to her distaste for his frontier postings. See *ITJ*, pp. 432–33n and index. Dodge was relieved as aide-de-camp by S.O. 163, HQA, July 15, 1882, which was reprinted in *ANJ*, July 22, 1882, p. 1183.

115. RID to AG, August 11, 1882 (AGO LR); *ANJ*, August 19, 1882, p. 52.

he preferred not to make the move.[116] On July 31 he addressed a letter to the adjutant general, Brigadier General Richard C. Drum, informing him that he could see no reason for the transfer other than to gratify the wishes of a junior officer who wished to remain in Washington. He informed Drum that he had asked the senators of his home state, Kentucky, to exert their influence to secure revocation of the order.

Taylor assured the general that he had no wish to conceal his effort to enlist this political assistance.[117] Nevertheless, his appeal to the senators contravened a directive issued two years earlier by Sherman forbidding evasive actions of this sort.[118] A military trial to consider the infraction was thus called for. The judgment of the court, under the presidency of Brigadier General Christopher C. Augur, was awaited with interest, since Taylor's behavior could be considered a test case. Private and semi-official correspondence among army officers often dealt with dissatisfactions such as Taylor had expressed, and as all knew, the practice of seeking political support was pervasive. Inasmuch as Taylor's letter to General Drum was open and above board, exactly how reprehensible was his misconduct?

In sessions over three days the court considered two sets of charges and specifications against the accused officer. To the first charge, that his correspondence with the senators was prejudicial to military discipline, Taylor held that his action was not subject to trial under the Articles of War, and the court sustained him. To the second, that the letter to General Drum manifested "contempt and disregard" for his orders and so was conduct prejudicial to good order and military discipline, he pled not guilty, but the court disagreed. Wisely, however, it recommended a light sentence: Taylor was "[t]o be reprimanded in orders by the General of the Army." Sherman issued his public rebuke

116. *ANJ*, August 12, 1882, p. 17; August 26, 1882, p. 72.

117. J. H. Taylor to General Richard C. Drum, July 31, 1882 (*ANJ*, September 9, 1882, p. 128). Taylor had appealed for assistance not only to Senators James B. Beck and John S. Williams of Kentucky, but also to a congressman from that state, John G. Carlisle. Moreover, as son-in-law of Brigadier General Montgomery C. Meigs, the recently retired quartermaster general, Taylor may have had access to yet further intervention.

118. *ANJ*, August 26, 1882, p. 72; see also July 15, 1882, p. 1155.

on August 31, Taylor reported to his new duty station,[119] and there the test case—but not abuses of influence more flagrant than the court had considered—ended.

Following the Taylor trial, Dodge returned to Washington for a few days before departing for Fort Snelling, Minnesota, headquarters of the Department of Dakota, where he was to report to his new commander, Brigadier General Alfred H. Terry. Sherman was himself about to depart with his family and the Tidballs for a few days of relaxation at Lake Winnipesaukee, New Hampshire. During his final days of service at army headquarters, Dodge no doubt expressed to the general his gratitude for various good offices, in the preparation of *Our Wild Indians* and in other ways. To his satisfaction, Sherman promised to make him a member of the following summer's official tour as far as Fort Missoula, at the western boundary of the Department of Dakota.[120]

It had become the general's custom to address letters of thanks to departing members of his staff for whom he felt special regard. In full, the letter he wrote to Dodge appears below:

Headquarters Army of the United States,
Washington D.C., Sept. 2d, 1882.

Dear Dodge:

When McCook was promoted to the 6th Infantry, from my staff, I endeavored to frame a General Order congratulating him on his promotion, and thanking him for his services as A.D.C. on my staff, but the more I thought of it, it seemed tame and unprofitable;[121] for peace does

119. GCMO 54, HQA, August 31, 1882 was reprinted in full in *ANJ*, September 9, 1882, p. 128. In his reprimand, Sherman defined the issue at stake in the Taylor trial: "To seek outside influence, or to accept outside influence when a sure mode of redress for all real grievances is given by the statutes and usages governing the Army, is destructive to all good discipline, and the higher the officer, the more exalted his reputation and fame, the worse the example. If Major Taylor may with impunity defy any orders, regulations, and usages, and resort to irregular and forbidden methods, other officers will surely do the same, with equal if not greater impunity."

120. WTS to General Alfred H. Terry, May 20, 1883 (HQA LS).

121. In G.O. 82, HQA, December 17, 1880, Sherman paid tribute to Colonel McCook and Colonel Whipple on their departure from his staff and also announced the three new staff members—Dodge, Tidball, and Morrow. The portion of the order he found wanting was as follows: "The General thanks these distinguished officers for the zeal and fidelity manifested in the long period during which they have served near his person, and he wishes them eminent success in their new and most important spheres of action."

not afford those opportunities for personal distinction which war does, and the duties of an A.D.C. in peace are, as you have discovered, more social than military. I do, however, congratulate you on your promotion to so good a regiment as the 11th, which is serving near the Indians, our only enemy, and where you can have many opportunities to apply your extensive knowledge of these aborigines, which you have already gained by a long experience with them. I shall endeavor during my remaining short period of command to strengthen existing companies by more "privates"; to encourage company officers to stay with their proper commands, and to collect our soldiers in larger garrisons at strategic points of the country where good comfortable permanent barracks should be built.

To reach this most desirable conclusion you can, at your new post of duty, aid me quite as much, if not more than if you remained here in Washington. Nevertheless I am none the less obliged for the assistance you have afforded me by your familiarity with the personnel of the Army, and the usages and customs which have grown up on our frontiers, as well as by the cheerfulness and good feelings you have inspired about you.

Wishing you eminent success in your new rank and sphere of action, I am

Sincerely your friend,
W. T. Sherman,
General

With this memento safe in his baggage, Dodge boarded the first in a succession of trains that took him to St. Paul, Minnesota, adjacent to Fort Snelling, and then to Pierre, Dakota Territory, within a few miles of his new posting. On September 12 he arrived at Fort Sully, headquarters of the Eleventh Infantry, where on the next day he assumed command of the post and the regiment.[122]

At Headquarters and in the Field

Dodge's new duty station was situated on an elevated plain near the east bank of the Missouri River, approximately twenty-five miles north of Pierre, a town that had sprung up on the completion of the Chicago and Northwestern Railroad to that point two years

122. Fort Sully Post Return, September 1882; Eleventh Infantry Regimental Return, September 1882.

before.[123] Established in 1863 by Brigadier General Alfred Sully during a campaign against the Sioux Indians, Fort Sully had remained a fixture in the army's effort to control the tribe.[124] By a treaty ratified in 1868, the great Sioux reservation, encompassing more than one-third the territory in present-day South Dakota and much additional land to the north, extended west from the opposite shore of the Missouri River. A subpost, Fort Bennett, adjoined the Cheyenne River Indian agency nine miles north of Fort Sully. During the years of most serious Indian agitation, the threat of violence at the agency had necessitated maintaining a larger garrison at Fort Bennett than at the main post, but those conditions no longer prevailed. Fort Sully now housed four companies of army troops, and Fort Bennett, one—all of the Eleventh Infantry.

Like most frontier posts, Fort Sully bore a double responsibility, to protect residents of its vicinity from mischief by Indians and other malefactors and, reciprocally, to help ensure that the treaty rights of the Indians were respected and that they were not victimized in other ways. Owing to an influx of settlers nearby, the latter duties often devolved on troops at the fort. An effort by the federal government to induce the Sioux to permit homesteading on their treaty lands had just been rebuffed, and would-be farmers were disposed to take the law into their own hands.[125]

As post commander, Dodge performed duties essentially the same as at the numerous other western forts where he had served in that capacity. Only two features of this assignment significantly distinguished it

123. Originally known as Fort Pierre, the town was the point of embarkation for stage and freight lines westward to the Black Hills. In the summer of 1881, Pierre consisted of about one hundred buildings but was growing steadily. Valleys and lowlands in its vicinity near the east bank of the Missouri River were attracting settlers. Stock ranches already dotted the area, which was said to include "the finest agricultural land in the north-west, especially for the growth of wheat and other grains" (*ANJ*, July 30, 1881, p. 1093).

124. Frazer, *Forts of the West*, pp. 137-38. General histories of this important frontier post include Schuler, *Fort Sully: Guns at Sunset* and Hoeckman, "The History of Fort Sully." See also *ANJ*, January 3, 1880, p. 424; October 9, 1880, p. 180; November 27, 1880, p. 331.

125. Schuler, *Fort Sully*, pp. 17-18. In the summer of 1881 two companies of troops from Fort Sully were temporarily stationed at Pierre as a precaution against efforts to defy federal law.

Fort Sully, Dakota Territory, with the Missouri River in the background (U.S. Army Military History Institute)

from those in his earlier career. First, this was the first time he had been stationed in the Department of Dakota, northernmost of the four departments that policed the Great Plains.[126] Extremes of weather were endemic to the entire region, but they were worst in this sometimes forbidding country. Like many career officers of the line, Dodge had begun to suffer from rheumatic joints, the result of prolonged exposure to inclement conditions. How his constitution would respond to a climate where winter temperatures dropped to forty degrees below zero Fahrenheit for nights at a time was a matter for anxious doubt, especially since he was otherwise in vigorous physical condition.[127]

The other new feature of Dodge's posting at Fort Sully was the concurrent command of a full regiment. The degree of responsibility was nothing new in itself, for during his nine years as a lieutenant colonel he had often commanded the Twenty-third Infantry in the absence of its regular chief officer, Colonel Jefferson C. Davis, sometimes for months at a time. However, the continuing discipline and development of the Eleventh Infantry was now his to ensure. Just as a company of soldiers took its tone from the captain who led it, so a regiment bore the impress of its field officers, especially the colonel. Dodge looked forward to establishing a working relationship with the officers and men who would come under his leadership during his last years of army service.

After almost a month at his new post, he wrote a letter to General Sherman in which he summarized his impressions. No doubt mindful of Major Taylor's recent comeuppance, he began by assuring the general that "I would not presume to address you a personal letter, but for your request that I do so."[128] The prefatory disclaimer was more than mere punctilio, for he at once proceeded to discuss a matter of admin-

126. These were the Department of Texas, the Department of the Missouri, the Department of the Platte, and the Department of Dakota. Dodge's service had been chiefly in the first two, more southerly departments. For a map showing the boundaries of the departments, see Hutton, *Phil Sheridan and His Army*, p. 116.

127. On January 20, 1883, Dodge informed his wife that the recent weather at Fort Sully had been "absolutely stunning. The ther[momete]r dont think anything of going down to 20° below zero." On December 20 of that year he reported to her that the temperature that morning had been 18° below zero, "a temperature that would kill off half New York" (RID to Julia Rhinelander Paulding Dodge, Dodge Papers, Yale).

128. RID to WTS, October 7, 1882 (Sherman Papers, LC).

istrative policy in which he felt himself potentially aggrieved. In forthright but respectful terms he reminded Sherman of an earlier conversation in which the latter had mentioned the possibility of an exchange of stations between the Eleventh and the Twenty-first regiments of infantry. "Recent papers," he continued, stated that the Tenth Infantry, then stationed at Fort Wayne, Michigan, would exchange with the Twenty-first, then at Vancouver Barracks, Washington Territory, probably in the fall of 1883.[129] "I don't think that will be fair," he wrote. "According to received Army opinion, 'the Lakes' [for example, Fort Wayne] is the best station, Vancouver the next best. It does not seem just to the other Reg[imen]ts that the 10th & 21st should oscillate between the two best stations."

Advocating the claim of his new regiment, Dodge pointed out that the Eleventh had seen service in the Department of Dakota for the past six years and in Texas and the Indian Territory for seven years before that. In his view, "no other regiment has a better claim for second choice"—meaning, apparently, after the Twenty-first, which had served in Oregon, Washington, and Idaho for ten years and in Arizona for three before that.[130] Dodge admitted that his informal appeal had a personal side. The recent death of his mother had severed the last of his close ties to the east, and having always desired service in the Columbia River region, he wished for it now more than ever. In what remained of his career he hoped to accomplish "something besides mere guard duty." However, lest he grow importunate, he dismissed the subject with a wry but apt quotation from Milton: "They also serve who only stand and wait."[131]

129. See *ANJ*, September 30, 1882, p. 196. The anonymous source summarized remarks recently made by Sherman during a visit to Fort Porter, New York. The exchange of stations eventually did occur as anticipated. See *ANJ*, August 4, 1883, p. 53; September 1, 1883, p. 92.

130. Alternatively, Dodge's reference to "second choice" may signify not the second most eligible regiment but the second most desirable regimental station—namely, Vancouver Barracks, in the Department of the Columbia. In its issue for February 23, 1889, the *Army and Navy Journal* published a useful table summarizing the stations of infantry, cavalry, and artillery regiments since 1865 (p. 511).

131. Dodge quoted the concluding line of John Milton's sonnet, "When I Consider How My Light Is Spent."

Dodge pronounced his regiment "a fine one," but in need of new blood and the salutary experience of service outside the confines of a post. The companies he had seen thus far showed the ill effects of a "long tour of mere guard duty, at posts so small that officers & men could not well be spared for those scouts, marches, & hunting expeditions which are absolutely necessary to teach officers & men *field duty*—to take care of themselves under all possible circumstances of danger, whether from the elements, or from human enemies." Moreover, many of his officers were permanently disabled and ought to be retired.[132] Dodge went on to describe the rapid pace of change in the vicinity of Fort Sully, relating his comments to the debate about federal Indian policy that had engaged him and Sherman in the months surrounding publication of *Our Wild Indians*. Not only was the region being settled by outsiders, but Indians native to the area seemed anxious to establish farms and begin following "the white man's road." He confessed his amazement at the progress these people had made in adopting customs of the American culture that impinged on them. Optimistically, he looked forward to an end of federal mismanagement:

> This whole Indian business is now so easy of solution, that it seems strange that no statesman can be found, to place it in its proper light before the people. Every senator seems to regard the Indian from the standpoint he gained while a boy at school. The truth is that the Indian has progressed in his way as rapidly as the white, & all the old-fashioned notions & arrangements are now obsolete. A little common sense, fair dealing & courage enough to fight the Indian Ring, are all that can be wanted to settle the Indian problem forever. So rapid is the progress of these people that though constantly studying & writing about them for years, I as constantly find myself behind. And this progress is due not to schools churches or instruction but to their enforced contact with whites, & their inability from lack of game, to live their old usual style of life.[133]

132. In years to come the perceptions that prompted both these statements led to programs for strengthening the regiment. For example, see afterword, pp. 178–80.

133. RID to WTS, October 7, 1882 (Sherman Papers, LC). By the "Indian Ring," Dodge referred to all those who profited by manufacturing and supplying goods for use on Indian reservations, a politically powerful group who, it was alleged, hypocritically supported the Indian Bureau to serve their own ends. A recent novel by T. H. Tibbles, an investigative journalist, purported to lay bare in fictional form the methods of the Indian Ring. It was entitled *Hidden Power: A Secret History of the Indian Ring, Its Operations, Intrigues, and Machinations* (1881).

First-hand experience confirmed the thesis Dodge had recently advanced in print, that in a few years the formerly "savage" inhabitants of the plains would be ready for productive citizenship. Sherman's response to this thoughtful letter has not survived,[134] nor has additional correspondence between the two men during the next few months, if indeed there was any. Each was fully occupied in his own sphere of action, Dodge adjusting to his new command and Sherman leading the army while quietly making arrangements to end his active service.

For several years prior to his tour of duty in Washington, D.C., Dodge had employed as household servants an African American couple, Joe and Laura, with whom he had formed a close personal attachment. To their infant daughter, Ida, he was "Grandpap."[135] The family arrived at Fort Sully soon after he, and with the able assistance of Laura, Dodge established himself comfortably in the post commander's residence. Social calls and evenings at the home of the commander were staples of the modest menu of entertainments at frontier posts, and on these occasions he became better acquainted with the officers' wives and families. A complimentary supper and dance arranged in his honor on December 5 marked his progress in winning the regard of his subordinates, who had served under their former colonel for twelve years.[136] But in truth Dodge, who enjoyed amusements like dancing, billiards, and card games and took pleasure in testing his skill as a flirt at parties, was finding garrison life at Fort Sully a bit dull.

To his wife Julia, who continued to reside in New York City, he wrote in January 1883 that neither the officers nor the ladies of his post entirely suited him thus far. Though "good duty men," the officers were "very poor sticks socially," almost all being married and with their wives in residence. As for the women, with a few exceptions they were "the most inveterate tattlers I ever knew . . . no *scandal*, but simply *tattle*. Some of the women seem to know what everybody has for dinner

134. Beneath Dodge's signature at the end of the letter Sherman did write "Ansd —" for "Answered," a formula notation he employed regularly.

135. See *PREJ*, pp. 52–53, 170; *ITJ*, pp. 20, 98–100, 147–48, 390–95, 403.

136. *ANJ*, December 16, 1882, p. 440. Colonel William D. Wood had retired on his own application after thirty years of active service (*ANJ*, July 1, 1882, p. 1109).

every day."[137] Dodge had formed close friendships with several of the officers and ladies of his former regiment, the Twenty-third Infantry, but that closeness had not yet developed with those of the Eleventh. More satisfying were his occasional jaunts in quest of rabbits or grouse, accompanied by Joe, an orderly, and perhaps a fellow officer or two.[138]

More actively than most field officers of his time, Dodge interested himself in the welfare and discipline of the enlisted men under his command. Though far from lax in his exercise of authority, he took satisfaction in the low rates of occupancy in the guardhouses at posts where he was stationed, the result he believed of fair and impartial treatment. He deplored the employment of private soldiers as in effect poorly paid laborers, and so far as practicable he ensured that the men were assigned tasks not always wanting in interest and variety.[139] Dodge also supported initiatives for amusement, once a day's drill and other duties were completed. He permitted hunting parties, both to diversify company menus and to ensure the familiarity of his men with terrain in the vicinity. He actively promoted athletic events, including competition by a post baseball team, the Sully Blues, and he encouraged use of the post library. On February 20, 1883, he must surely have attended the inaugural performance of the Fort Sully Minstrel and Variety Troupe, comprised entirely of enlisted men, which played to an overflow house. A published account of this evening's entertainment predicted additional performances monthly, "if the fortunes of war permit."[140]

During the winter and spring of 1882–1883, Dodge's chief initiative as regimental and post commander was to encourage his men in regular target practice on the post's firing ranges, at two hundred, three hundred, and six hundred yards. Stimulated by publication of

137. RID to Julia Rhinelander Paulding Dodge, January 20, 1883 (Dodge Papers, Yale).

138. "On good days I take horse & gun & Joe," Dodge wrote his wife. "Large game is not to be found, but my last hunt of three hours gave me 1 grouse and 28 rabbitts. These rabbits are delicious. Ida & I ate a whole one at dinner today & quarrelled over the remnants" (RID to Julia Rhinelander Paulding Dodge, January 20, 1883—Dodge Papers, Yale).

139. RID, "The Enlisted Soldier," pp. 282–83, 316.

140. Schuler, *Fort Sully*, pp. 160, 162–63; RID, "The Enlisted Soldier," p. 317; *ANJ*, September 24, 1881, p. 163; March 10, 1883, p. 724. The quotation is from the latter article.

Colonel Theodore T. S. Laidley's *Course of Instruction for Rifle Firing* (1879), a program for improvement in marksmanship was by now a prominent feature of the army's effort to strengthen the professional ability of its troops.[141] Captain Stanhope E. Blunt, ordnance officer for the Department of Dakota, was an active participant in the movement. He administered a system of testing to certify levels of accomplishment, and he also organized an annual tournament at Fort Snelling wherein representatives from posts in the department vied for gold medals. Two of the four medals awarded at Fort Snelling in 1883 went to men from Fort Sully, and the overall performance of the Eleventh Infantry was the best in the entire army.[142] Skill at rifle firing was of course an acquirement that had long interested Dodge. On May 17 he scored an average of 83$^1/_3$ percent in firing at the three standard distances, earning the right to wear the official Marksman's Buttons.[143]

That spring Dodge came into arm's-length official contact with General Sherman, as the result of a letter he wrote drawing attention to a problem that beset his regiment, namely, the low number of officers listed on its roster who were actually available for service with it. Forwarded through official channels, from the Department of Dakota to General Sheridan at the Division of the Missouri and then to the Adjutant General's Office in Washington, once the letter reached army headquarters it elicited a testy reaction. Dodge had pointed out that, of thirty-three officers assigned to the Eleventh Infantry, only sixteen were on hand for company duty. Four others were physically present at their posts, but owing to one infirmity or another they were performing "light duty" only, thereby creating an embarrassment and a source of dissatisfaction.[144] In his endorsement to the letter, Sheridan

141. The implementation of this initiative is described by McChristian in *An Army of Marksmen*, pp. 41–79. For G.O. 44, HQA, May 10, 1881, establishing annual marksmanship competitions within the army, see *ANJ*, May 14, 1881, p. 847.

142. *ANJ*, December 13, 1884, p. 385; Schuler, *Fort Sully*, p. 105.

143. Certificate No. 35, Office Chief Ordnance Officer, Headquarters Department of Dakota, May 17, 1883 (Dodge Papers, Graff).

144. The original of Dodge's letter, dated March 26, 1883, has not been located. Its date and contents are noted in a summary that precedes the text of Sherman's endorsement of it as copied into the general's collected papers. See Endorsement No. 87, April 14, 1883 (Sherman Papers, LC). The Regimental Return of the Eleventh

had noted that, of the remaining thirteen, only one officer not serving with his company could possibly be ordered back to it. This was Captain Warren C. Beach, the commander of Company D, who for more than a year had been assigned "temporarily" to a comfortable station, the headquarters of the Department of the East in New York Harbor.

Dodge's letter with its endorsements touched on three areas of potential abuse by officers that especially provoked Sherman: not serving with their regiment, avoiding regular duty or obtaining sick leave on flimsy pleas of illness, and obtaining comfortable tours of duty through political influence.[145] Though fluent in the formal parlance of official interchanges, the general was not shy of delivering his opinions "with the bark on." In an endorsement of his own, he commented on the situation to Secretary Lincoln: "Respectfully submitted to the Hon. Secy. of War, inviting his attention to the fact that by his orders Capt. W. C. Beach, 11th Infantry, has been for a year on temporary duty at Genl. Hancock's Headquarters. There is no earthly reason for his being there except for his personal convenience—his father residing at Brooklyn. Being Capt. of a company of infantry he should be with it."

Turning his attention to the four officers who seemed to be accepting only those assignments they found congenial, Sherman exercised his delegated authority as the officer empowered to regulate the discipline and control of the army. He directed the adjutant general to inform all post commanders that "when officers are ordered to be at their posts for light duty, it is for the Com'dg officer, with the advice of his post Surgeon, to determine what that light duty shall be. The officer must obey orders, and he is not to be the judge of what constitutes 'light duty.'" He ended the endorsement on a sardonic note: "If we

---

Infantry for March 1883 confirms these statements, except that only three officers were shown on the report form as performing "light duty": Captain William E. Kingsbury and First Lieutenant Charles F. Roe of Company B, and Captain Mason Jackson of Company K. A fourth officer, Captain Theodore Schwan, Company G, was listed as sick in quarters since March 27.

145. G.O. 114, HQA, December 12, 1877, regulating the award of sick leaves, was reprinted in *ANJ*, December 22, 1877, p. 307. See also *ANJ*, November 19, 1881, p. 345; January 7, 1882, p. 493; March 4, 1882, p. 680; July 15, 1882, p. 1155.

cannot have able-bodied officers for duty, we must get along the best we can with the halt and the lame."[146]

The effort to suppress political meddling with the assignments given well-connected army officers was a constant struggle. In the present case, a War Department order dated April 26 directed Captain Beach to rejoin his company at Fort Sully. However, a few days later the *Army and Navy Journal* announced that, under recently issued new orders, Beach would continue as a member of General Hancock's staff.[147] The influence of Beach's father, a prominent lawyer active in the Democratic Party that had nominated Hancock for the presidency in 1880, quite possibly caused the original directive to be revoked. Beach remained on duty at New York Harbor until March 1885, when at last a new order to rejoin his company held firm. One year later he resigned his commission.[148]

After his arrival at Fort Sully, Dodge remained in regular contact with his publisher, A. D. Worthington, in regard to sales of *Our Wild Indians*. Worthington had invested heavily in the volume, but he was confident that the attractiveness of the product and the sales momentum created by his marketing efforts would yield a rich reward. Following the initial campaign to create public awareness of the book, he next sought to reach grassroots clients through saturation advertising. In a mass

146. Endorsement No. 87, April 14, 1883 (Sherman Papers, LC). Secretary Lincoln was sympathetic to Sherman's efforts to combat the influence of special interests on behalf of commissioned officers. A Washington, D.C., correspondent of the *Chicago Inter-Ocean* reported in July 1882 that Lincoln had "ruthlessly set aside quite a number of pleasant arrangements where the beneficiaries of some previous favoritism had settled down into what they considered a pleasant thing for life" (quoted in *ANJ*, July 22, 1882, p. 1181).

147. *ANJ*, April 28, 1883, p. 889; May 5, 1883, p. 901. Early in August, Captain Beach was reported spending a brief vacation at Saratoga Springs, New York, a fashionable watering place. In December he obtained a month's leave of absence for a honeymoon tour (*ANJ*, August 4, 1883, p. 53; December 8, 1883, p. 379).

148. *ANJ*, March 14, 1885, p. 645; Heitman, *Historical Register*, 1:201. The death of his father, William Augustus Beach, in June 1884 had deprived Captain Beach of a powerful advocate. Nevertheless, in later years an unsuccessful effort was made to restore him to the active officer corps so as to permit his retirement at the rank of captain, an action that would entitle him to a pension (*ANJ*, March 7, 1891, p. 480; April 2, 1892, p. 559). Curiously, when he died in 1923 Beach left an estate valued at over $4 million, but his chief published claim to memory was having been stationed at Governors Island "for many years" (*New York Times*, January 23, 1923, p. 13).

mailing to the editors of some seventeen hundred country newspapers, he offered to each, free of charge, a leather-bound copy of *Our Wild Indians* in return for placement in that newspaper's columns of an advertisement whose text he supplied. No fewer than 1,460 editors accepted the offer and so printed in their pages a notice that began "WANTED! AGENTS! AGENTS! AGENTS! for Gen. Dodge's bran' new book." With characteristic disregard of literal truth, Worthington announced to prospective door-to-door solicitors that "*thousands of* EMINENT MEN" had subscribed for the work, the forty-third thousand copies of which were then in press. Persons interested in collecting additional orders were invited to contact the publisher in order to receive an informative circular that further described the book.[149] Not surprisingly, that four-page pamphlet, printed on an extra-large sheet, heralded *Our Wild Indians* as "A Standard, Superb Work of Great Value and Interest."[150]

Worthington was determined, he told Dodge in October 1882, to give the work "such a lift as no book has ever received." He had sent out copies of the circular "by the cartload," but his corps of agents, many of them young boys, had not yet produced quite the results he had anticipated. The reasons for the shortfall eluded him, especially since persons who did order the work were well satisfied. He thought perhaps "there have been so many cheap miserable blood & thunder Indian books sold" that the public had lost its taste for the subject. In any case, he still hoped to sell at least twenty thousand copies, which would enable him to recoup his investment. Meanwhile, he wrote, he was glad to learn from Dodge of some likely new outlets for distribution.[151]

Following up on his earlier interview with the quartermaster general, Dodge proposed to that official that 150 copies of *Our Wild Indians* be purchased by the federal government and then sent to army posts. This suggestion, forwarded with a favorable endorsement to the secretary of war, prompted an inquiry to Worthington as to what

149. A. D. Worthington to RID, October 24, 1882 (Dodge Papers, Graff). A printed copy of the newspaper advertisement is attached to the letter.

150. A. D. Worthington & Co., "Thirty-Three Years' Personal Experience Among Our Wild Indians" (Dodge Papers, Graff).

151. A. D. Worthington to RID, October 24, 1882; December 30, 1882 (Dodge Papers, Graff).

price he would require for that number of copies. The publisher submitted a bid he thought low, but in the end Secretary Lincoln decided against the expenditure. Dodge was informed in November that the secretary did not "feel justified in authorizing the purchase of *this* book."[152] Though surprised, neither he nor Worthington were especially disappointed at the negative outcome. The publisher liked Dodge's suggestion that he attempt to enlist as agents the civilian traders at army posts across the country. He would "go for them red hot," he wrote. Judging from Dodge's success in selling copies through the post trader at Fort Sully, Worthington thought thirty to fifty copies might be worked off at all other posts, a sales response out of all proportion to the modest purchase the secretary of war had declined to make.[153]

By the end of 1882, 18,072 copies of *Our Wild Indians* had been sold, yielding Dodge a goodly harvest of royalty payments that totaled approximately one-half his annual salary.[154] Worthington was within range of breaking even on his investment and now hoped for sales of perhaps twenty-two thousand copies, but he was no longer very optimistic. Sales were "really about over," he informed the author on December 30. It was some satisfaction to receive praises of the book from many quarters, but he had grown short of funds. Protesting that he had done everything possible to market the book but had spent too much on it from the beginning, he asked Dodge to consider foregoing his royalty payments on future copies sold. When Dodge declined, forwarding still another order from the Fort Sully post trader and observing that Worthington seemed to him too pessimistic, the publisher assured him that any hopes of many more sales were doomed to disappointment.[155]

152. Alexander J. Perry, Deputy Quartermaster General, to RID, November 18, 1882 (Dodge Papers, Graff). The emphasis on "this" in the quoted passage is problematical. Secretary Lincoln may have considered *Our Wild Indians* too openly political in its approach to warrant patronage—and tacit approval—by the federal government.

153. A. D. Worthington to RID, December 30, 1882 (Dodge Papers, Graff).

154. Statement of Account, A. D. Worthington & Co. with RID, January 1, 1883 (Dodge Papers, Graff). As a colonel with less than five years' experience at that rank, Dodge earned thirty-five hundred dollars per year (*ANJ*, July 22, 1882, p. 1185).

155. A. D. Worthington to RID, December 30, 1882; January 19, 1883 (Dodge Papers, Graff). Not mentioned in either of these letters was the publisher's acute need of funds to finance an upcoming publication, *Our Famous Women*, which appeared in the spring.

Nevertheless, in April 1833 Worthington declared his intention to mount one more campaign on a new front, one he had considered a lost cause. He would "salt" the religious press, he said, and take his chances. After all, at this late date the editors' hostility could do little harm.[156] Whether by this means or, more likely, through the activity of copublishers he had enlisted in Chicago, Cleveland, and St. Louis, in the weeks that followed sales figures soared and swept away Worthington's mood of hopelessness. By August 1, 1883, a total of 30,149 copies had been sold, and the renewed surge in orders had not yet abated. *Our Wild Indians* was a resounding sales success.[157]

Meanwhile, the knowledge that General Sherman would soon retire from the army redoubled the attentions lavished on him in the national capital and elsewhere. At the president's annual reception on New Year's Day the greetings Sherman received from fellow officers brought tears to his eyes. On February 8, his sixty-third birthday, friends in Washington arranged an informal dinner in his honor. Responding in that month to an invitation to attend a meeting of the Society of the Army and Navy Officers in Cincinnati, he begged off, even though he

156. A. D. Worthington to RID, April 20, 1883 (Dodge Papers, Graff).

157. Statement of Account, A. D. Worthington & Co. with RID, August 1, 1883 (Dodge Papers, Graff). The statement of July 1, 1884, showed 38,185 copies sold (Dodge Papers, Graff). On March 10, 1884, Worthington wrote Dodge that *Our Wild Indians* "has 'taken the cake' from every other 'Indian' book published the last 30 or 40 years."

> "Belden, the White Chief"—issued in the years when everything was booming, and when it was just as easy to sell 10,000 books to 1,000 now, reached only 21,000; and it sold at a much less price than ours, too. Buffalo Bill's book, issued only three years or so ago, sold about three or four thousand, though I believe if I could have had his book & been allowed to shape it, I could have made a great success of it. He was here with his "show" about a year ago, and I called on him and presented him with a copy of "Our Wild Indians." *His* book, by the way, was wretchedly brought out; and while he expressed unbounded delight at the appearance of our's, he did not conceal his intense disgust at the appearance of his own, though it is doubtful whether its shortcomings would have ever suggested themselves to him had he not seen "Our Wild Indians." (Dodge Papers, Graff)

The two books referred to by Worthington are George P. Belden, *Belden, The White Chief; or, Twelve Years Among the Wild Indians of the Plains*, edited by James S. Brisbin (1870), and William F. Cody, *The Life of Hon. Wm. F. Cody, Known as Buffalo Bill* (1879).

enjoyed such gatherings. His "social obligations," he wrote, had become "simply overwhelming and imperative."[158] When in public, Sherman sought not to draw attention to himself, never appearing in uniform except when necessary and at some times even wearing a pair of large tortoise-shell glasses that partially concealed his features. Nevertheless, at theaters in the evenings he would often be recognized, applauded, even asked to say a few words.

Though well-intended, spontaneous marks of respect like these grew tiresome. Late in 1881 Sherman had declined an invitation to a dinner at Delmonico's Restaurant in New York City, making it no secret that he was weary of responding to toasts to the army. The story was circulated that once, when the strains of "Marching through Georgia" burst out at a dinner party he was attending, he began to weep. Turning to General Grant, who sat at his side, he explained that he had now heard the song for the three million, three hundred and eighty-seven thousandth time. He regretted ever having marched through Georgia and helped bring the song into existence.[159] Inevitably, Sherman's peaking popularity gave rise to renewed speculation that he might soon enter politics. For example, the *New York World* observed that, when seated at his desk in the War Department, the general could see the White House directly before him across the lawn. "Can he prevent his thoughts?" the reporter slyly inquired.[160] But the general gave no encouragement to speculations of this kind. In one of his more measured responses on the subject, he assured an interviewer that he would never "soil my military record" by participation in politics.[161]

Sherman maintained his usual daily schedule at headquarters, but he insisted that with his experienced aides on duty the affairs of the office could on most days go on smoothly without him. For a time at least, the clamor for generalships had moderated, Pope and Mackenzie

158. *ANJ*, January 13, 1883, p. 525; January 27, 1883, p. 576; February 10, 1883, p. 625.

159. *ANJ*, December 24, 1881, p. 481.

160. *ANJ*, January 6, 1883, p. 504. The observation was acknowledged as from the *New York World*.

161. *ANJ*, November 18, 1882, p. 348.

having been nominated to fill two vacancies.[162] The next scheduled retirement of a general officer would be his own. In the meantime, he pursued long-term initiatives for the army that he had determined upon in earlier years. Wishing to promote professional education, he approved a new set of regulations governing the Artillery School at Fortress Monroe, Virginia; addressed the graduating class at the recently organized School for Application in infantry and cavalry tactics at Fort Leavenworth, Kansas; and continued his efforts to adjust the curriculum at West Point toward practical military training and away from the long-standing emphasis on engineering. To reward the accomplishments of officers who, like Dodge, in these times of peace had directed their energies to worthy projects not specifically military, he made judicious use of public recognition. Upon receiving an account of Captain John G. Bourke's forthcoming study of a southwestern Indian tribe, he responded graciously with congratulatory comments, some of which echoed the letter he had written to Dodge for publication in *Our Wild Indians*.[163]

Sherman's relations with Robert T. Lincoln, son of the fallen president and since 1881 the secretary of war, were friendly and marked by mutual respect. So little distrust marred their working relationship that on occasions when Lincoln was absent from his office, sometimes for weeks at a time, by agreement the general simply performed the secretary's duties. The arrangement prompted Sherman to remark during one such interval that "for the first time since I came to Washington there is a perfect harmony between the General of the Army and the Secretary of War."[164] Lincoln, though an able administrator who took his responsibilities seriously, had little military experience. Unlike some previous secretaries, he was glad to receive bits of discreet tutoring, and Sherman was pleased to provide them, especially on matters that touched on his own authority and official prerogatives. One such

162. Pope was nominated for promotion in place of Major General McDowell, who was retired by law on October 26, 1882; Mackenzie was nominated in place of Pope on the list of brigadier generals (*ANJ*, March 25, 1882, p. 767; December 9, 1882, p. 416; Heitman, *Historical Register*, 672, 798).

163. WTS to General Philip H. Sheridan, April 23, 1883 (HQA LS). Bourke's *The Snake-Dance of the Moquis of Arizona* appeared in 1884.

164. *ANJ*, June 16, 1883, p. 1032.

incident occurred in March 1883, when he informed Lincoln of a dispute that had broken out between senior officers of the staff and line.

Recently Brigadier General Robert Macfeely, the commissary general of subsistence, had written two department commanders, Generals Augur and Pope, directing them to explain their reasons for issuing certain orders that ran counter to War Department policy for the commutation of rations—that is, cash payment in lieu of meals not regularly supplied through the commissary department. Both Augur and Pope took umbrage at the demand, or implied order, from Macfeely; they denied his right to question any action they had authorized in their official capacities. Sheridan, their immediate superior, concurred in their objections, and Sherman now forwarded the whole correspondence to Lincoln since it involved a principle of governance.[165] At issue was delimitation of the spheres of authority exercised by the General of the Army and the secretary of war.

General Macfeely, Sherman explained, was chief of a branch in the War Department, but in that position he possessed no authority to command within the army, whose discipline and control were instead the responsibility of himself, the General of the Army. Nor could he command in the name of his immediate superior, the secretary of war. The secretary's power was delegated to him by the president, and by a well-established legal doctrine it could not be further delegated. Thus, when an officer like the commissary general required information or explanation from a department commander, he could only request it though a common superior, the secretary of war, for no department commander need account to him for acting within the limits of his discretion. In short, while the secretary ought to hold every commissioned officer accountable for official acts falling within his sphere of duty, "this is his office and not that of the Commissary General."[166]

165. Sheridan forwarded the objections of Augur on February 21 and those of Pope on February 27, 1883. Beginning in October 1882, General Macfeely had aroused ire by disallowing requests for commutation of rations on behalf of enlisted men traveling under orders (AGO Reg LR). His directives to Generals Augur and Pope brought the matter to a head. The consolidated file of correspondence on the subject is 2032 AGO 1883, available in NARA microfilm publication M689, Roll 214.

166. WTS to Robert T. Lincoln, March 3, 1883 (HQA LS).

Of course, Sherman and many others believed that staff officers like Macfeely ought to perform their duties under the immediate supervision of the General of the Army, not the secretary of war.[167] However, lacking that arrangement, Sherman at least established a mutual understanding with the secretary that helped curb the inclination of staff departments to elevate themselves into fiefdoms. Presently a directive from the War Department resulted in publication by the adjutant general of a general order regulating the commutation of rations for soldiers traveling under orders—the matter that had aroused the suspicions of General Macfeely. A circular letter of instruction to division and department commanders accompanied the order.[168]

In the latter months of 1882 an unusual demand had been made on the resources of General Sherman's staff, a request that impinged on his plans for an inspection tour the following summer. Sir John Douglas Southerland Campbell, the marquis of Lorne, governor general of Canada, and husband of Princess Louise of England, asked the general's cooperation in arranging a tour through the western United States for himself, his wife, and a small official party.[169] Sherman decided that the best way to answer the imperial call for assistance was to offer the marquis the services of an aide-de-camp throughout the royal presence in the United States. The natural candidate to perform such an office was Colonel Tourtelotte, a well-traveled bachelor of considerable social address. However, Tourtelotte was at that time on leave of absence, so Sherman summoned Colonel Tidball into his office, briefly explained the situation, and informed him that he had been selected instead. Tidball was horrified at the news. Two years earlier he had doubted his ability to conduct himself with due decorum even in Washington, and now to travel in the presence of royalty for weeks at a time was out of the question. In quiet panic, through a series of telegraph inquiries

167. See Marszalek, *Sherman*, pp. 384-88, 434; Utley, *Frontier Regulars*, pp. 28-33, 41-43; *ITJ*, pp. 111-12.

168. G.O. 34, HQA, May 22, 1883 (AGO Reg LR). The text of the order was reprinted in *ANJ*, May 26, 1883, p. 969.

169. WTS to Marquis of Lorne, August 14, 1882; WTS to General H. G. Wright, August 14, 1882; WTS to Colonel F. De Winton (aide-de-camp to the marquis), August 14, 1882 (HQA LS).

he managed to locate Tourtelotte at a resort on Lake George, in upstate New York, and thus to throw off the onus of attendance on the "exalted persons," as the general called them.[170]

Tourtelotte was issued orders to meet the royal party at Chicago on September 6 and accompany them for as long as His Lordship might wish. As it happened, that period proved to be lengthier than Sherman had anticipated. Shortly after his arrival at San Francisco, the marquis took ship for Victoria, British Columbia, leaving Tourtelotte to await his return, but that event did not occur until mid-December. However, a railroad journey back across the continent brought the aide's errand to a close, and on January 27, 1883, the marquis was guest of honor at a state dinner in Washington, D.C.[171] The table talk between him and Sherman must have included the general's plans to visit British Columbia with his escort in the summer to come.[172]

By that time Sherman was updating his arrangements for the more physically challenging portions of his anticipated western tour. Developments in recent months had made clear that in order to perform a reconnaissance now regarded as necessary, he would need to cross the international boundary into Canada. Fort Colville, in northern Washington Territory, had recently been abandoned, but amidst some uncertainty. If in fact it was to be given no further military use, then

170. "On General Sherman's Staff as Aide-de-Camp," pp. 67–71, John C. Tidball Papers, USMA; WTS to Colonel John E. Tourtelotte, September 1, 1882 (HQA LS); *ANJ*, September 16, 1882, p. 141.

171. WTS to General John M. Schofield, December 5, 1882; WTS to Colonel John E. Tourtelotte, December 11, 1882 (HQA LS); *ANJ*, September 9, 1882, p. 115; October 14, 1882, p. 237; November 25, 1882, p. 377; December 23, 1882, p. 460; January 13, 1883, p. 535; January 27, 1883, p. 576.

172. A few months earlier, Canadian officials had ruled that any U.S. military organization wishing to visit Canada must first make application to the secretary of war in the United States. If that official approved, he was to forward the request to the governor general of Canada through the British ambassador in Washington (*ANJ*, September 30, 1882, p. 188). On April 10, 1883, Sherman therefore officially informed Secretary Lincoln of his desire to enter Canada accompanied by a military escort and requested that the matter be laid "before the Dominion authorities of Canada, or it may be, the proper authorities in London" (HQA LS). On the same day, Lincoln forwarded Sherman's letter to the secretary of state, requesting that he make the necessary contact with Canadian officials (SW LS). By early June Sherman had been granted the permission he sought (WTS to General Nelson A. Miles, June 4, 1883—HQA LS).

a new post would need to be established to replace it. According to the imperfect maps of the region then available, the most eligible sites for such a post were either near the point where the Columbia River crosses the international boundary or else to the west, in the Okinakane Valley. In either case, if Sherman were to examine that country, a mountain range yet further west would necessitate his passing into Canada in order to avoid great delay by backtracking. He therefore directed General Schofield to determine whether an old road, shown on maps as leading from near the region he proposed to reconnoitre toward Fort Hope, on the Fraser River in British Columbia, was still in good enough condition for use by his party.[173]

Schofield's inquiries would require a few weeks, but by early March, Sherman had otherwise "pretty well staked out" the remainder of his itinerary.[174] As planned the year before, he would leave Washington in mid-June and be absent until about October 1. The members of his party would be few, including Justice Waite and possibly justices Gray and Harlan, with two aides-de-camp, Colonels Bacon and Tidball. Other persons would join the tour and then drop away as it moved from region to region. Passing from Buffalo, New York, to Duluth, Minnesota, via the Great Lakes, the group would board a Northern Pacific train for St. Paul, Minnesota, where a reception was planned at Fort Snelling. From that point, augmented by General Terry and persons traveling with him, the party would continue by railroad to Fort Ellis, from which they would proceed south by pack train through Yellowstone National Park, following the course marked out the year before, then back to Missoula, Montana Territory, which the Northern Pacific had reached by this time.[175]

The month of August would take the travelers through northern Idaho and Washington Territories and into Canada, then by sea aboard a U.S. revenue cutter back to Vancouver Barracks, headquarters of the Department of the Columbia. Following a series of events being planned

173. WTS to General John M. Schofield, February 17, 1883 (HQA LS).

174. WTS to General Alfred H. Terry, March 7, 1883 (HQA LS).

175. WTS to General Alfred H. Terry, March 7 and May 20, 1883; WTS to General Philip H. Sheridan, May 20, 1883; WTS to Colonel Thomas H. Ruger, May 29, 1883 (HQA LS).

there, the party would continue south, by a route yet to be determined, to San Francisco, California, where it would remain for a few days before proceeding by railroad to Los Angeles. It would then cross the southwestern territories to Santa Fe, New Mexico, and zigzag northwesterly to Salt Lake City, Utah, setting out from that point on the final leg of the journey back to Washington.[176] In all, the tour would cover approximately eleven thousand miles.

Sherman looked forward to visiting two stretches of country he had not yet seen, the region north of Fort Coeur d'Alene, Idaho Territory, and much of the rugged mountain terrain between Santa Fe and Salt Lake City.[177] Only months before, the Denver and Rio Grande Railroad had completed a narrow-gauge line that connected Pueblo, Colorado, and Salt Lake City—a bold feat of engineering and entrepreneurship. Writing to William J. Palmer, president of the Denver and Rio Grande, Sherman confessed himself "even yet incredulous" at the thought of rapid commercial travel in that "hitherto inaccessible" section of the country.[178]

Fortuitously, the Sherman tour in the summer of 1883 would coincide almost exactly with the completion of three major railroads, the Northern Pacific, the Denver and Rio Grande, and the Atlantic and Pacific, the latter connecting Needles, California, and Albuquerque, New Mexico. In view of Sherman's emphasis on railroad transportation as a key element of future army policy, this conjunction of events seemed fitting, the final links being established just as he rounded out his career.[179] To register his sense of the railroads' crucial role in the

176. WTS to General Alfred H. Terry, March 7 and May 20, 1883; WTS to General Philip H. Sheridan, May 20 and June 2, 1883; WTS to General John M. Schofield, May 20, 1883; WTS to Colonel Thomas H. Ruger, May 29, 1883 (HQA LS). Plans for the summer tour were made public in *ANJ*, March 31, 1883, p. 798, and June 23, 1883, p. 1069.

177. WTS to General John M. Schofield, May 20, 1883; WTS to General Philip H. Sheridan, June 2, 1883 (HQA LS).

178. WTS to William J. Palmer, May 21, 1883 (HQA LS).

179. Sherman appreciated the historical symmetry suggested here, as he indicated in his annual report for 1883: "The recent completion of the last of the four great transcontinental lines of railway [the Atlantic and Pacific] has settled forever the Indian question, the Army question, and many others which have hitherto troubled the country" (*Report of the Secretary of War* [1883], p. 46). See also Athearn, *William Tecumseh Sherman and the Settlement of the West*, pp. 343–48.

development of the nation, he directed Colonel Poe to prepare a report describing the construction of the transcontinental lines and the implications of their presence for military operations. Poe's discussion would be published as part of the general's annual report to the secretary of war for 1883.[180]

Early in June, Sherman informed the post commander at Fort Ellis, Montana Territory, Major David S. Gordon, Second Cavalry, of the arrangements he wished made there prior to his arrival on July 1. "I fear too much preparation rather than too little," he wrote, but in the directions he issued to Gordon and others he inclined to the former extreme. He specified the number and type of wagons, pack mules, and escort troops to be assembled, and declining an offer of overnight hospitality at Gordon's residence, he indicated the site on the post grounds where he wished to make camp. Once away from the railroad, he hoped to travel in relatively spartan fashion. "What I and all my party . . . want is to get away from dinners, parties and civilization; we are 'blasees,' and want to come down easily and gracefully to rations, to hard work, and in contact with nature." While at the fort he would borrow a camp table and stools and perhaps a few other conveniences, but these were the only "luxuries" he would sanction.[181]

Of course, he would need to consider the needs of the judges who proposed to accompany him. Waite was sixty-seven years of age and unaccustomed to mountain travel, while Gray, though twelve years his junior and something of an outdoorsman, was a mountainous man, standing six feet five inches and weighing over three hundred pounds. He would require a sturdy horse. Meals on the pack-mule journey would consist of foodstuffs issued by post commissaries of subsistence, supplemented by whatever else could be bagged or purchased along the way.[182]

180. Poe, "Report on Transcontinental Railways, 1883," in *Report of the Secretary of War* (1883), pp. 253–330.

181. WTS to Major David S. Gordon, June 3, 1883 (HQA LS).

182. Sherman wrote to General Terry on May 20: "I want to put these Judges on army diet, for they are over fed now, and I want them to experience the usual privations of camp life. . . . The nearer we get to 'first principles' the better will I be pleased" (HQA LS).

Official welcomes would necessarily occur at Fort Ellis and at other points, but these brought a certain satisfaction to all and, Sherman felt, need not be strongly discouraged if kept within due limits. Receptions and testimonial dinners at towns and cities along the way were also part of the bargain, inseparable from his office and his fame. Having developed considerable skill in fashioning impromptu remarks before large audiences, he rarely failed to hit upon an observation or two that delighted those who came out to see him.[183] However, a genuinely painful feature of his public appearances was the succession of bear-trap handshakes given him by admirers. On more than one occasion the repeated pressure had forced him to break up a receiving line, briefly address all those present, and make his exit.

That a superabundance of hearty handshakes posed one of the worst threats to the general's well-being on a tour over three months in duration indicated the profound peace that prevailed along the proposed route of travel. Though escorted by only a small troop of soldiers, whose main function was to conduct the pack train and attend to camp duties, Sherman was confident of traveling in security even in the northwestern wilderness. True, Indians on the Colville reservation in Washington Territory had recently been aggravated almost to violence by incursions of illegal settlers, but the general was reasonably confident of a friendly reception from their representatives. Similarly, his reconnaissance of that region was in part to ensure its defensibility in the event of armed conflict, presumably with Canadian or British forces, but his reception by civil and military officials in British Columbia was expected to be cordial. In every regard, the inspection tour promised to be one long journey of good feeling.

A newspaper interviewer observed "a beam of satisfaction" in Sherman's eye as he outlined the plans for his now imminent escape from the stresses and distractions of life in Washington.[184] He and his aides would leave the city on Wednesday, June 20. The core group

183. Dodge later alluded to Sherman's "numerous speeches (wonderful for their 'infinite variety')" ("The Enlisted Soldier," p. 286). The quoted phrase within Dodge's parentheses is from *Antony and Cleopatra* II.ii.244.

184. ANJ, June 30, 1883, p. 1082. The article was acknowledged as from the *Washington Republican*.

of travelers had decreased by one, Justice Harlan having decided not to attempt the journey, but General Terry and his guests would still join it as far as Missoula. One member of the Terry party would be Colonel Dodge, Sherman having informed the department commander of the promise to include him in the initial weeks of travel.[185] All was in readiness when, on June 19, a last-minute complication arose.

The wife of Colonel Bacon, who was under orders to accompany the general on his entire trip, fell so ill as to preclude her husband's leaving Washington. Advised of the difficulty, Sherman remedied it promptly. He telegraphed Terry that Dodge would replace Bacon and join him for "the whole round."[186] An order issued that day from army headquarters therefore incorporated a reference to Dodge in an unanticipated new role:

> The General of the Army, accompanied by one aide-de-camp, Colonel *John C. Tidball*, will proceed from this city [Washington, D.C.] along the northern frontier of the United States to Fort Colville, Washington Territory; thence to Fort Mojave, Arizona Territory; thence to Fort Lewis, Colorado, &c., on public business, and on the completion thereof will return to this city. Colonel *Richard I. Dodge*, 11th Infantry, now at Fort Sully, Dakota Territory, will report in person to the General of the Army on the 28th instant, at Fort Snelling, Minnesota, and will accompany the General thence, as escort, until relieved. The travel, as herein directed, is necessary for the public service.[187]

Sherman directed Terry to inform Dodge of his new assignment, but for some reason Terry failed to do so. Hence, when Dodge left his post on September 23 to board a train for St. Paul, he looked forward eagerly to joining the Sherman-Terry expedition, but he had no inkling of the revised orders. A fateful coincidence had destined him for daily association with the General of the Army during a summer that Sherman regarded as in a sense the capstone of his career.

185. WTS to General Alfred H. Terry, May 20, 1883. See also WTS to General Philip H. Sheridan, May 20, 1883 (HQA LS).

186. WTS to General Alfred H. Terry, June 19, 1883 (HQA LS); *ANJ*, June 23, 1883, p. 1059.

187. S.O. No. 140, HQA, June 19, 1883 (Dodge Papers, Graff).

The 1883 Inspection Tour

According to plan, Sherman and Tidball set out from Washington on June 20. At Buffalo, New York, they were joined by Justice Gray and took passage on a Great Lakes steamer, the *Nyack*. Two days later Judge Waite boarded ship at Detroit, Michigan, making the core traveling party four-fifths complete. At this point the general began performing his official duties by inspecting Fort Wayne, a facility important for its strategic location between Lakes Erie and Huron. Here too, as he had done while on tour in 1882, he began writing a series of letters to the secretary of war in which, with much other material, he reported his observations and reflections on the nation's military preparedness. He recommended constructing additional stone barracks at Fort Wayne, making it capable of housing six companies of artillery and infantry. It might now seem "absurd to contemplate a period of war ahead," he wrote, but in the event of a military conflict with Canada the expenditure would repay itself in a single day. On June 25 the general inspected a smaller post, Fort Brady, which guarded a canal joining Lakes Huron and Superior. After stops at Minnesota ports and visits by the party to the Hecla and Calumet copper mines, the *Nyack* reached Duluth on June 27, almost exactly on schedule. Sherman judged the first week of the journey "most successful and agreeable."[188] That night the party boarded a train for St. Paul and Fort Snelling, where they were expected the next morning.

By this time Dodge had reached Fort Snelling and learned of his new orders. He would have charge of the mess arrangements and general outfitting of the camps—light duties for a colonel of infantry, especially since most of the camp equipment had already been provided for. As he remarked privately, it was a "very Bully" turn of events.[189] Whatever the circumstances that had dictated it, the assignment was a valued mark of the general's regard, and the summer to come promised additional satisfactions. Though widely traveled in the central and

188. WTS to Robert T. Lincoln, July 2, 1883 (HQA LS). Sherman's letters to the secretary of war during the summer of 1883 are available in NARA microfilm publication M857, Roll 9. Recopied texts of the letters form part of the William T. Sherman Papers (LC).

189. See Journal One, June 25, 1883.

southern plains, Dodge had never yet visited Yellowstone National Park, the Pacific Northwest, Canada, or even San Francisco. The itinerary would thus introduce him to regions already winning renown as attractions for privileged tourists,[190] and it would also enable him to revisit places he had come to know in earlier years. He would have ample opportunity for hunting and fishing, two of his favorite pastimes, in locales said to abound in fish and game. And at post after post he would renew contact with former comrades and acquaintances. In all, his participation in the Sherman tour promised to be for Dodge the journey of a lifetime.

With anticipations like these, on June 23 he began compiling a daily journal of his experiences, the first such record he had kept since his service in the Ute campaign in Colorado during the summer of 1880. In the eight years since he had begun writing them, his collection of journals had served him in various ways. Some were themselves documents with multiple uses, including data to be incorporated in official reports along with entries on scenes, ideas, events, or persons that interested or concerned him. Others, especially those written during his Indian Territory posting in 1879 and 1880, were what he called "diary books," intended to afford his parents and other family members some notion of his daily life.[191]

In the present instance, however, most of the purposes served by the earlier journals no longer governed his practice. He would not be called upon for a description of his movements, as in a military campaign, and his parents were no longer alive to serve as a reading audience. Two powerful motives for compiling a journal remained, however—his sheer enjoyment of expressing himself, and his belief that

190. Hiram Chittenden noted in *The Yellowstone National Park* that 1883 was a "banner year" for distinguished visitors to the park. "The list . . . includes the President of the United States and a member of his cabinet; the Chief Justice and an associate justice of the United States Supreme Court; the General, Lieutenant General, and a large number of other distinguished officers of the army; six United States senators; one territorial governor; a prominent railroad president; the ministers from Great Britain and Germany; the President of the Admiralty Division of the High Court of Justice, England; three members of Parliament; and a considerable number of other eminent personages, both from this country and abroad" (p. 93).

191. *ITJ*, pp. 169, 205.

the weeks to come would prove worthy of a personal record. As in earlier years, he had no plans to publish any part of the journal account.

From Fort Snelling onward, the progress of the Sherman entourage received steady journalistic coverage, first in newspapers published at the towns and cities it visited, and later in eastern newspapers through reprinted articles and the reports of correspondents. The *Army and Navy Journal* served up a steady sprinkling of anonymous reports from army posts and also quotations from articles in newspapers gleaned through exchange. Because no correspondent accompanied the touring party from place to place—an arrangement that would have been unthinkable to Sherman—successive newspaper reports often included similar material: description of the travelers' appearance and mood, especially those of the general; an account of a reception, inspection, or some other special event; a list of attendees; and sometimes a summary of remarks made on the occasion. The progress of the tour was thus national news, but the newspaper coverage emphasized its social or civic, rarely its military, character, and conveyed no sense of its day-to-day flavor.

The chief news event in the northwest during the approximate period of Sherman's presence there was a ceremony on September 9 at Last Spike, Montana Territory, marking completion of the Northern Pacific Railroad.[192] The driving of a final spike, witnessed by President Arthur and other distinguished guests, including representatives of several foreign nations, was an occasion for celebration and a full measure of what Sherman had acerbically termed "second wind oratory."[193] Asked to speak a few words, the usually taciturn former President Grant observed that railroads in the United States might have amounted to little even yet, had not Civil War veterans like Henry Villard, president of the Northern Pacific, sought out the western territories as their

192. Witnessed by approximately thirty-five hundred persons, the ceremony received wide newspaper coverage. For examples, see *San Francisco Chronicle*, September 9, 1883, p. 8; *Chicago Inter-Ocean*, September 10, 1883, p. 1; *New York Times*, September 9, p. 2, and September 10, 1883, pp. 1–2. The regional competition and business alliances that at last resulted in completion of the Northern Pacific are surveyed by James B. Hedges in *Henry Villard and the Railways of the Northwest*.

193. *ANJ*, May 27, 1882, p. 982. The topic under discussion was Sherman's brisk style of presiding at meetings.

new field of enterprise. The old soldier had added his mite to the self-gratulatory themes that defined the occasion, and his remarks earned three hearty cheers.[194]

General Sherman was not present at the ceremony, but he also took satisfaction in the completion of the Northern Pacific, viewing it within a yet wider historical perspective. To him, the dreams of visionaries and surveyors in the 1840s and 1850s that had assumed solid reality in the great east-west railroads symbolized "a period of change." "The trapper, the Hunter, the miner, the buffalo, elk, deer, and antelope are gone," he wrote Secretary Lincoln on August 30. "Soon the Indian will disappear, or be absorbed as have been the Mexicans and Greasers of 1846." Some persons might view these almost magical evanescences in a more sober light, but Sherman expressed satisfaction at the "miraculous" changes that brought with them the prospect of stable prosperity throughout the land.[195]

Of the five travelers who comprised the Sherman party, three—Sherman, Tidball, and Dodge—wrote day-to-day accounts of the entire summer, each characteristic of its author and serving a purpose distinct from the others. Sherman's letters to the secretary of war emphasized military matters—officers he encountered, forts he visited and their place in future army policy, recommendations for appropriations from Congress. Tidball's narrative, prepared at the general's direction for publication with his annual report,[196] was the lengthiest and least personal. Pleasant but not lively in tone, it expatiated with workmanlike industry on the history and associations of the various places visited. Whatever his private thoughts might have been, Tidball sought to include some gracious or at least diplomatic remark about every par-

194. *New York Times*, September 10, 1883, p. 1. The portion of the *Times* article dealing with Grant was reprinted in *ANJ*, September 15, 1883, p. 133.

195. WTS to Robert T. Lincoln, August 30, 1883 (Sherman Papers, LC). On the other hand, from a more personal point of view Sherman regretted the disappearance of more primitive modes of travel. See Athearn, *William Tecumseh Sherman and the Settlement of the West*, p. 348).

196. John C. Tidball, "Report of Journey Made by General W. T. Sherman in the Northwest and Middle Parts of the United States in 1883" (hereafter cited as "Report"), *Report of the Secretary of War* (1883), pp. 203–52. The report has been reprinted, but with some inaccuracies, in *Travel Accounts*, pp. 152–213.

ticipant on the tour and almost every other person who came into significant contact with it. Individuals of foreign extraction and non-white race sometimes received less generous mention, however. Dodge's record was the most candid of the three about his impressions of scenes along the way and his personal likes and dislikes. One or more periods of note-taking by the three men often formed part of a day's activities as the journey proceeded. Similarities between the accounts suggest that their authors shared ideas and perhaps even compared notes on occasion.[197]

Despite differences in purpose and point of view, in some respects the three chroniclers of the inspection tour reacted similarly to their shared experiences of travel. For example, all commented on the rapid pace of change in the settled regions they visited. Sherman's chief points for reference in this regard were his journey through some of the same territory in 1877 and his recollections of California in the 1840s. Dodge drew upon a smaller budget of experience for comparison, but he also marveled at the developments in places he had visited not many years before. Thus Pueblo, Colorado, which he had known in 1870 as a sleepy Hispano-American trading center, was now a bustling seat of industry, "improved out of my knowledge."[198] Tidball interpreted the development or decay of rural communities he passed through as manifesting the inexorable laws of history. Writing of the area near Bannock City, Montana Territory, he described an old wagon road, the Bannack Trail, running alongside a railroad that had rendered it obsolete. A decade earlier, he wrote, the trail had been dotted at intervals by stage stations, with blockhouses for protection against marauding Indians. But the Indian had since disappeared without a trace. "Civilization withered him up as flax is consumed by fire, and no one mourns his loss."[199]

197. For example, compare Dodge's journal entries for July 16–19, 1883, with the corresponding accounts by Tidball, in "Report," pp. 219–22, and Sherman in his letter to Robert T. Lincoln, July 29, 1883 (HQA LS).

198. Journal Two, September 20, 1883. A few years later, Pueblo's Board of Trade promoted the city as the "Pittsburg of the West," a center for industry "better situated to control the trade of Colorado than Denver" (*New York Times*, April 28, 1889, p. 10).

199. Tidball, "Report," p. 222.

The three officers reacted similarly to the scenes of nature they witnessed, their written responses ranging from pleased appreciation to awestruck wonder. As the summer passed, Dodge's journal entries registered his passage through a cycle, from dismissive skepticism toward degrees of enthusiasm whose intensity must have surprised him. As the train moved through country west of Bismarck, he dismissed journalists' breathless descriptions of the terrain as *"bosh."* Later, viewing the lakeside location of Fort Coeur d'Alene, he exclaimed "Lovely - Lovely - *Lovely*."[200] Eventually, sated with beauty, he lapsed into simply naming the places he had seen without further comment. The impossibility of conveying in words the strange splendors of Yellowstone National Park had already become a commonplace of published descriptions, but it was confirmed in experience by each of the three men. Sherman resorted to superlatives when, writing from Fort Coeur d'Alene, he avowed that if offered the whole world to choose from, he could ask for nothing better than the place where he then sat.[201] Perhaps with a touch of irony, Tidball described a fall landscape in the Wasatch Mountains of Utah Territory as so beautiful that Judge Gray, "with aesthetic tastes . . . readily admitted that there was nothing in or around Boston to excel it."[202] The greatest disappointment of the tour began a few miles north of Fort Coeur d'Alene and continued until the party's departure from Vancouver Barracks more than three weeks later. During this entire period, the visibility was severely limited by smoke from immense forest fires.

At other times, as witnessed by these appreciative travelers, the western landscape opened to view two distinct varieties of scenery. One was the unaltered land, primitive nature. The other, admired with equal intensity, was the result of bold design and engineering that had placed a human imprint on the natural scene. Thus Tidball described a railroad bed that had been cut through a precipitous canyon as a feat of "engineering skill" that was "simply marvelous." The canyon itself, formed by a tributary of the Rio Grande in northern New Mexico, he

200. Journal One, June 30 and July 30, 1883.
201. WTS to Robert T. Lincoln, July 29, 1883 (HQA LS).
202. Tidball, "Report," p. 250.

characterized with less ardor as "wild and rocky."[203] Similarly, the travelers expressed wonder both at the bountiful natural resources of the regions they passed through and also at the ambitious efforts being made to extract them. All three men repeatedly employed words like "ample," "abundant," and "unlimited." Sherman remarked that the earnings of the mines he visited in Minnesota "must simply be infinite" to warrant the expenditures necessary to design and construct the machinery he saw in operation there.[204]

Indeed, infusions of financial wealth were bringing about the removal of a wealth of mineral deposits. None of the three expressed concern that these seemingly boundless resources were finite and ought to be drawn upon with discrimination—with a single exception. Sherman, distressed at the uncontrolled forest fires, affirmed that the great stands of timber around Puget Sound were a mine of wealth nearly equal in value to the gold fields of California. He was dismayed to witness the forests being consumed as surely as the numberless herds of buffalo had been swept away a decade before. "Unless some means be adopted to extinguish these fires," he warned, "we may have to import lumber from Europe."[205]

Especially in California, where they were guests at the estates of wealthy bankers and industrialists, the party's shared impression of the far West as a place of almost unparalleled prosperity was clear. Hundreds of acres planted in orchards and vineyards, fields of wheat in view for mile after mile, the Bessemer Steel Works at Pueblo turning out three hundred tons of fine steel rails per day—the dimensions of volume and velocity were almost disorienting. After a day spent visiting lavish residences near San Francisco, Dodge wrote a terse summary analysis: "Power of money."[206] Unlike Henry Adams, who a generation later would symbolize industrial civilization as a whirling

203. Ibid., p. 246.

204. Sherman "hinted to the superintendent that the owners ought to be pretty sure of the extent of their underground, unseen bed of copper to warrant such outlays, and he said they had two miles of ore which would employ this present machinery a hundred years" (WTS to Robert T. Lincoln, July 2, 1883—HQA LS).

205. WTS to Robert T. Lincoln, August 30, 1883 (HQA LS).

206. Journal Two, September 1, 1883.

dynamo, moving at vertiginous speed and generating incalculable, perhaps anarchic energy,[207] these observers reacted to the displays of wealth and harnessed power with confidence and pride. "All honor say I," Sherman wrote of the completed Northern Pacific Railroad, "to the men who conceived this most important enterprise, and even more to those who have achieved the vast labor and work."[208] Confidence and mutual regard prevailed throughout the tour. Just as the general thought of the crowds, many of them Civil War veterans, who packed town halls and streets to meet him as "his" people, so they considered him theirs. The accommodations made available to him—a Palace Pullman car, rooms at the Palace Hotel in San Francisco, a day trip to Flood's Palace in Menlo Park, California—seem distinctly regal.[209]

In its passage through towns and settlements, the Sherman party did glimpse scenes that qualified the controlling impressions of peace, prosperity, and good feeling. In San Francisco, Dodge met an old friend, Gus Bibby, who had come west with her late husband to make their fortune, but she had been disappointed. In the same city he thought it prudent to hire a policeman as his escort on a walk through Chinatown. On the whole, however, the potential for violence from any source was minimal. In Washington Territory the aggrieved Colville Indians called on Sherman, not with threats, but with a request that he render them whatever assistance he could. One week later, at Esquimault Harbor in British Columbia, he was warmly greeted by Admiral Sir Edmund Lyons, who commanded the formidable British naval squadron in the northern Pacific. Both officers knew that the warships were capable of steaming into American waters virtually without resistance and quickly leveling the settlements on Puget Sound, but neither saw the slightest likelihood of such an attack. Upon disembarking from the admiral's flagship, Sherman received a sixteen-gun salute, a tribute

207. Adams, *The Education of Henry Adams: An Autobiography*, pp. 344, 378–90, 490–98.

208. WTS to Robert T. Lincoln, July 29, 1883 (HQA LS).

209. In September 1876 Sherman assured an appreciative audience at the Palace Hotel in San Francisco that the building they occupied was "superior to the Grand Palace Hotel of Paris or of Vienna, at both of which places I have been a guest." He foresaw a time in the future when the city "will have a hundred of these palace hotels" (*ANJ*, October 7, 1876, p. 138).

of respect to the vice-regent of a friendly nation. Near the end of the tour he reported to the secretary of war that it had all gone smoothly, "without any real danger or trouble."[210]

His inspection tour of 1883 confirmed Sherman's belief that the United States was on a steady course of development in its western states and territories. More effectively, he felt, than the army and the Indian Bureau combined, the advancing system of railroads had made possible the advance of civilization, opening up to peaceful development first the central region, then the south and the north. In his final letter to Secretary Lincoln he held up Denver, Colorado, "the peer of any City of the Great West," as a worthy product of the nation's enterprise. It offered "elegant hotels, thousands of fine brick stores and dwellings, lighted by electricity, with bountiful supply of purest water, and every thing that can make life agreeable."[211]

Dodge described the summer tour within a less encompassing historical perspective than either Sherman or Tidball. In fact, he attempted almost no analysis of the sort, contenting himself with recording scenes and incidents from day to day. However, what his journal entries lacked in breadth of perspective, they gained in attention to sometimes revealing moments and details. Unlike the other accounts, Dodge's record captured the flavor of interactions between members of the party and included characteristic glimpses of the individuals themselves, including "the Old Man" in charge.[212] At times Dodge represented the foibles of his companions with irony. For example, during the first weeks of the journey he referred to the outsized Judge Gray as the "Baby," a nickname taken up among themselves by other members of the party who disliked his boastfulness and tendency to find fault. However, the judge gradually moderated his claims to superior skill as an outdoorsman and became more willing to accept the discomforts of cross-country travel as he found them. Dodge later admitted, though without enthusiasm, that Gray had "been very good"

210. WTS to Robert T. Lincoln, October 1, 1883 (HQA LS).

211. WTS to Robert T. Lincoln, October 1, 1883 (HQA LS). For a survey of Denver's development as a regional center, see Paul, *The Far West and the Great Plains in Transition*, pp. 94–104.

212. Journal One, July 5, 1883.

on the whole.[213] He concealed neither his affectionate regard for some companions, such as Judge Waite, nor his irritation or amusement at others, such as Brigadier General Nelson A. Miles, whose arrival at Fort Coeur d'Alene initiated yet another test of equanimity for Sherman, related to Miles by marriage.

Dodge's companionable instincts led him to pass several evenings "gassing" with officers or other persons, fortified by glasses of whisky. According to his journal, as commissary to the party he had purchased "a few gallons" at St. Paul for consumption en route.[214] Some portion of the keg's contents remained available for consumption as the pack train approached Canada, but once across the border he was pleased to discover Robertson's Irish Whisky for sale at a trader's store, a valued reserve supply. Two weeks later, after an official function at Portland, Oregon, he and a group of fellow officers adjourned to a nearby saloon where they imbibed "quantities of lush,"[215] with sickly results the next day. Sherman and Tidball made no mention of evenings like these, nor did they touch upon more essential matters such as the long hours of rest at night that were necessary to ensure sufficient energy for the next day's travel. More than once Dodge recorded in his journal sending visitors on their way in order to let him get some sleep.

Inevitably, Dodge's own personality and tastes expressed themselves in his daily notes on the summer's experiences. His love of outdoor life, his conviviality and capacity for friendship, his unawed respect for General Sherman, his pride in his profession, his zest for life and curiosity about topics of all kinds—all come into view. Written as they were for his own eyes, the journal entries are sometimes laconic, referring to matters all but unintelligible to an unaided reader. Yet his impulse to capture experiences in words often results in apt distillations, as when at the end of a day touring the estates of the wealthy, he described himself as "gorged with splendor."[216] His wry humor is also regularly in evidence. At the Roman Catholic mission of St. Francis

213. Journal One, July 6 and August 4, 1883.
214. Journal One, June 28, 1883.
215. Journal One, August 25, 1883.
216. Journal Two, September 2, 1883.

Regis, in Washington Territory, Sherman and the rest of the party witnessed songs and speeches by Indian children dressed in colorful costumes. After the performance, Dodge noted, the general "showed his usual taste, & kissed the 2 prettiest girls."[217]

Fortuitously, in the summer of 1883 Dodge was given the opportunity to accompany Sherman on a journey which most Americans could undertake only through imagination. Published here for the first time, his journals provide a new perspective on the summer tour, even as they detail his responses to the succession of new sights and experiences. Taken together, they capture in writing a period without precedent or recurrence in his career. Probably he would have described the summer of 1883 much as he had the summer of 1875, when he commanded the Black Hills Expedition, as "the most delightful summer of my life."[218]

217. Journal One, August 7, 1883.
218. Turchen and McLaird, *The Black Hills Expedition of 1875*, p. 92.

Journal One
June 23–August 29, 1883

June 23, 1883[1]

Left Ft Sully at 10.30 am enroute for Ft Snelling "to report in person to the Dept Comdr" by my own order,[2] no information having reached me as to how I was to join Genl Sherman's party.

The day was very hot & I made the driver go slow, so we only reached Spring Ck at 1.30 pm. I had given Joe & Laura the chance for "an outing" to Pierre where they wanted to make some purchases.[3] We had a nice lunch at Spg Ck & got into Pierre about 4 pm. The Marvellous progress of the Country is well exemplified by this short journey of 25 miles. When I went to Ft. Sully Sepr/ 82, there was a little settlement of some four or five houses in a valley some four miles from Pierre just under a high hill. Today I stopped on that hill & counted in sight with the naked eye, 101 farm houses

1. The manuscript journal measures 3 1/4 by 5 9/16 inches and contains 60 unnumbered leaves. It consists of brown flexible cardboard covers at front and back, secured to the pages inside by a strip of tape at the top. The endpapers are of unlined, cream-colored paper flecked at random with blue ink; the inner leaves are lined horizontally in light gray ink. On the front cover Dodge has written in black ink "No 1[/] Trip with [/] Genl Sherman." The remaining text is in pencil. Pages [1] and [60R] are blank, and page [60V] includes notations written with the notebook in reversed position. The text begins on p. [2R].

2. As a post commander, Dodge had authority to order his own absence from his duty station for a period of up to seven days without consulting his department commander.

3. Dodge's domestic servants Joe and Laura had accompanied him from post to post since 1874.

On a rise just south of Spring Creek I had stopped & counted 96 farm houses. All this in eight months of winter.

Stopped at the Reed House in Pierre - & got as good rooms as they have. Was visited by several people & one invited me to play a game of billiards, which I can never resist.[4] Though tired, I played several games, but when I wanted to stop it was pouring rain, so kept on playing. About 12.30 am it let up enough for me to get to my hotel without a ducking, & I took advantage of it, to be very soon wrapped in the Arms of Morpheus.

June 24. Pierre, Dakota Territory

The tramping around in the shell of a hotel woke me early. Got up, & took breakfast about 5.30 am. Joe Laura & Ida saw me to the train, & <at>soon after 6 am I bade them good by.

The rain had made everything green, there was no dust, & I had a very quiet but pleasant trip, arriving at Kasota 11 pm.[5] Had to room with an "entire stranger" but the hotel is a fairly good one. Got supper & went to bed at once.

June 25, 1883. Fort Snelling, Minnesota

Left Kasota at 7.40 am after a good breakfast. Asked a hotel porter this am where I could find the bootblack. "Bootblack" exclaimed he, "there is none in this town" - Reached depot at St Paul's 11.30 am, & was met by Col Rucker[6] with ambulance &c to take me to Ft Snelling. Over a hour's ride. Col R. handed me at depot a letter which proved to be from Tidball telling me that I am to go the whole trip - as caterer & general camp outfitter - very Bully.[7]

4. Dodge was a superior billiards player, rarely beaten and rather vain of his skill. His journal entries often describe the surprised discomfiture of his opponents. For example, see the entry for August 23, 1883, and *ITJ*, pp. 98 n, 103, 241, 389.

5. From Pierre, Dodge traveled approximately 320 miles east on the Chicago and Northwestern Railroad to Kasota, Minnesota, where he would transfer to the Chicago, Minneapolis and St. Paul line for a sixty-mile run north to the latter city.

6. Lieutenant Colonel William A. Rucker, deputy paymaster general for the Department of Dakota.

7. In the days that followed, Dodge set about making necessary arrangements and purchasing supplies. A preliminary list of articles to be obtained is in Journal Two; see Journal Two, following the entry for September 28, 1883.

On arrival at post reported to Genl Terry, & found I had orders, to go the whole trip.[8] Mrs Bacon was sick, & B. could not go – a score in woman's favor.

Met Mrs Rucker & was installed in a nice room of their nice house. Everything is very beautiful inside & out –

Met many Off[icer]s. Strolled down to post club in evening When I got back found I had missed several visitors

Went to bed about 11 pm.

June 26, 1883

Went to Hd Qrs & spent the morning buzzing the different heads of Depts in behalf of my post. There is a Boom in economy & I fear they have cut off Ft. Sully utterly.[9] But there is a chance for change of station of the Regt.[10] Had many visitors at night. After dinner rode out to Minne Ha Ha Falls with Col Rucker.[11] Visited the post, & took a general look at everything. Met my old Winter Campaign friend Smith of the Art[iller]y,[12] & had a drink with him.

Was very busy all day with official matters & there is nothing to record, except that all are pleasant & disposed to help me.

8. See introduction, p. 74.

9. In his annual report, dated October 8, 1883, General Terry criticized the program to conserve quartermaster's funds: "The allotment of money to this department from the diminished appropriation for general supplies is necessarily so small that the troops and their animals could not be maintained upon it. It has been found necessary to obtain a part of the necessary fuel and forage by the labor of the men." That makeshift arrangement, he warned, "not only creates dissatisfaction and leads to desertion, but . . . affects injuriously their drill and discipline and seriously impairs their efficiency" (*Report of the Secretary of War* [1883], p. 117).

10. This rumor proved unfounded. As further described below, p. 177, the headquarters of the Eleventh Infantry remained at Fort Sully through July 1887.

11. Located in Minneapolis, Minnehaha Falls was the fifty-foot cascade of a creek of the same name, the outlet of Lake Minnetonka. Falls and creek both took their names from Longfellow's *Song of Hiawatha* (1855).

12. Captain Frank G. Smith, Fourth Artillery, commanded the single company of artillery troops then stationed at Fort Snelling, Light Battery F. His unit had served under Dodge in the Powder River Expedition of 1876; see *PREJ*, pp. 58, 76, 114.

June 27, 1883

Directly after Breakfast Penrose (A.C.S.) & I started to Town.[13] Bought a lot of stores for the mess of our party - also some things for myself.[14] Made preliminary arrangements to get a cook & waiter - but am not sure of taking them. Met my old classmate Sub Johnson, now a retired General.[15] Bought everything the mess will want, & am arranging to have it go on same train with us.

Visited Genl Terry & family in evening as soon as I could for my own visitors Had a pleasant call. Blunt & wife & several other Offs called on me.[16] Genl Sherman is at Duluth tonight & there is going to be a ——— of a time here tomorro.[17]

June 28, 1883

Just as we were finishing breakfast the boom of the guns announced the arrival of the General at the bridge & in half an hour, escorted by 4 Cos 25th Infy & 1 Battery Arty,[18] he reached Genl Terry's house where all the Hd Qr people & myself were standing to receive him. There was great cordiality and handshaking for a few moments, & then (as one of the Ladies down the line remarked) the circus was over. The visitors went to Bkfst, & we to our several homes.

13. Captain Charles B. Penrose, chief commissary of subsistence for the Department of Dakota, had charge of the commissary depot at Fort Snelling. As a commissioned officer, Dodge had the privilege of purchasing foodstuffs stocked by the commissary department at 10 percent above cost.

14. The "stores" Dodge purchased at the commissary depot are listed in Journal Two, following the entry for September 28, 1883. The twenty-one items he purchased for himself follow that list.

15. Richard W. Johnson, Dodge's fellow West Point graduate in the class of 1848, had been awarded brevets through the rank of major general of volunteers for his Civil War service. He retired from the regular army in 1875 at the lineal rank of brigadier general.

16. Lieutenant Colonel Matthew M. Blunt, Twenty-fifth Infantry, was in command of his regiment in the absence of its colonel, George L. Andrews. On July 3 Blunt was promoted to the colonelcy of the Sixteenth Infantry, headquartered at Fort Concho, Texas.

17. The general and his party had arrived at Duluth, Minnesota, at 5 P.M. Learning of his presence, local citizens at once arranged a reception that evening at the St. Louis Hotel. At 9:30 P.M. the party boarded the train for St. Paul, arriving at 7:30 A.M. on June 28.

18. These five units comprised the entire garrison of Fort Snelling.

<Got> Drew my milage from Pierre. Went to town - slowest place I ever saw, things promised last evening were not forthcoming. I actually waited until 4 pm for the stores I bought yesterday - & for two hours more for the delivery of a few gallons of whisky.[19] Did not get to post until 7. pm - found an invitation to dine with Genl Terry - at half past six.

It was too late, but the invitn of a Dep[artment] Comdr is like that of the Presdt in the nature of an order. So I went & had a real nice dinner -

Before we got through the whole country was filled with old soldiers come to see the Genl. He shook hands with some thousands & then announced that he was tired out & in lieu of hand shaking would speak to them. He made one of his characteristic speeches No eloquence but full of plain good sense[20] Then Genl Terry was called for, & he rather botched it - for a lawyer he is a poor extempore speaker. Chief Justice Waite & Justice Grey each made a few remarks which were well received.[21] After all that fuss was over, or about 10 pm, I came home bade goodby to all who have been so kind to me, & went to packing. I am just through about 12 pm.

I took a mid day dinner with Wheeler of the Q M D,[22] who helped me a great deal -

The store-keepers of St Paul are very slow, & it was after 5 pm. before I got all my things, into the cars On arrival at post was informed by Mrs Rucker that I was invited to dinner by Genl Terry. I was half an hour late but had to obey of course Slipped on my undress coat & went over. Nice dinner, pleasant time General T's

19. Expenses of thirty-one dollars for "Ralegh Lamme 70" and "Lamme &c" recorded in Journal Two, following the entry for September 28, 1883, probably refer to bottles of champagne and this goodly supply of whisky.

20. Later in the year the *Army and Navy Journal* expressed admiration for Sherman's versatility as a public speaker: "What reunion of veterans is complete without his crisp and racy humor, and his stirring words evoking all the glory of the past—never the bitterness? Who can make such after dinner speeches? He is to prose what Dr. Holmes is to poetry, the man for occasions always rising to the situation" (October 27, 1883, p. 250).

21. Dodge consistently misspells the surname of Justice Horace Gray.

22. The quartermaster's department. Captain Daniel D. Wheeler of that department had been stationed at St. Paul since December 1881.

family delightful & cultivated people - Old Bach brother & 4 old maid Sisters - touching - but seems a waste[23]

Grand parade of Old Soldiers just after dark Genl got tired of hand shaking - so made them a speech - then Genl Terry, Ch. Just Waite & Just. Grey were called out. Crowd very nice and well behaved Sort of a reception afterwards. I got away at 10 pm, & spent two busy hours getting all my traps packed.[24]

June 29, 1883

Woke up early - as we were to leave the post at 7 am was invited by Genl Terry to Breakfast so as not to disturb Rucker & family. Got ready to start, & on time all were off - to the sound of cannon. Got our car & found everything all right & at 8.35 set out all in splendid order except Genl S. who is a little sick. N.P.R.R. gave us passes & a splendid Pullman all to ourselves, & we make our start under the most favorable auspices. At Crow Wing ran out of the oak into the pine region - & sandy soil.[25] Hot as Tophet & suffocating dust. Excellent eating car. Genl Terry & I played whist against the two Justices, & were shamefully beaten.

Terribly hot, & very dusty. Took dinner & supper on eating car - both good.

June 30

Nothing of special importance except that the extravagant praises of the scenery by tourists & writers is *bosh*[26] The bad land scenery

23. General Terry's brother was J. R. Terry (*ANJ*, November 17, 1883, p. 309). His four sisters were Polly, Betsey, Fanny, and Caddy, but according to John W. Bailey the latter was married to Captain Robert P. Hughes, Third Infantry, Terry's aide-de-camp (*Pacifying the Plains*, p. 135).

24. In his journal entry for this busy day, Dodge set down much of the same information twice.

25. From St. Paul the southern spur of the Northern Pacific Railroad followed the Mississippi River north to Brainerd, a few miles beyond Crow Wing, where it met the main east-west line.

26. Dodge refers to the promotional literature generated by advocates of tourism, settlement, and industry along the railroad. A representative example is Robert E. Strahorn's *The Resources of Montana Territory and Attractions of Yellowstone Park*, issued in 1879 by the Montana territorial legislature: "Entering Montana . . . the tourist

might be remarkable to one who had never seen anything of the kind before, but it is tame to monotony as compared with that on White River Nebraska.[27]

The ride was excessively hot & very monotonous.[28] At 9 pm halted for 1/2 an hour at Keogh to see the Offs. All the Comd was out with the band, & we had quite a Celebration.[29] Met many old friends

July 1

Tidball turned over to me $200. of the money in his hands contributed by the party. Still due $134.91.[30] First view of snow-clad peaks.[31] Diminishing river, & narrowing valley. Judges Waite & Grey went on to Helena.[32] Lost our car at Boseman, but were permitted to

---

hardly crosses the line ere objects of interest to the purely aesthetic taste plead for attention to the right and left. Then he may wander over all this marvellously beautiful domain, from the bad land region of the lower Missouri and Yellowstone at the extreme east, to the grandly rugged and often iridiscent summits of the Bitter Root range at the western boundary, and, at the close, confess in his bewilderment that nature charmed so irresistibly at different steps, it would be difficult which spot to favor in a second ramble" (p. 44).

27. Dodge compares the "bad lands" of the Little Missouri River to country he had seen on his expedition to the Black Hills in 1875; see *BHJ*, pp. 231-34.

28. According to Tidball, the party was informed at Glendive, on the Yellowstone River in eastern Montana Territory, that the temperature that day had reached 128 degrees Fahrenheit and that a fierce wind had blown for the past four days ("Report," p. 206).

29. Fort Keogh, on the Yellowstone River just west of Miles City, Montana Territory, was headquarters of the Fifth Infantry, the regiment Dodge had been expected to command in 1882 when he instead succeeded to the colonelcy of the Eleventh. General Sherman had telegraphed the commanding officer at the fort, Colonel John D. Williams, that his party would stop at the nearby railroad station for only an hour. Accordingly, on the arrival of the train at 10:30 p.m. Williams and his large garrison—eight companies of infantry and one of cavalry—were formed in line to welcome him. The general left the train and reviewed the troops by the light of lanterns.

30. These funds were payments on the mess account, which Dodge administered.

31. The initial glimpse of the Rocky Mountains occurred just as the morning mists cleared away (Tidball, "Report," p. 207).

32. The two judges' temporary separation from the main party had been planned for several weeks. On their return from the territorial capital they were accompanied by a colleague, Senator George F. Edmunds of Vermont, the man whom Dodge had quoted on the title-page of *A Living Issue*; see introduction, p. 39. At Fort Ellis Senator Edmunds and his nephew, Lieutenant Elliott J. Arthur, U.S. Navy, were invited by Sherman to accompany his party on the coming tour through Yellowstone National Park. Edmunds agreed at once and purchased for himself a "cow-boy suit" of leather colored duck, a fishing outfit, and other sportsman's supplies. Tidball observed that the

ride in the car of the Officers of Road. Snow mountains all around - rivers very high - fear we are too early in the season. Very heavy grade in Bozeman's pass 216 feet to mile. They are making a tunnel 3700 feet[33] Most excellent dinner at Merchants Hotel Bozeman

Arrived at Ellis 4 pm & went immediately to camp which Hughes had already pitched[34]

Took supper with Gordon Comdg Off. A heathen Chinee[35] as cook - sent him to hunt up another as waiter.

All of our luggage & stores arrived safely, & were put off the train at Ellis, though checked for Bozeman.

We have been very fortunate & had a glorious start so far.

July 2. Fort Ellis

Got sub[sisten]ce stores for trip - also mess furniture.[36] Hired another Chinese as waiter. Ordered stove, gridiron & lunch box - all to order.[37] Spent several hours in Bozeman - a very flourishing place. <had> Started our mess with an excellent dinner by our "Chinee".

---

senator proved an able campaigner and an enthusiastic sportsman, so that "his singular outfit was entirely appropriate" ("Report," p. 208).

33. This pass, over the Belt Range, separated the Yellowstone River watershed from that of the Gallatin River to the west. The steep grade was on a temporary railroad track for use only until the tunnel was completed. Extra locomotives were required for the ascent.

34. Fort Ellis was then occupied by three companies and was under the command of Major David S. Gordon, Second Cavalry. Tidball briefly described the layout of the fort, the scenery surrounding it, and the position of the visiting party's temporary camp: "The railroad runs directly through the post, separating the cavalry stables from the rest of the garrison. All around, except to the westward, are mountains, with intervening foot-hills; to the westward, beyond the Gallatin Valley, is the Gallatin Range. About 4 p.m. we reached the post. The General was received with a salute, and we at once took possession of our camp, which . . . was most delightfully located on the high ground immediately in rear of the post, on the south side" ("Report," p. 207). Captain Robert P. Hughes had directed the preparations.

35. A popular phrase from Bret Harte's comic ballad "Plain Language from Truthful James" (1870).

36. The foodstuffs Dodge purchased at Fort Ellis are listed in an undated entry on pp. [48V]-[48R] of Journal Two, p. 158. On May 20 Sherman had informed Terry that he hoped to borrow a mess kit from some officer at Fort Ellis, "else we must buy" (HQA LS).

37. The expenditures for "Stove &c" ($22.90) and "Gridiron" ($1.50) are included in a list of supplies purchased at Bozeman; see Journal Two, following the entry for September 28, 1883.

July 3

Repetition of above – very busy. Vice Presdt Edmunds[38] & a Lt of Navy joined or agreed to join our party. Genl Terry takes charge of them. Could start in morning if necessary.

July 4, 1883

Pretty much everything ready for our start tomorrow morning. Senator Edmunds & Lt Arthur of Navy arrived about 3 pm and were taken in charge by Genl Terry

Genl Sherman, Chf Justice Waite Asst Justice Grey Col Tidball & myself were invited to take our 4th July Dinner with Major Gordon 2d Cavy Comdg this post. Had a really excellent dinner & we all enjoyed it very much.

Had tressle bedsteads made for the party but the General "scorns them with his heels"[39] – He is the only man I know who takes a positive delight in discomfort. He was watching the Cavy Compy get off yesterday.[40] <The> A wagon was being loaded with comfortable rolls of bedding when he turned to me, "Why Dodge look at that, every private soldier has as much as a Major Genl ought to have"

July 5, 1883. Camp on Trail Creek

Was waked about 4 am by the patter of rain on my tent. Laid still & took another snooze, uncertain whether the General would start. About 5 am I heard his voice, & got up but it was raining so fast that he was uncertain what to do. However he soon determined to go

38. Following the death of President Garfield in 1881, George F. Edmunds was appointed president *pro tem* of the Senate, thereby becoming first in succession to the presidency after Garfield's successor, former Vice President Chester A. Arthur. On his arrival at Fort Ellis he was greeted with the vice-presidential salute.

39. An adaptation of *Much Ado About Nothing* III.iv.50. On July 2 Sherman informed the secretary of war that, owing to "the presence of the two distinguished judges, we will carry tents and a few more of the ordinary comforts of life than I usually approve on such trips" (HQA LS).

40. Company D, Second Cavalry, under Captain Thomas J. Gregg, left Fort Ellis on July 3 with a pack train of forty mules. This unit had been designated the escort to the Sherman party while in Yellowstone National Park, and its early departure enabled it to make advance preparations. Later, while passing over the park trails, members of the general's group would make use of mounts loaned them by the company.

rain or no rain, but it was a very slow business to pack, & load the wagons.[41]

We got off at 9.15.[42] The rain had penetrated the soil about an inch making it very slippery & the travelling was simply wretched. The wagons could not keep up, & we had to stop frequently to wait for them. At a ranche on Trail Creek we waited until nearly 4 p.m. & the "Old Man" was reluctantly forced into camp about one mile below the ranche at 4.15 pm. Tried fishing but failed to get a bite. Creek too high and muddy. Pretty camp 5500 feet above tide water & 16 miles from Fort Ellis. Cleared off in afternoon though clouds still hang around -

July 6, 1883. Donohue's Creek, Yellowstone River

Made a good start, & travelling over fair road reached Bottler's ranche on Yellowstone about 12 m.[43]

Here the General made a halt to renew acquaintance with Bottler. Judge Grey & I went on about a mile to the river to fish. It was very hot & the fat old Baby gave it up after a few casts. I had splendid sport taking 9 fine trout & 18 white fish (not very good eating but a vigorous biter).[44] Hughes tried to get the old man to go on to a creek

41. Always an early riser, Sherman imposed this discipline on his party during the portions of the summer journey made by wagons and on horseback. Ordinarily reveille was at 4:00 a.m., breakfast at 5:00, and departure from camp at 6:00 (Tidball, "Report," p. 208).

42. Accompanied by a sergeant and ten infantry soldiers, the travelers rode on four spring wagons. Four additional wagons carried the camp equipment and baggage.

43. Frederick Bottler and his brothers Philip and Henry owned a ranch and lodging place along the Yellowstone River which in recent years had become a landmark for visitors entering the national park from the north. Sherman had made cordial acquaintance with the Bottlers during his 1877 visit. His aide-de-camp at that time, Colonel Orlando M. Poe, described the ranch as "beautifully located" and its irrigated crops abundant: "One field of wheat contained 90 acres, and was the best I had ever seen up to that time. General Sherman and myself walked into it, in company with one of the Bottlers who estimated the yield at 50 bushels to the acre, an estimate which did not seem to me at all extravagant" (*Travel Accounts*, p. 98).

44. Tidball reported that during the two-hour stay at Bottler's ranch Dodge filled his twelve-pound basket with trout and "graylings": "Colonel Dodge was the principal fisherman of our party, and from this day on, until we reached the Fraser River, in British Columbia, kept our mess well supplied with delicious trout" ("Report," p. 209).

where there was good fishing but he went into camp about 2.30 p.m. on this creek, where there is no fishing, & poor grass. Several of the party tried fishing in river but got nothing. I tried & lost an excellent double leader & three fine flies. I also lost today my old Conroy reel, which I valued very highly.

July 7, 1883. Mammoth Springs

Made a good start this am. The road is up a sharp Canon of the Yellowstone & is very steep & narrow, sometimes overhanging the water. About noon arrived at Park City, a new town of one half a street. It is built on one long line, 15 feet from the line of the national park. The houses are tumbled down among the rocks, & all is as primitive as possible.[45]

Four miles of steep road brought us to Mammoth Springs - an immense deposit of lime &c from boiling watter. It is very wonderful, but has been greatly over written -

We camped on a high plateau overlooking the valley & spring, & all rode on horseback to *do* the springs. After this I went to work. Genl Sherman & the wagons go from here direct to the lower geyser basin, while all the rest of us take horse & pack mule train for the falls & canon. Was very busy separating the eatibles &c. Genl will mess with Capt Gregg, while we take Lieut Erwin.[46] Immense Hotel.[47]

45. Park City was to be the terminus of the railroad then under construction from Bozeman to the entrance of Yellowstone National Park. It consisted of "one half a street" because the south side of the one thoroughfare lay within the government reservation. Tidball remarked that businesses were housed in "every conceivable manner of shanty, the majority of which are drinking saloons" ("Report," p. 209).

46. One-half the cavalry company, with the wagons, was to go into camp with General Sherman. The other half, with the infantry detachment, remained with the other dignitaries and managed the pack mule train as it passed over mountain trails all but inaccessible to wheeled vehicles. Second Lieutenant Francis G. Irwin, Jr., Second Cavalry, had charge of the latter unit.

47. Then under construction, the Mammoth Hot Springs Hotel was a three-story frame structure capable of accommodating five hundred guests—far more than the trade at that time warranted. Tidball commented that the building "has the disadvantage of occupying the most uninteresting site to be found within the limits of the park" ("Report," p. 209). Writing in 1895, Hiram M. Chittenden summarized the short career of the company that in 1883 was erecting this "pretentious but ill-conceived structure": It quickly went bankrupt, and for a time the hotel remained unfinished. "In

July 8. Baronett's Bridge

Got under weigh about 9 am The trail or road is for wagons but rough, & very steep. Camped near this Bridge about 4 pm, after a long & hard march The bridge is historic - Joseph & Howard passed over it on the celebrated campaign.[48] Nothing remarkable today.

July 9, 1883. Falls of Yellowstone

Broke camp quite early. The trail leading up the river is very steep, sometimes dangerous. The river flows in a canon 6 or 800 feet deep, with almost perpendicular sides, & the trail is dizzily near. Tower Creek 4 miles below Baronetts bridge runs in a gorge, but where the trail crosses it is not so deep by several hundred feet. It is however a very steep nasty & dangerous trail. All got down in safety, & went below to look at Tower Falls, over which the creek plunges into the river chasm. Coming up the mountain on south side the Chief Justice'[s] saddle slipped back, his horse began to kick It was a bad, steep place, & the Chf was thrown or fell off & badly hurt. Fortunately there happened to be a party of tourists camped very near, among whom was a Dr. He said that one & possibly two of Judge Waite's ribs were cracked. He put on a bandage, the Judge re mounted & pluckily came on - changing horses with Hughes.[49]

1885 the tourist season began with the building in possession of unpaid workmen who held it under guard until their wages were paid. Subsequently a new company, the Yellowstone Park Association, acquired the property and completed the hotel, which has remained in operation since" (*The Yellowstone National Park*, pp. 115-16).

48. The bridge's claim to historic status had been established six years earlier. Named after C. J. Baronett, "Yellowstone Jack," a well-known scout and guide who built it, the bridge was the first to span the Yellowstone River. In his pursuit of the fleeing Nez Perce Indians under Chief Joseph from Washington Territory, on September 5, 1877, Brigadier General O. O. Howard and his army force repaired and crossed the bridge, which had been partially burnt by the Nez Perces the day before. See Beal, *"I Will Fight No More Forever,"* pp. 180-81.

49. Tidball's account of this incident adds details to the one by Dodge: "Soon after starting . . . while ascending a steep bluff, the saddle of the Chief Justice slipped, causing his horse to buck; the saddle then turning, the Chief Justice fell heavily to the ground, but fortunately in a place free from rocks or logs. At first he thought himself uninjured, but as he was about to remount he felt something wrong about his side. Within a few yards from the spot there happened to be a party of excursionists, and among them a physician, Dr. King, who, being called, pronounced a fractured rib as

At Tower Creek we commenced the ascent of Mt Washburn the trail ascending its side to nearly 9000 ft. At the highest point of trail, Terry Tidball & Hughes left the rest of us to go to the summit.[50] I wanted to go, but thought I ought to stick to the Chf Justice. By a boggy trail, through great masses of snow, we passed between Mts Washburn & Dunraven,[51] down an extremely steep grade & finally struck the river exactly between the falls, & went into camp, after a most exciting day, of wild scenery - distance 21 miles. There is no doing justice to falls & Canon in words.

Bagged 2 pine grouse & 1 blue grouse. The pine grouse most delicious eating

July 10, 1883. Mud Geysers

The party got off about 7. am The Chief Justice Tidball & myself remained to *do* again all the points of interest.

The view of Falls & Canon from Point Lookout is indescribably grand & beautiful. Fish hawks nest. Chf Justice feeling much better, but very sore. At upper falls we found a good wagon road - along the banks of the Yellowstone, here very placid and beautiful flowing through lovely meadows & full of huge trout rising languidly. I could

---

the result of the fall. He ingeniously extemporized a bandage and skillfully bound up the injured parts, after which the patient remounted and we proceeded on our way" ("Report," p. 212).

50. Named after Henry D. Washburn (1832–1871), an early explorer of the Yellowstone region, this peak is the highest on the west side of the Yellowstone River. The trail from Mammoth Hot Springs to the Upper Geyser Basin ran athwart its slope, leaving only a strenuous three-mile hike to its summit. The effort yielded a magnificent panoramic view. In the report of his 1877 visit to the national park, General Sherman wrote that from the summit "is plainly seen, as on a map at one's feet, the whole of the National Park and the mountains to the south of the Yellowstone Lake, whence flow the waters east, west, north, and south. . . . [A]ny man standing on Mount Washburn feels as though the whole world were below him. The view is simply sublime; worth the labor of reaching it *once*, but not twice" (*Travel Accounts*, pp. 50–51). Tidball, Terry, and Hughes had no difficulty making the ascent except for trouble breathing at that high altitude.

51. The latter mountain was named after the Earl of Dunraven, Windham Thomas Wyndham-Quin (1841–1926), a friend and hunting companion of Dodge. See *PREJ*, p. 52. Dunraven explored Yellowstone National Park in 1874 and described it enthusiastically in *The Great Divide* (1876), one of Sherman's favorite books about the West.

not stand it. Tidball had a short line I tied it to the end of a pine stick, put on a grasshopper & soon got out a pounder. He was wormy so I threw him back. Took another with a like result, & quit. At Hot Sulphur Spgs we saw our first mud Geyser - very beautiful & curious. Camped early after only 16 miles. After a look at the mud geysers I took Judge Grey's fly rod went to the river, & in a short time took 13 trout, 1 1/4 to 1 1/2 pounds - 6 of which were good.[52]

It was intended to go to the lake tomorro, but all agreed to go away from the Yellowstone to where we could get good fish.

Jack Bean killed a B.T. deer[53]

July 11, 1883. Alum Creek

Started late, & marched only 10 miles. During the last two days <whe> we have scarcely ever been out of sight of a smoking boiling spring - passed many today & camped about 2 miles from a group, which Senator Edmunds & I visited. Found every body out fishing when I got to camp, so took my rod & went to work - Killed 16 very pretty little fellows 6 to 8 inches long.

Chf Justice Waite had a very bad turn today. We are only about 10 miles from Genl Sherman & the Comd, so General Terry sent a courier for the Dr. who arrived about 9. p.m.[54] He says no ribs are broken, but the Chf. Justice must go back. We have all fallen in love with the old man, & it has cast a gloom over the whole party.

July 12, 1883. East Fork of Firehole

Waited for a long time in camp for an ambulance which had been sent for the Chf Justice, but which passed us in the night, we being

52. In his account of the 1877 visit, Sherman wrote that below Yellowstone Falls, where the river flowed quietly between grassy banks, the trout were healthy and good eating; but above the falls, owing to warmer water from geysers and mineral deposits, they were sometimes wormy and inedible (*Travel Accounts*, p. 52). Tidball made the same observation in his 1883 narrative ("Report," p. 214).

53. A blacktail. A longtime resident of the vicinity who had accompanied Dodge's friend William Blackmore on a tour of Yellowstone National Park in 1872, Jack Bean was the guide to the party with General Terry.

54. The physician was Acting Assistant Surgeon J. C. McGuire, a civilian assigned to Fort Ellis who was accompanying the cavalry escort.

off the road. After packing all my things I took my rod & went again after the trout. In about an hour took 24. Tried fishing in a beautiful lake (Mary's) on the divide but there appear to be no fish in it. Arrived at General S.'s camp on east fork of Madison about noon.[55] No fishing - bagged 4 young ducks which were very excellent.

Tidball & I were lying in our tent, when who should ride up but McCook.[56] He of course met with a most cordial reception. He is with a party on a flying visit - Dr. & Mrs Curtis of N.Y. (Mrs C is Mc[Cook']s sister) Mcs daughter & a Miss Philips, a friend of the Chf Justice.[57] Dr. Curtis at once went in to examine the Chf Justice, & the two Doctors tell him he must go back. General S. went this am to the upper Basin, so we have not seen him. McCooks party camped near us, & he, Tidball & myself made a night of it. He goes to the Falls today, & expects to rejoin us tomorrow. All the Command is together again (except Genl S).

July 13, 1883. Upper Geyser Basin

As soon as I had packed, I made out Ch. J. Waite's account, & paid him $130, the balance due him after deducting his expenses

McCook's party got off before we were up. We got off at 7 am. About 9 reached Lower Geyser Basin[58] & found the General waiting for us, looking rugged & well, & glad to see us. Here we all bade

55. The general had arrived at this point in three days' easy march from Mammoth Hot Springs but was absent at the time Dodge and the rest of the party arrived. He had arranged a room for Judge Waite at the National Park House, a modest stopping place at the Lower Geyser Basin kept by G. W. Marshall and his wife. Attended by Dr. McGuire, the chief justice was being given a period of rest in hopes he would be able to continue the journey (WTS to Robert T. Lincoln, July 29, 1883—HQA LS).

56. Colonel McCook, Sherman's former aide-de-camp, was stationed at Fort Douglas, Utah, adjacent to Salt Lake City. He and his party had reached the national park via the Utah Northern Railroad, leaving the train at Beaver Canyon approximately one hundred miles west and proceeding thence by wagon. A visit to Fort Douglas later in the summer formed part of the general's itinerary for this inspection tour; see Journal 2, September 22, 1883.

57. Dr. Curtis, a brother of the author George William Curtis, was professor of physiology in the College of Physicians and Surgeons, New York City (*ANJ*, August 25, 1883, p. 65). According to Tidball, the McCook party also included a Mr. and Mrs. Yerbe of Salt Lake City ("Report," 216).

58. Dodge meant the Upper Geyser Basin.

Alexander McD. McCook (U.S. Army Military History Institute)

good by to the old Chief Justice, who almost shed tears over the parting, & all of us were touched. He was so genial, so kind, so winning, took everything so well, was so manly under all the novelty of camp life, & bore his hurt & pain with such plucky fortitude, that he had endeared himself to every one of us.[59] He is the exact contrast to Judge Grey, who is a selfish grumbler, thinking only of his belly. If *he* had had the tumble & hurt, not a man of our whole party would have cared, & we would have regarded the parting as a good riddance.

59. For a time Chief Justice Waite had hoped to rejoin the Sherman party at San Francisco, but in deference to the wishes of his wife he abandoned the idea. By late August he had almost recovered from his injury (*ANJ*, August 25, 1883, p. 65).

It was decided that the Chf Justice should go to the hotel at Lower Geyser Basin, & be put to bed for perfect rest. Genl S. & the Dr. went with him. We left the pack train at the Lower Basin, but all else came on to Upper. Three miles from Lower Basin came to Hell's Half Acre, which is most wonderful.[60] From there to this camp is one succession of springs & geysers. We camped at 12m, within 200 yards of Old Faithful, which spouts regularly every 65 minutes. From my tent door, where I sit I can see the steam arising from 30 or 40 geysers & springs. Almost the whole valley is occupied by them & their deposits. The Giantess went off three days ago,[61] & her

60. Tidball wrote:

> This is a pool covering half an acre, inclosed in a depression some 30 feet deep. The lower side next to the river is somewhat broken away, and all around the shaly geyser rock is giving way, huge masses caving down until it looks dangerous to approach the edge. The center of the pool is in the most violent state of boiling, heaving up in great billows. At irregular and rare intervals the whole pool is said to go up in one gigantic geyser, rising to a height of over 400 feet. The water flowing into the river raises it a foot or more, and makes it too hot for fording for several miles below. This geyser pool is evidently making its way rapidly up to the larger and higher pool; and when the break between the narrow strip separating the two finally takes place, there will probably be a commotion of hot elements rarely witnessed of late on this planet. ("Report," p. 217)

61. Nathaniel P. Langford, a member of the Washburn exploring party of 1870, was among the first white men to witness an eruption of the Giantess, on September 19 of that year:

> Ascending a gentle slope for a distance of sixty yards we came to a sink or well of an irregular oval shape, fifteen by twenty feet across, into which we could see to the depth of fifty feet or more, but could discover no water, though we could distinctly hear it gurgling and boiling at a fearful rate afar down this vertical cavern. Suddenly it commenced spluttering and rising with incredible rapidity, causing a general stampede among our company, who all moved around to the windward side of the geyser. When the water had risen within about twenty-five feet of the surface, it became stationary, and we returned to look down upon the foaming water, which occasionally emitted hot jets nearly to the mouth of the orifice. As if tired of this sport the water began to ascend at the rate of five feet in a second, and when near the top it was expelled with terrific momentum in a column the full size of the immense aperture to a height of sixty feet. The column remained at this height for the space of about a minute, when from the apex of this vast aqueous mass five lesser jets or round columns of water varying in size from six to fifteen inches in diameter shot up into the atmosphere to the amazing height of two hundred and fifty feet. This was without exception the most magnificent phenomenon I ever beheld. We were standing on the

periods are two weeks. We will not likely see any of the very grandest, that is those which throw very great volumes of water. We have seen the "Grand," the "Castle -" the "Bear" - but Old Faithful is the reliable & beautiful.

Sat up late chining with Arthur -

July 14, 1883. Old Faithful

Remained in camp under the shadow of Old Faithful The Genl arrived about 11 am & we all took to horse & visited all the Geysers & Springs in the immediate vecinity.

About 1 pm McCook & party came in & camped near us Genl returned to the hotel in Lower Basin in evening to look after Chief Justice -

I strolled out in afternoon in hope of finding something to shoot, but was nearly eaten up with musquitoes.[62] Saw the Grand, the Splendid & many others. Most beautiful of all is the Bee Hive -[63]

> side of the geyser exposed to the sun, whose sparkling rays filled the ponderous column with what appeared to be the clippings of a thousand rainbows. These prismatic illusions disappeared, only to be succeeded by myriads of others which continually fluttered and sparkled through the spray during the twenty minutes the eruption lasted. (*The Discovery of Yellowstone Park*, pp. 111-12)

62. This region was proverbial for its mosquitoes and blackflies. Anticipating their assaults, on June 18 Sherman had telegraphed Terry asking him to order five mosquito nets for use by members of the party (HQA LS).

63. Robert E. Strahorn included in *The Resources of Montana Territory and Attractions of Yellowstone Park* a description of the Beehive in eruption, written by Harry J. Norton of Virginia City:

> In the middle of the afternoon an eruption took place without a moment's warning. The column of water ejected filled the full size of the crater, and was shot up fully 200 feet. So nearly vertical does the stream ascend that on a clear day nine-tenths of the volume would fall directly back into the aperture. From this cause, probably there is no mound of any consequence built around it. At the time we witnessed its action, the ascending torrent was interposed between us and a bright, shining sun, and through its cloud of spray there formed a rainbow of magnificent proportions, lending the fountain a crowning splendor and glory that it could not otherwise possess. (p. 73)

July 15, 1883. Lower Geyser Basin, Head of Madison River

Broke camp at 8.30 a.m. Tidball & I left camp much earlier, so as to give a parting visit to the wonders.

Arrived at the Hotel at Lower Geyser (Marshall's House) we found the Genl & Chf Justice. Terry had determined to go in & as soon as they could get their dinner the whole party set out. General Terry & Hughes, Chf Justice Waite, Senator Edmunds & Lt Arthur, Capt Gregg & Lt Erwin. Only four of us left, Genl Sherman, Judge Grey, Tidball & myself —[64]

McCooks party came up about 12m, & camped near us. We are all to go together from here for 3 days. We had a very pleasant reunion & dinner at the Hotel, previous to which I had had a most glorious bath. Bought some elk & bacon. Yesterday one of the men borrowed my gun & killed a very curious animal which he called a Mountain Hare - dark color - not so large as a Jack Rabbitt - ears much smaller, but enormous splay feet, & toes two inches long[65]

July 16, 1883. Tarbee Pass[66]

The very middle day of summer, yet we found the thermometer at 22° when we got up or -10° below freezing, with ice in our buckets & wash basins Got off about 6 am McCook ahead. The road is a

64. The group with General Terry took with them the pack train and cavalry escort, leaving with General Sherman and his party the wagons and the infantry. The latter detachment would remain with them on the next leg of the journey, 454 miles from the Lower Geyser Basin to Missoula, Montana Territory.

65. In a report on the geology and natural history of the Big Horn Mountains based on observations during General Sheridan's reconnaissance of that region and the Yellowstone Valley in 1877, First Lieutenant W. L. Carpenter, Ninth Infantry, identified the species described here by Dodge as Baird's rabbit (*Lepus Bairdii*). "This animal may be looked for in the dense pine-forests at an altitude of about 9,000 feet; rarely below this elevation. It will be recognized by its large size, which is fully equal to the 'jack-rabbit' of the plains; by its dark color in summer—it is probably white in winter; and the broad and remarkably thick-furred hind feet, which spread out to a great breadth, thus affording the animal sure footing in the deep snow which surrounds its abode." Lieutenant Carpenter was unable to secure a specimen to confirm the report by F. V. Hayden in 1872 that the male of this species, furnished with well-developed mammary glands, suckled the young (*Travel Accounts*, p. 30).

66. Also known as the Tahgee or the Targhee Pass.

very heavy grade rising about 1000 feet in about 6 miles[67] - then came to a tremendous drop down (a road made by Howard when in pursuit of the Nez Perces) to the Madison Valley, & at 12 miles came to Riverside Station.[68] Thus far I had ridden on my horse, but here I took position in McCooks wagon & we started ahead in search of game. But we could'nt keep ahead & when we saw a deer, and had a good chance to bag it, we found the whole party on top of us, & the deer *got*. McCook & I stopped to fish on West Fork of Madison I got 6 good grayling, but no trout. Mc got *one* G. Scenery, road, everything lovely. Camped after crossing the backbone of the Continent[69]

July 17, 1883. Potter Creek

Got off at 6 am. Rode in ambulance with Genl. Wont do it again if I can help it - for he has a miserable narrow wagon - very uncomfortable in every way. Passed Henry Lake early & escaped musquitoes, but had six or eight miles of miserable roads. Stopped for half hour on Snake river (Henry's Fork) & saw a young Moose, & the skin of the mother[70] At second crossing of Snake River, I stopped to fish, & had the very best sport I ever had in that way. Took only seven fish, but they weighed at least 8 lbs, 2 of them going 1 1/2 pounds. Broke my rod & had to quit. Judge Grey who was with me got 3 little ones.

Camped on a small tributary of Snake & took 19 more, mostly small, but one 1 1/4 pounds.[71]

67. Named the Norris Road after its builder, P. W. Norris, an early superintendent of the national park, this trail was completed on a severely limited budget. Yet, Tidball wrote, "For a road newly cut and through dense timber this is a very good one" ("Report," p. 219).

68. A log house on the east bank of the Madison River. For the steep descent, see Beal, *"I Will Fight No More Forever,"* pp. 162-66.

69. That is, the western continental divide.

70. Probably this observation derives from the party's surprised awareness that almost no big game was being encountered. See the journal entry for August 17.

71. Alluding to Dodge and reproducing a wry observation of his, Tidball wrote of the fishing on this day: "The most expert of our anglers complained that the trout of this Western country, although so beautiful and delicious, are clumsy at taking the bait; that although they strike with vigor, it is in an awkward country-like manner, entirely inferior to the more accomplished fish of the East" ("Report," p. 221).

July 18, 1883. Beaver Canon

Rode out on horseback ahead of party, which did not catch me until I had gone 6 miles.

Saw several sage hens, & took two shots at a big old cock, but did'nt get him. Saw a young Curlew. Road over long uninteresting flats - sacred to the musquito & horse fly. Reached Utah Northern R.R. at 12 m & followed it for 4 miles to Beaver City, & camped. Passed yesterday & today immense herds of cattle being driven from Oregon to Miles City Montana - in all about 10,000 head & very fine stock with very numerous young calves[72]

Shot a wolf from the ambulance, and caused the poor tender baby's (Judge Grey's) head to ache.

McCook invited us all over to the station house, & opened up his last five bottles of champagne. About 10 we bade them all good by & went to camp & to bed. They take the cars here at midnight & will be at Salt Lake tomorro night.

July 19, 1883. Willow Creek, Near Spring Hill

Took horse & rode ahead. Delightful morning, but the McCook champagne left only unpleasant effects. Rather sick at stomach for some hours. Got into camp about 12 m. Went fishing & worked hard for 3 hours with very poor results 3 trout & 2 white fish. Had a good nap. The road has been uninteresting <T>the mountains on either side being obscured <with> by a mist.[73]

July 20, 1883. Horse Prairie

Felt rather badly this a.m. so kept to the ambulance. Nice bracing morning, but cool for comfort. Stopped at Red Rock for an hour then came on. This creek well settled & fenced Grass inside of

72. General Sherman remarked that the chief enterprise of this vicinity was now cattle ranching, which had displaced the placer mining that reigned only a few years before. Miles City, site of a stockyard, was approximately 300 miles north east from Beaver City.

73. Tidball observed that the party was now following "the old emigrant trail to Oregon" over whose "weary miles had toiled thousands of pioneers, with their trains and families, in search of homes on the distant Columbia" ("Report," p. 222).

fences very fine. Cattle numerous. Misty, therefore poor views tho' mountains on either side. Alkaline dust - sage brush - no game, no fish as this is a mining stream & muddy. Spring chickens, fresh butter, milk & cream for dinner. Judge Grey in good humor

July 21, 1883. Head of Big Hole

Got off a little late, 6.30. In eleven miles reached Bannock City, a played out town of about 100 inhabitants. Once the proud capital of Montana, with 10,000 inhabitants.[74] Old mines in every direction. A few are yet worked, but yield but little. Stopped an hour - bought lots of things - pushed on up Grasshopper Creek & by a long but not difficult pass crossed divide to Big Hole Bagged 4 young sage hens.[75] Judge a fraud as a shot. Took about 20 nice trout after getting in camp - cold.

July 22, 1883. Crossing of Big Hole

Late again this morning Very bad road - scarcely traced. Ten miles to Sulphur Spgs. Then 18 miles to crossing of Big Hole. Very uninteresting day. Jolted to death.[76] Killed 31 fine fish in Big Hole - from 1/4 to 1/2 pound - 2 trout, 20 grayling, & 8 white fish. Took all but one with fly. Good camp, but no wood. Judge Grey took 11 fish & Tidball 4 -

Quite cold at night Magnificent views

74. On July 29 Sherman described Bannock City to Robert T. Lincoln as "once of note as the place where Gold was first discovered in Montana, and as the Capital of the Territory reduced to a County seat, but now even that distinction is taken away, for the County seat is moved to Dillon on the Railroad" (HQA LS). Selected as seat of the territorial government in 1864, in the following year Bannock City was supplanted by Virginia City. That town remained the capital until 1875, when it too was displaced, by Helena. Tidball noticed at Bannock City "numerous signs of banks, assay offices, 'gold dust bought here,' still clinging to the decaying houses [that] attest the business activity . . . in days not long gone by" ("Report," pp. 222–23).

75. Tidball wrote: "During this day, and from this on, we saw broods of blue grouse, better known as *fool hens*, on account of their extreme stupidity. The young were at the age corresponding to spring chickens, and were a great addition to the variety of our mess" ("Report," p. 223).

76. Tidball added an explanation: "The road, never a very good one, is now but little used, and is exceedingly lumpy from the many badger and gopher mounds made by these industrious animals" ("Report," p. 223).

July 23. Camp on Trail Creek

Left camp on horseback half an hour ahead of party Took a musket & had hope of an antelope Got a 400 yd shot at one running, & another about same distance at one standing overshot him by 2 inches Road very crooked - passed Gibbons battle ground[77] about 11 am, crossed Pioneer Ck, & turned up Trail Creek. Rode it on horseback - beautiful camped near top of mountain - Flies terrible. No fish - 5 grouse.

July 24, 1883. Camp on Bitter Root Near Edwards Ranche

Very cold last night Ice an inch thick. Started on horseback ahead. Beautiful ride to top of pass - then 2 1/2 miles of plunge into an abyss. The steepest road I ever went over. I should say 1000 feet to the mile. Terribly tired - waited for ambulance at Ranche on Ross Ck but wished many times I had kept on my horse though it was very hot. Road through canon as bad as possible to be passable. The very hardest days march we have made, both on men & animals tho' only about 26 miles[78] Beautiful camp on bank of Bitter Root.[79]

77. On August 9-10, 1877, Colonel John Gibbon, Seventh Infantry, fought a pitched battle in the Big Hole Basin against the Nez Perce Indians under Chief Joseph. Both sides suffered heavy casualties, and Gibbon himself was wounded. His official report of the engagement is in the *Report of the Secretary of War* (1877), pp. 501-05; see also *ANJ*, August 18, 1877, p. 21, and Beal, *"I Will Fight No More Forever,"* pp. 112-27. A monument commemorating the battle and the men who died there was subsequently constructed. However, in 1883 it had not yet been placed on the battlefield, owing to difficulty transporting it from the Northern Pacific Railroad.

78. Sherman agreed with this assessment of the day's travel. The fourteen miles through a canyon in the afternoon he considered "the worst part of the whole Road" thus far (WTS to Robert T. Lincoln, July 29, 1883—HQA LS).

79. The contrast between the difficult travel on this day and the excellent camp at the day's end marked a twofold transition in the character of the journey. First, the Bitter Root Mountains, their peaks outlined by sunset, were now behind the party. Henceforward, smoke from forest fires cut off all distant views, ordinarily a great satisfaction of mountain travel. Second, in the valley of the Bitter Root River the evidences of a more temperate climate were everywhere. As Sherman wrote with some exaggeration, the party seemed "positively on the waters of the Pacific" (WTS to Robert T. Lincoln, July 29, 1883—HQA LS). The valley was fenced and under cultivation with tomatoes, corn, berries, and other crops that could not survive in places like those just passed, where frosty nights occurred throughout the year. See Dodge's journal entry for July 25; Tidball, "Report," pp. 224-25.

Nine Trout, none over half a pound - 5 grouse - elegant little fellows. Judge took 3 trout

July 25, 1883. Camp on Bitter Root Near Mitchel's Ranche

Broke camp at usual hour. Nine miles to Skelkaho, an embrio town of some 4 or 5 houses - Then ten miles, some of it bad road to Corvales - a town of probably 100 people.[80] Got some oats, & a few things for mess. Also got some Vegetables lettuce potatoes onions &c - & <also> some chickens - from a farmer this side

This valley is destined to become a very rich community - soil good only needing water & there are numerous irrigating ditches —

Camped at Mitchels. He took us into his farm on river, & put us in a beautiful camp Took 7 very fine trout Judge took 4 little ones

Very hot in sun but a fine day, with beautiful scenery -

July 26, 1883. Fort Missoula

Broke camp at our usual (lately) late hour - 6.30 Bagged 3 fine young grouse in Mitchels field.

Arrived at Stevensville about 8.am - an ambitious village. Near site of Owen's old Fort, & with a mission established by Father de Smet - now merely an asylum for played out priests[81]

The scenery along Bitter Root very fine, but the way was long & very dusty. Twenty six miles below Stevensville we arrived at Fort Missoula General recd. his salute, & we drove up to Hd Qrs to shake hands with Comdg Off, and tell him that we were going into

80. "Small as the place is," Tidball wrote, "it supports a school, at which we stopped for a few minutes, and found twenty-three children busy at their lessons." He described Corvallis as "a village with three small stores, a church, and quite a number of neat, private residences. Barber-poles and baby-carriages indicated that we were again within the limits of civilization" ("Report," p. 225).

81. Fort Owen, on the south edge of Stevensville, was an adobe structure built years before by an Indian trader named Owen as a combined fortification and trading post. St. Mary's Mission, on the north side of the village, was established in 1843 by Fr. Pierre-Jean de Smet (1808-1873), the indefatigable Jesuit missionary to the Indians of the Plains and the Northwest.

camp.[82] All hands invited to dine with Maj Jordan, & all accepted except myself who went off to dine with Thompson.[83]

The Offs of 3d apparently very glad to see me.[84] Disappointed in Ft Missoula It is not nearly so pretty a post as Sully, & I think badly arranged. (Genl Sherman says he planned it, so I dont say this out loud)[85] The only advantage over Sully is the hunting & fishing. All invited to Jordans at 9 pm to meet Offs & Ladies of the garrison. After I got through went to Thompson & got a drink or two.

T. went with me to my camp, & was disposed to owl me,[86] but I told him to clear out & let me go to sleep –

82. The party arrived at Fort Missoula at about 1:30 P.M., ending what General Sherman considered the first major stage of the summer tour. Arrangements were made for the return to Fort Ellis of wagons, ambulances, some camp equipment, and the infantry escort. On confirming that the western section of the Northern Pacific Railroad was in service as far east as Missoula, five miles distant from the fort, it was decided to board a train there at 9 A.M. the next day for Rathdrum, Idaho Territory, the station nearest the next army post on the itinerary, Fort Coeur d'Alene.

The post commander at Fort Missoula, Major William H. Jordan, Third Infantry, had planned to lodge the visitors at his own home and in his other officers' quarters. However, as Sherman reported to the secretary of war on July 29, "we were so used to tents that we preferred to stick to camp, and accordingly pitched our tents inside the Fort enclosure near the river bank" (HQA LS).

83. Dodge had enjoyed the hospitality of Major Jordan in 1875, near the end of his expedition to the Black Hills (see *BHJ*, pp. 115, 239). Dodge's host this evening was First Lieutenant John P. Thompson, Third Infantry; see *BHJ*, p. 157.

84. Between 1869 and 1873 Dodge was major of the Third Infantry and saw field service with several officers who were still attached to the regiment.

85. The general had directed major changes to Fort Missoula during his Yellowstone tour of 1877. In the absence of a railroad route across the continent at that latitude, he then regarded the town of Missoula as "the door of the western frontier." Accordingly, he modified plans for the nearby fort to permit its enlargement and use at need by a full regiment of infantry. Even if its site was a compromise, necessitated by prior civilian settlement in more desirable locations, in 1877 Sherman regarded Fort Missoula as of permanent military importance, "a strategic point that will remain forever, made so by the conformation of the rivers and mountains. These will force all roads to converge here, and four hundred men here will equal a thousand at any point within 400 miles" (*Travel Accounts*, pp. 47, 63). But the imminent completion of the railroad now lessened the importance of the fort.

86. Though recorded in no dictionary, Dodge's "owl" is clearly a transitive verb meaning "to cause to stay up late at night."

July 27, 1883. On Cars, from Missoula

Up at 4 am - got all our things seperated - sent back matrasses &c but brought our messing outfit. Left Fort M. at 7 am. Got all my baggage cared for, then we loafed about town until 9 am, when the train started.[87] Several Offs down to see us off & found Baldwin on board, in charge of Moses & some Indians just retd. from Washington[88] Delightful trip in cars through a wonderfully beautiful & romantic country. Mountain streams & lakes, all beautifully mixed

Arrived at Rathdrum 10.52 pm. Found Wheaton & others waiting for us with ambulances & wagons.[89] After a tedious & chilly ride of 10 miles reached Fort Coeur d'Alene. Tents all ready,[90] - got baggage

87. Tidball sketched Missoula as "a town of great business activity, combined, as we were informed, with an unusual amount of wickedness of every variety. It is prettily situated on a plateau facing Hell Gate River. . . . The streets, decorated with worn-out cards from the saloons, were picturesque with roughly clad miners, Indians with their squaws and papooses, flashily dressed gamblers, and the ubiquitous Chinaman. Less conspicuous were more worthy citizens, many of whom paid their respects to the General at the store of Mr. Baldwin, a pioneer of the place of twenty-two years' standing" ("Report," pp. 225-26).

88. Under escort by Captain Frank D. Baldwin, Fifth Infantry, Chief Moses and other head men of the Indian tribes north of this place, including Tonasket, Sussopkin (Sarsopkin), and Lot, had visited Washington, D.C., to discuss incursions by American citizens on their ancestral lands and a recent executive order by the president mandating a reduction in the size of their reservation. An accommodation had been reached on July 9. The events leading to Chief Moses' visit to Washington D.C., and the agreement that resulted from it are described by Ruby and Brown in *Half-Sun on the Columbia*, pp. 198-211.

Captain Baldwin, an experienced troubleshooter, was judge-advocate of the Department of the Columbia and aide-de-camp to its commander, Brigadier General Nelson A. Miles. For a biographical sketch, see Robert C. Carriker, "Frank D. Baldwin," in *Soldiers West*, ed. Paul A. Hutton, pp. 228-42.

89. The railroad journey, described by Sherman as "thirteen hours of absolute comfort," covered 230 miles (WTS to Robert T. Lincoln, July 29, 1883—HQA LS). Tidball noted that although the road was in good condition, it was not yet finished and "gangs of Chinamen were at work; the woods appeared to swarm with them, and the road was lined with their squalid camps. In the evening after the mosquitoes had assumed sway in the land, it was interesting to witness the activity exercised by these Asiatics in protecting their yellow legs and shaven heads from the ravenous attacks of these insects" ("Report," p. 226).

Colonel Frank Wheaton, Second Infantry, was post commander at Fort Coeur d'Alene, the headquarters of his regiment.

90. General Sherman described Fort Coeur d'Alene and the preparations made there for his party:

in, then went over to Jacksons,[91] got a lunch supper of Pacific Codd fish & good drink of whiskey, then bed

July 28, 1883. Fort Coeur d'Alene

All our party had a magnificent breakfast at Wheatons. Post & surroundings lovely beyond compare.

This is certainly God's Country - & I would gladly compromise on it for my Heaven.[92]

Got a cook - temporary. My bed lost off wagon last night - worried - found by mail carrier on road & brought in. Wrote letters all day. Concert to Genl at night, & a nice time with the ladies.

Put out washing -

July 29, 1883. Fort Coeur d'Alene

Post lovelier than ever. Wrote letters until dinner time. Dined with Wheaton - all hands - nice dinner - near quarters - everything lovely.

Jolly time at night with Wheaton & the bachelors - telling stories. Wheaton & I are old compadres at El Paso in the days of /56.[93]

Wash returned about as dirty as when sent out.

General and Mrs. Wheaton are noted for their refined hospitality, but I had written him that we were travellers, and preferred for the time being our tents, asking him to pitch a Camp for us on the Lake shore where we could be at perfect ease, and not be a burden to a family. He construed my wish as an "order," and on arrival we found a beautiful camp prepared for us, not literally according to Army Regulations, but still most convenient. He has three Hospital tents with floors and bedsteads, one for Judge Grey, one for me, and the third for Generals [*sic*] Dodge and Tidball. These are on the margin of this beautiful Lake Coeur d'Alene, and inside the area of the Fort, which consists of seven double sets of officers quarters facing the Lake, and four sets of men's quarters forming the sides of a Rectangle open towards the Lake. (WTS to Robert T. Lincoln, July 29, 1883—HQA LS)

91. Captain James Jackson, First Cavalry, commanded Company B of his regiment, the unit designated to escort the Sherman party on its journey north as far as Fort Colville, on the Columbia River.

92. Tidball, Sherman, and many others agreed with Dodge in his assessment. See *ANJ*, October 30, 1880, p. 241; April 22, 1882, p. 860; Tidball, "Report," pp. 226–27. Sherman wrote that "General Dodge" pronounced Fort Coeur d'Alene "perfect, as near Heaven as he ever expects to get" (WTS to Robert T. Lincoln, July 29, 1883—HQA LS).

93. In 1856 Wheaton and Dodge were both first lieutenants, the former attached to the First Cavalry, the latter to the Eighth Infantry. Wheaton transferred to the infantry arm in 1866. In 1883 he was the senior colonel in the Department of the Columbia,

July 30, 1883. Coeur d'Alene

Lovely - Lovely - *Lovely*.

Fishing in the afternoon with Jackson, who rowed the boat. 41 beauties in 3 hours - one 2 pounder *Rainbow Trout* - a fish peculiar to the River outlet of the lake.

July 31

<Trout> Miles & party arrived.[94] Went up lake on Steamboat. Lunch on board. Took five trout, Dr. Wood rowing me [-] not much but all that were taken by 3 so called skilful fishermen.[95] A so called lunch at Rowels, which in reality was a huge dinner only that being at 3 pm it was not proper to call it a <lunch> dinner.[96]

Elegant party at night Flirted with all that would flirt, most desperately & I think carried away all the honors as flirt. Kept it up until 2 am[97]

---

and in the absence of its regular commander, General Miles, he commanded the department.

94. The party with General Miles had left Vancouver Barracks, Washington Territory, on July 28. It included Major John Moore, medical director of the Department of the Columbia; Second Lieutenant John S. Mallory, Second Infantry, aide-de-camp to Miles; and Mr. Saurin, first secretary of the British legation at Washington, D.C. First Lieutenant George W. Goethals, chief engineer officer for the Department of the Columbia, had just returned to Fort Coeur d'Alene from a reconnaissance tour through the region General Sherman would traverse after leaving the fort. He and his assistant had journeyed on horseback about 550 miles and by ambulance about 350, "not to mention the long miles on foot" (*ANJ*, August 18, 1883, p. 47). Lieutenant Goethals had prepared a full set of maps for use by the general. He would accompany the Miles and Sherman parties until they reached Vancouver Barracks after passing through parts of Canada.

95. The steamboat had been constructed by men at the post. Dodge's fishing companion was the post physician, Assistant Surgeon Marshall W. Wood.

96. First Lieutenant Charles W. Rowell, Second Infantry, was regimental adjutant. He would also accompany the Sherman party on the journey into Canada.

97. A full account of this entertainment appeared in the *Portland (Oregon) News* and was summarized in the *Army and Navy Journal*. According to the latter source, the post hall was "handsomely decorated" and the music of the regimental band excellent. "One very agreeable feature of the evening . . . was the evident enjoyment of Gen. Sherman, for he entered into it with the zest of a young man, and at 3 o'clock (the last dance), his eye was just as bright and keen as at 11 p.m." (August 25, 1883, p. 65).

August 1

Still lovely - lovely - Busy all day getting ready for our start tomorro. Have everything we need. Inspected transpn [-] all right. Had escort moved into camp near us

Went the rounds after ladies - & bade good by to all. They are exceptionally charming, & I have lost a heart to not less than half a dozen of them.

Packed up, & finished of[f] all business. As I went to my tent, I heard the pleasant sounds of a *musicale* - but I was not to be tempted. Had a siege of it in getting packed, as I always do when I stop for a day or two.[98]

August 2. Spokane Falls

Up very early, & got breakfast Wagons reported 4.30 am To my disgust found one 1/2 loaded with things belonging to the Miles party. Reported to the Genl & was further disgusted when he said, "Well all right, let him have it"[99] "But," I said, "we will have to leave half our own things" - "Well it dont make any difference - let it go" -[100]

That was just like him ready to be put to any inconvenience by any one who had cheek enough - but I did'nt see it. I went off & ordered another wagon without his knowing it. All this delayed us about an hour but we got off soon after 7 am - all the Offs being down to see us start. I dont think I ever left a post with so much regret.

98. From Fort Coeur d'Alene to the crossing of the Columbia River, a distance of 324 miles, the party was to be transported in ambulances, with its camping equipment carried in wagons.

99. Dodge wrote an unnecessary pair of quotation marks after "right," and before "let."

100. Sherman was inured to the aggressive officiousness of Miles, which he deplored despite recognizing his sterling qualities as administrator and commander in the field. Sherman had once told Miles with irony that his ambition seemed inexhaustible. There seemed no way to satisfy it, he said, "but to surrender to him absolute power over the whole Army with President and Congress thrown in" (Robert M. Utley, "Nelson A. Miles," in *Soldiers West*, ed. Paul A. Hutton, p. 222).

Traveled by a very good road to Spokane Falls. Arrived 1 pm. Dined at Hotel. Lovely camp fine falls. Thriving town,[101] Genl. S. recd. the people at night in Cannon Hall. I was tired & begged off.

Mr. Cutter was very polite[102] - wanted me to fish - also to visit his charming wife who I met at the ball at Fort Begged off all

August 3. Deep Creek

Gen S. & Terry with Tidball left at 5 am for Camp Spokane.[103] I took Dr. Moore, Mr Saurin & Mr. Willis into my party for the

101. Sherman and Tidball shared Dodge's impression of Spokane Falls. The general characterized its location as "a most picturesque spot, where is begun what promises to be one of the future Cities of Washington Territory" (WTS to Robert T. Lincoln, August 30, 1883—HQA LS). Tidball dilated on the scenic, commercial, and industrial advantages of the town, noting that it "soon hopes to become the Minneapolis of the Pacific Coast" ("Report," p. 228). First Lieutenant Thomas W. Symons, of the Engineer Department, explored the upper Columbia River in the fall of 1881 and declared Spokane Falls "unexcelled in the whole world as a town site" (*Report of an Examination*, p. 118).

102. Kirtland Kelsey Cutter, who had recently taken up residence in Spokane after study in New York and Europe, was at the beginning of a distinguished career as an architect, chiefly of commercial and public buildings (Durham, *History of the City of Spokane*, 2:448–50).

103. Dodge's "Terry" was an error for "Miles." The three officers were en route to Fort Spokane, sixty-five miles west. They planned to make the entire distance by ambulance on this day and on the next day to meet the northbound party with Dodge, taking advantage of a trail north across the mountains that intersected with the road to Fort Colville. The purpose of the side excursion was official: to inspect Fort Spokane with regard to its role in future military operations along the northern frontier. Sherman's account of the journey and his observations are given here from his letter of August 30 to the secretary of war:

> Accordingly early on the morning of Aug. 3rd, with a single ambulance drawn by four horses, we drove rapidly. . . . From appearances the whole country south of the Spokane from the Lake to its mouth is being rapidly settled up, and there will be no difficulty in supplying Forts Coeur d'Alene and Spokane with forage, flour and meat. There has been great controversy about Fort Spokane as to its necessity and the fitness of location. We found it a well built Post of four companies, located on a bench or plateau about a mile above the mouth of the River, in sight of the Columbia. This bench is about 400 feet above the Spokane River, and about a 1000 feet below the surrounding Country, the hill sides are well covered by pine forests. On a bench immediately above the Post is a prolific spring, which supplies the Post abundantly with the best quality of water; and near this spring is the Post saw mill, which has supplied all the lumber for the Post.

time.[104] They belong to Miles - Started 7 am Easy march 16 miles to Deep Creek. <F> Small brook - a few fish - small Pedragal[105] everywhere - but some good fields.

August 4. Chamokane Creek

Started 7 - slow road - hot & dusty. Tried fishing at Spokane Bridge - no go - only two little ones Came on to Haines Ranche got

---

There are four good barracks, and six sets of officer's quarters but none of them are finished, that is not plastered, which should be done as the winters are severe though the country abounds in firewood. Five (5) more sets of officers quarters are needed to complete the Post, when it will compare favorably with Coeur d'Alene, or any other in the Department. Lt. Col. Merriam [Henry Clay Merriam, Second Infantry] is in command, and seems peculiarly qualified for building a Post, as this one has been constructed without an appropriation by Congress out of driblets furnished out of the usual appropriations for Barracks and Quarters. There was a Government bridge across the Spokane just below the Post, but this was swept away by last winters unprecedented freshet, and here all wagon roads pointing north cease. With this bridge established, and a ferry across the main Columbia near by, the troops at Spokane could reach any point in the Spokane, Colville, and Moses Reservations, so that this Post would answer all probable uses for ten years to come, and would give great encouragement to the people, who are fast settling up that Region, at least such parts of it as are eligible, and not embraced in any of the Indian Reservations. I think twenty five thousand dollars will finish the Post, and two thousand would rebuild a better and safer bridge than the last, as well as a ferry boat for the Columbia, when Fort Spokane would answer all the purposes of the Fort contemplated further North, and obviate the necessity of any new Post in the Department of the Columbia. On the morning of the 4th, we took riding horses, descended to the River bank about two miles above the Post, crossed the Spokane in boats the horses swim[m]ing, and with a small escort struck across the country 25 miles north east to a small prairie, where we met an ambulance which next morning conveyed us to the main Colville Road, and overtook our main party before it reached Brown's at the Colville River Agency. (HQA LS)

104. By "party" Dodge meant "mess." The last named person was Bailey Willis (1857–1949), son of the New York journalist Nathaniel Parker Willis. The younger Willis was a geologist, then exploring the region on behalf of the Northern Pacific Railroad in search of coal deposits. Willis remained with the group as far as Lake Osoyoos, on the national boundary. He recounted his participation in the Sherman tour in *A Yanqui in Patagonia*, pp. 20–23.

105. "The word 'pedregal,' like the word 'canyon,' has been introduced into our language from the Spanish as designating a feature of the topography more clearly and tersely than any word or phrase in our language. As by the word 'canyon' the idea of a ravine between walls of rock is conveyed to the mind, so by the word 'pedregal' we understand an irregular volcanic surface of basalt, trachyte, etc., more or less broken by upheavals from below, and cracked and fissured in the process of cooling" (*ANJ*, April 19, 1873, p. 565).

forage - & yet came on 7 miles to a good camp on this creek except that the grass is very poor. But having got oats at Haynes, dont care. Judge tried to take comd. but I did'nt see it. He has been very good. A few little fish.

August 5, 1883. Brown's Ranche, Chewalla

Broke camp 6.30 Came slowly, for near 12 miles through a region heavily wooded with pine - a branch parallel to the Chamokane Creek, up which we are traveling. Crossed a low divide to Sheep Ck at 5 miles from camp <At Loon Ck 6 miles further> Here came in the trail by which the Genl is to come[106] This & Loon Ck form the heads of Colville River. The Vally is very fine, & noted in the Terr[itor]y.[107] In many places it is 3 miles wide a perfect level almost all under fence, & in grain & grass. Oats & wheat both poor.

Arrived at Browns 11.30 & ten minutes later the Genl came in - in Judge Grey's ambulance - both mad - the Genl because I had not camped last night at Haynes, & the Judge because he was crowded in ambulance[108]

106. Tidball estimated the distance of this junction from Hayne's (or Haine's) ranch at sixteen miles ("Report," p. 229).

107. In his *Report of an Examination*, Lieutenant Symons wrote:

> The Colville Valley, one of the pleasantest and finest valleys anywhere in the Northwest, has been retarded in its settlement and advancement many years by the fact that it is occupied and the lands held in large quantities by Indians and half-breed descendants of the old Hudson Bay fur-traders. These people, owing to the way they have been treated and the insecure tenure on which they hold their lands, are shiftless and unprogressive, make no effort to improve and beautify, and are a stumbling block in the way of civilization. When the land is surveyed and can be taken up according to the laws of the country, and titles be obtained, settlers will assuredly flock into the country, and Colville Valley will take the high rank that it deserves to hold among the most productive, pleasant, and beautiful regions of the earth. (p. 21)

Tidball described the region as "a fine, rich valley, well settled and well cultivated. Most of the settlers are old employés of the Hudson's Bay Company, who, when in 1846 the privilege of trading over this territory was withdrawn from that company, remained as farmers. These men, after the manner of most of the Hudson's Bay Company people, had taken to themselves wives from among the Indians, and their piebald descendants swarmed about their habitations" ("Report," p. 229).

108. At Brown's, Sherman spoke with Mr. Simms, the Indian Bureau's agent for the Spokane, Colville, and Moses Indians who inhabited the region. In a letter of August 30 to the secretary of war he recorded his impressions: "No single man can be Agent

This is a fine wide valley, but very marshy. Here is the site of an old Indian Mission.[109] Went into camp, - & a very good one. Went fishing - got 10 trout rather small.

Gave an excellent dinner to my party at 6 pm which put all in a good humor, & we passed a pleasant evening. Took the very coldest of cold baths, in the ice cold brook

August 6, 1883. Fort Colville

Broke camp 6.45. Road fairly good, except around bases of rocky mountains - great slopes of loose rocks 500 feet high giving a feeling of insecurity, as we wind through the narrow path at their foot.

The river is a fraud disseminating itself in great Tula ponds & Lakes & getting smaller as we go down. - We were too slow for Miles who passed us en route (by permission) - sailed away in his usual break neck - or more properly kill-horse style

At the town of Colville stopped half hour to have a mule shod. Bought some groceries & vegetables. Arrived at the Abandoned Fort 1 pm.[110] Took 14 trout for dinner - then a good nap - then a splendid dinner

---

for all these tribes. They are a type of Indian totally different from the Sioux, Cheyennes &c &c. They have no tribal relations, but are cut up into families; they have farms, or work on the farms of white men for wages; they do not confine themselves to their Reservations, but make little farms of their own, and take no steps to getting a title from the land office, and are consequently displaced by some white man, who makes the entry, and enforces his title. This is the sole and only cause I heard of for the threats of war, which sometimes reached the military Posts" (HQA LS).

109. Tidball described the scene at midday: "The Catholics have a mission here, and as it was Sunday, and the Indians, all pious, they were out in force, in all their gorgeousness of scarlet blankets and fancy calico. After church the young bucks showed off by riding furiously around. The young squaws, in bright handkerchiefs and many beads, made themselves attractive to their beaux" ("Report," p. 230).

110. The question whether to refurbish the recently abandoned Fort Colville or to establish a new post in a more strategic location to guard the national frontier and control violence between citizens and Indians had been much discussed in the past two years. At the urging of General Miles, fifty thousand dollars had been earmarked for construction of a new post. However, General Sherman wished these funds to be used most effectively in view of probable military needs, and he inspected Fort Colville with this priority in mind. On August 30 he described the post to the secretary of war:

Our cook is sick & the substitute spread himself Soup - Trout - Bacon & cabbage corn, new potatoes -

25 miles - pretty place

August 7, 1883. Opposite Old British Fort Colville[111]

Broke camp 6.30 am. Our road led back to the new town of Colville - where we stopped for half an hour. I bought a good quantity of vegetables

About <10>9 am arrived at the mission of St Francis Regis. The Indian agent was at the front gate & asked us to go in. The General consented with great reluctance, <but> as he hates to stop en route. But we had a surprise. The children were dressed up in grand style, & welcomed us with songs & speeches, & finally a character part by a little Indian girl, who sang & acted a little beggar girl, (in English). The Genl showed his usual taste, & kissed the 2 prettiest girls. Color is no object to him. Remained 1 1/2 hours. It is a Jesuit Mission, founded by Father De Smet.[112]

> It is situated on Mill Creek, a tributary of the Colville about 1 1/2 miles back, on a level plot of land, surrounded by hills covered with pine trees. It was built before the Civil war in connection with the Boundary Survey; the mens quarters were of round logs without any stone foundation, and are in consequence tumbling down, and not fit for occupation; same of stables, corrals &c &c, but the storehouses and quarters for officers are better built and in better condition. I think it will be well to maintain possession of the site, as it is as good if not better than any I found north or west of it, beside before reaching Colville we passed a wagon carrying a Steam Yawl, destined for the Columbia River above the "Little Dalles" twenty seven miles north of Fort Colville, and I was informed that this little steam Yawl or launch was the Pioneer to a larger Steam boat, which would navigate the Columbia River 300 miles north of the "Little Dalles", and quite up to the Canadian Pacific Railroad, now under rapid construction. If such be the case, Fort Colville may again come into requisition, and some of the buildings are worth saving. (HQA LS)

111. According to Tidball, this post had been built in 1858 about thirty miles south of the international boundary to house the British surveyors, engineers, and laborers who were running the boundary line ("Report," p. 231). At that time, the American surveying party had made use of the Fort Colville that Sherman had examined on August 6.

112. Tidball described both the mission, supervised by Fr. Caruana and Sr. Bernardina, and the reception:

> It was the season of summer vacation, and the boys, 50 in number, were absent, and so likewise the girls (also about 50) except 20, who, expecting us, had been

Columbia
Arrived at ∧ river 1 pm - wagons up soon after. Got our things on the ferry boat - & a really good boat, taking everything at one load.[113] River 480 yards wide, quite rapid though but 1100 feet above tide.

Arranged all our baggage for pack mules tomorro.[114]

A small town on south bank

August 8, 1883. Camp in Woods

Broke camp 7 am - with all our things on pack mules In the hope of getting some game, I started ahead with Mr Saurin & Lieut Rowell & two orderlies. Willis, a geologist of the N.P.R.R., & his assistant were with us. We crossed Kettle River & rode gaily forward (killing some ducks - that is I killed 2 mallard) Our destination was a forage pile hid somewhere up Dead Mans Creek - said by the Engineers to be 7 miles up it. We found the marks of a large camp about one mile up, looked everywhere for the forage but finding none went on. Looked all along but found no forage. The trail was utterly abomin-
ten
able, & when we had travelled <eleven> ∧ hours, I felt sure we had passed our camping place. Held a council of war. To go back meant good fare, & a good bed, but a terrible road - & we finally decided to take our chances on the ground with our saddle blankets & the game we had killed, & rely for our breakfast on overtaking

---

arrayed in all their finery, neat, clean, and civilized. They were paraded in two semi-circular lines, the smallest in front, and received us with songs of greeting, accompanied by music on a parlor organ. After the songs little speeches of welcome were pronounced in succession by several of the children, to which the General replied in appropriate words. The children ranged from four to fifteen years of age; some of them were half-breeds. After the singing one bright-eyed little girl, dressed as a beggar child, rehearsed a piece in the most effective and touching manner. ("Report," p. 231)

113. The fifty-mule pack train and the escort had already crossed the Columbia River; only the tents and baggage were yet to be ferried across.

114. The final leg of the cross-country journey, 222 miles north and west to Fort Hope, British Columbia, on the Fraser River, would be made using saddle horses and pack mules only. Lieutenant Goethals was the guide.

Abercrombie who is supposed to be repairing road ahead.[115] Crossed divide & camped after 12 hours hard march on a little brook

August 9, 1883. On Little Mountain Trail

Up with the earliest dawn & pushed forward to overtake Abercrombie. Caught him by 5 am, yet in bed - & all asleep. Got a good breakfast & then loafed round for all day. Last night was not unpleasant. I made a bed of pine boughs, & wrapped myself in my saddle blanket with saddle for pillow. Rowell constituted himself cook, & gave us an excellent supper of ducks & grouse, cooked on a tin plate, without salt, bread or coffee. The only serious annoyance was the abundance & pertinacity of the flies & musquitoes. Since we struck Old Fort Colville we have been beset by them Last night they were terrible until they were driven off by the cold.

Genl S. & party came up to us, about 1.30 pm.[116] I had been greatly worried lest all my things were broken up by the terrible trail, & it was a real surprise to find everything intact - even the demijohn of whiskey.

Camped at this point - Put whiskey into a keg, <& s> Chaffed mercilessly by all hands for *"getting lost"*. Mr Saurin nearly used up -

August 10, 1883. Imasket River

Broke camp at 6 am Had a delightful canter ahead with Genl Miles, who was equally with myself bound to get some game & fish.

115. Second Lieutenant William R. Abercrombie, Second Infantry, with a detachment of men was attempting to open the road ahead of the party, obviously with indifferent success. The forage pile, one of several along the trail south of the Canadian border, had been placed there under orders from General Miles.

116. Tidball described the party's overnight separation from the point of view of the Sherman group: "Upon leaving camp this morning, Dodge, Rowell, Saurin, and Willis, lured by the marvelous stories they had heard of the abundance of game in the country west of the Columbia, started in advance, for the purpose of hunting. In the eagerness of pursuit they had passed beyond the place for encamping, and, dreading to return to us over the trail which they found to be, as they expressed it, 'most damnable,' they encamped *al fresco*, and having secured during the day a couple of wood grouse managed to cook them for a frugal supper. Their absence from camp gave us no concern, for we knew that such veteran woodsmen were not to be lost" ("Report," p. 233). When all together, the General's party with its escort from the Columbia River crossing included eighty-one men, sixty-six horses, and seventy-nine mules.

I got 9 grouse & about 20 trout but all small. Miles beat me in weight but he got only 8 or 10 & a Lt Backus[117] beat us both badly, getting 17 fish that would go altogether up to some 8 or 10 lbs - one over a pound —

It was very hot, & I was tired out, fighting my beast of a horse, who insists on keeping his nose in the very tail of the horse in front, & rears, plunges & turns around, whenever the rider wishes to leave ranks.[118]

I went to camp about 1 pm Passed through a very pretty country, with some Indian Ranches. This is all the Reservation of the Colville Indians, & no white settlers are permitted unless they marry squaws - & there are a good many so married. Imasket a prominent Colville Chief.[119] Owns all this valley, & has large herds of ponies & cattle.

August 11, 1883. Myers Creek

Broke camp 8. am, to give a working party time to cut out a bad piece of fallen timber in front of us. Had a delightful ride - over a

117. First Lieutenant George B. Backus, Company B, First Cavalry, from Fort Coeur d'Alene.

118. Dodge was not alone in having trouble with his mount at this stage of the journey. Bailey Willis recounted two accidents, suffered in succession by Generals Sherman and Miles, who were thrown by the same horse:

> General Sherman rode a lively bay mare Kentucky-bred, a beauty of the Bluegrass. She was . . . not exactly the mount I would have picked for a mountain trail. . . . In one tangle she got mad, reared, plunged wildly, stumbled, and threw the General. He saved himself adroitly & was not hurt, but General Miles was furious at the mare. He mounted her and we rode on, General Sherman having protestingly accepted the exchange.
> Toward noon we bivouacked for lunch in a grassy meadow. Miles rode out before the group of officers and squad of cavalry and, drawing attention, he proclaimed in a loud voice, "Now I'll take it out of her!"
> He jerked hard on the cruel curb. As the mare backed and reared he whipped and spurred. She, utterly frightened to be thus suddenly attacked by the demon astride her, plunged as before and threw the doughty general . . . upon the grass, where he lay a moment, the breath knocked out of him.
> "That's it! that's it!" cried Sherman, in ecstasy. "That's just the way she threw me!" But he turned away to hide his delight. The cavalrymen dashed after the mare in a body. They could not restrain their laughter. (*A Yanqui in Patagonia*, p. 21)

119. Tidball spells the name of this chief Tenasket; in official records he is also named Tonasket or Tonaskit. He and a group of his people called on General Sherman at Osoyoos Lake on August 13. Tidball described him as "a respectable looking oldish man, resembling in appearance a Louisiana Creole planter" ("Report," p. 235).

beautiful country. Came over the very highest mountain of our whole trip - that is the highest rise in a short time - about 1500 feet in 2 or 3 miles. No accident or incident. 6 grouse - no fishing. The working parties killed many grouse with carbines Wagons waiting us here to take Genl S. to Osoyoos - but he wont -[120]

August 12, 1883. O-So-Yoos Lake

Broke camp as usual Miles' ambulance and wagons proved a failure, as the General would not use them. Miles loaded his things on them & pushed on. Consequently he got his own things into camp, some hour after we were in -

Went down to the Custom House[121] - afternoon to Smith Ranche.[122] Got plenty of seductions - apples, melons, & plenty of real Robertson Irish Whiskey

Very pretty lake - but nothing to induce a man to hanker after a station here. All sorts of things raised - wheat oats corn apples melons

August 13, 1883. Similkameen River

Got off about 7 am, which was good considering that all the pack trains had to be reorganized.[123] Four miles above the American, we came to the Brittish Custom House. The Collector Judge Haynes

120. Osoyoos Lake, which straddles the international border, was eighteen miles distant from Myers Creek. The transportation, two ambulances and two light wagons loaded with oats, had been sent from the lake by direction of General Miles.

121. Tidball and Sherman described in almost identical terms the unprepossessing appearance of this outpost of federal authority, contrasting it unfavorably with its Canadian counterpart a few miles north. Sherman wrote to the secretary of war on August 30: "The Custom House is a log building of a single room with a kind of back shed, in which the Collector, Mr. [C. B.] Bash, lives and transacts his business. This consists chiefly if not wholly in stopping Chinese emigration, and in collecting the tax of one dollar a head on cattle sent from British Columbia into the United States. The whole place is sandy, dusty, and forbidding, and in no sense suited to military uses" (HQA LS; see also Tidball, "Report," p. 234). Sherman noted that in arriving at this place the party had completed in five days the first eighty-five miles of its journey to Fort Hope, British Columbia.

122. Smith had settled on this spot about 1858, during the Fraser River gold rush. He traded principally with Indians in the vicinity.

123. A company of the Twenty-first Infantry had been sent here from Vancouver Barracks with forage. General Miles now gave orders that the forage be transferred to the pack mules and that some of the Sherman party's baggage be returned by wagon to Vancouver Barracks.

came out to meet us, & invited us all into his house, which is by far the most pretentious on this frontier.[124] Gave us a variety of drinks, though I confined myself to the Irish whiskey. When the pack trains were all up, we pushed on. Osoyoos narrows, & a man named
Kreuger
<Creyg> ∧ has built a bridge across the narrow place & charges toll. About 2 miles from Kreuger's bridge we had entered the British Territory. We stopped here for half an hour & took more of that Irish whiskey[125] Consequently when we took the trail again I was as drunk as I ever get - that is I could feel that I had been drinking. Crossed a high divide with lake & in ten miles reached the river - a stream of 100 feet wide - shallow & swift. Flies very bad, & the Yellow Jackets a perfect pest - biting & stinging - One poor blue grouse was all my bag & there were no fish - at least none that would bite. Poor camp no grass

August 14, 1883. Similkameen River

Broke camp 5.30 am Ten miles brought us to Price's Mill[126] - ten more to a pretty good camp on the banks of the river. No game. Beautiful scenery, but the air is so filled with smoke that little can be seen.

August 15, 1883. Similkameen River

Broke camp at usual hour. Six miles brought us to some very pretty fields, & a village of Indians. They live in houses, wear civilized clothing, & are Brittish subjects - with all the rights of citizens.[127]

124. The international boundary was marked by a pyramid of stones. The British custom house, operated by Judge J. C. Hayne, was two miles north of it. According to Tidball, unlike the custom house on the American side of the line, "this is a neat, comfortable frame building, with brick chimneys and broad piazzas. It occupies a beautiful site on the shore of the lake, which is here a clean sandy beach" ("Report," p. 236).

125. Sherman thought Kreuger, "a german, with a good hearty german wife and three children, a most worthy gentleman" (WTS to Robert T. Lincoln, August 30, 1883—HQA LS).

126. This mill adjoined an abandoned establishment of the Hudson's Bay Company.

127. Probably Dodge had in mind a contrast between the treatment of native inhabitants in Canada and those in the United States. The responsibility of the latter government to extend rights of citizenship to American Indians was a theme of both *Our Wild Indians* and *A Living Issue*.

Road pretty bad in places. The place indicated for camp was a wretched rocky hill side so we went on & after a while came to a large creek which is named Graveyard Ck on map.[128] - This indicates that we have made today about six miles more than we expected. Very hot. Camped on bank of River & took a fine lot of trout & White fish - enough for Dinner and Breakfast. Miles tried it but did not succeed very well.

August 16, 1883. Old Powder Camp

The Genl disgusted because he is ahead of programme. He is very curious in many respects. This a.m. he would not start until 6, though for the first time on the trip, all was ready by 5.30. Five miles brought us to Allison, a ranch occupied by a man wife & ten children - the oldest 14.[129] The nearest ∧ white neighbor is 40 miles away. They can raise no vegetables, & have a stock ranche with some 200 head of cattle & some horses - The first five miles of the trail very bad - Genl determined to go back to his programme - & make camp at Nine Mile Creek - but Miles got after him & fairly bullied him into going on. It had rained pretty heavily in the morning, the weather was cool, & delightful for traveling - & when we got to what we believed to be the 9 Mile Ck, it was a terrific gorge, with no camping place. We came on therefore & at 2.30 camped at what we take to be indicated on the map as Old Powder Camp. Trail on the whole good, but some very bad, steep & rocky

128. According to Tidball, this creek was named after an Indian burial place near its mouth, enclosed by a paling fence and ornamented with carvings ("Report," p. 238).

129. On contemporary maps this place was shown as Princeton, formerly the name of a gold mining development. Tidball took particular interest in Allison's family: "Allison himself was absent, being at Victoria, but his courteous wife received us with hospitality. She is a rosy-cheeked English woman, apparently about twenty-five, but is old enough to boast of ten children, healthy, handsome urchins, another instance . . . that the more distant and difficult of access the place, the more prolific are the human inhabitants. . . . She appeared cheerful, happy, and contented, in her isolated home" ("Report," p. 238).

August 17, 1883. Foot of Hope Mountain

Started at usual hour 6 a.m. - & made the summit of the pass in 3 hours. This is where we expected to camp tonight, & the Genl did not like to go on especially as there was good grass. Finally however he decided to take the Cañon trail (there being two) & to camp at the head of Canon. Before 12 m, the guide stopped & informed the Genl that we had arrived at the place.[130] We all wanted to go six or seven miles further & the General was now very anxious to go on - but the guide said it was the last camping place till we reached Lake House (sixteen miles he said) So we went into camp in a bad place with very little grass.[131]

One of the packers killed a deer.[132] Cold & very disagreeable crossing the Mountain - & a mixture of sleet snow & rain began to fall about 9 p.m. -

About 16 miles No game - no fish

August 18, 1883. Lake House

Waked rather late to find the whole camp buried in snow - not less than 2 inches deep cold raw & disagreeable & still snowing.

We got under weigh at 6.30, & such a journey![133] The trail was as bad as bad can be, barely passable in places, muddy boggy & very slippery, with rocks enough to make it dangerous - Sometimes on horseback, sometimes on foot, sometimes going up hill, sometimes down but always in rocks & bogs, we plodded our way not more than 2 miles an hour - making only about 9 miles by 1.30

130. The guide was a packer who had followed the trail to Fort Hope on one prior occasion. His information proved inaccurate.

131. In fact, the party was twenty-seven miles—a long day's journey—from the Lake House, intended to be the next night's camping place.

132. This was a rare success in the party's effort at hunting large animals. As Tidball observed, "we passed through regions abounding, no doubt, in large game, but saw none. Experts explained that it was because it had all taken refuge from gnats and flies on the tops of the mountains. In the Big-hole valley we had seen a dozen or so of antelope, but nowhere did we see buffalo, elk, or bear" ("Report," p. 239).

133. Dodge ended this exclamation with a question mark.

pm.[134] About six or seven miles from our camp we came to the true head of canon - & a very excellent camping ground Our guide had made a mistake yesterday - & a very serious one for us. We could easily have made the distance, & the road was comparatively good & dry. Now everything is covered with snow & slush.

The canon is the most marvellous I have ever seen.[135] Mountains rise very steep - 1500 to 2000 feet. Avalanches & water spouts have torn them, throwing great masses into the Valley, blocking out the stream for miles. One Water Spout very recent. They seem to be common in these mountains.

At 1.30 struck the old wagon road built years ago, by Her Majesty's Royal Engineers. It was a good road & cost a deal of money & labor, but is now barely passable for horses & pack mules.[136]

Ten miles of plodding brought us to the head of Suwallow River, at a shanty called the Lake House.[137] Arrived 5 p.m. - Everybody used up except Miles & myself. Packs came in half an hour after - all right. Went fishing in Lake after 6 pm - & in an hour bagged 30 fine trout - 2 grouse. Terribly hard day - only about 20 miles, but terrible trail.[138] No snow here Camp last night over 4000 feet elevation. Tonight 2250.

134. Tidball wrote: "The trail for the first 6 or 7 miles was through a dense forest of Norway spruce, over ground much of which was boggy[,] other parts of which were unspeakably rough from rocks, logs, roots, and broken corduroy. The snow caused the animals to ball badly, slip and stumble. The most veteran of our trail travelers emphatically pronounced it the worst traveling they had ever encountered" ("Report," p. 239). The *Oxford English Dictionary* defines the intransitive verb *ball* as "to become clogged, with balls (of snow, etc.)."

135. This was the Skeist River canyon, eighteen miles in length.

136. The long unused road had been intended to open up the interior valleys of the region for settlement.

137. Sherman commented on the sounding name of this outpost: "Lest some one who may follow us may construe the Lake House as a pleasant resort, surrounded by meadows of timothy hay, I will record it the rudest sort of clapboard shanty, whilst the grass and meadows are a mith [myth]" (WTS to Robert T. Lincoln, August 30, 1883—HQA LS).

138. Tidball concurred: "Taken all in all, this was the most disagreeable day's march that we had encountered in our entire route" ("Report," p. 240). However, Hope—or Fort Hope—was now only fourteen miles distant.

August 19. Fort Hope

Broke camp 8 am in order to give the animals time to feed. We are out of grain & the grass is very poor. The march today was very beautiful, through a deep canon, the sides scored by avalanches & waterspouts. The trail is an old wagon road, built at enormous expense by Her Majesty's Royal Engineers in 1861 - part of the work of the Boundary Commission. It is in remarkably good order considering that it has never had any repairs, but some of the bridges have been carried off & avalanches have overwhelmed some parts, so that it is by no means a wagon road at present. Arrived Ft Hope 2 pm.[139] Met a deputation from Yale, asking the Genl to visit that town. He Tidball & Judge Grey went & left me alone.[140] <Got>Pitched camp on

139. Dodge's laconic journal entry fails to register the relief felt by members of the party at the end of this cross country trek. Tidball noted that the animals, on short forage ration for the past several days, addressed themselves eagerly to the oats and hay that had been provided for them at Fort Hope. Despite minor accidents, men and animals were all in good condition.

Tidball and Sherman both expressed wonder at what the former termed the "marvelous endurance" of the horse that had carried Judge Gray from the Columbia River crossing to Fort Hope ("Report," p. 240). According to Bailey Willis, the judge was "no doubt wise in the law but not exactly happy on a horse (it took a dray horse to carry him)." During this stage of the journey he was under the particular care of Lieutenant Goethals and had been given the nickname "Goethals' Baby" (*A Yanqui in Patagonia*, p. 20).

140. The arrival at this small center of population brought with it invitations, some of which General Sherman felt obliged to accept. In his letter of August 30 to the secretary of war he describes these:

> During the day I received several invitations to visit Yale, 14 miles above, and the Headquarters of the New Canadian Pacific Railroad, also to dine with Mrs. Onderdonk that evening. She is the wife of Mr. Onderdonk the contractor for building the section of this Road from Port Moody on Pugets Sound to a point on Thompson's River sixty-eight miles above Yale. In the course of the afternoon a Committee of Gentlemen came down from Yale on the Railroad on the other side of the River, guided us to a ferry of Indian canoes in the upper part of Hope, by which General Miles, Col. Tidball, Judge Grey and I crossed over and went up to Yale, which is a thriving busy town with infinite prospects. We saw the town but it was too late to go up through the Rock Cuttings above the town, which are represented as extraordinary, some miles costing $300,000 per mile. Col. Bacon, relative of my A.D.C. of same name, who is an officer under Mr. Onderdonk, shew us everything visible in the smoke, which prevailed there as every where, and he dined with us at Mrs. Onderdonks in a house and at a table that would do credit to Washington. (HQA LS).

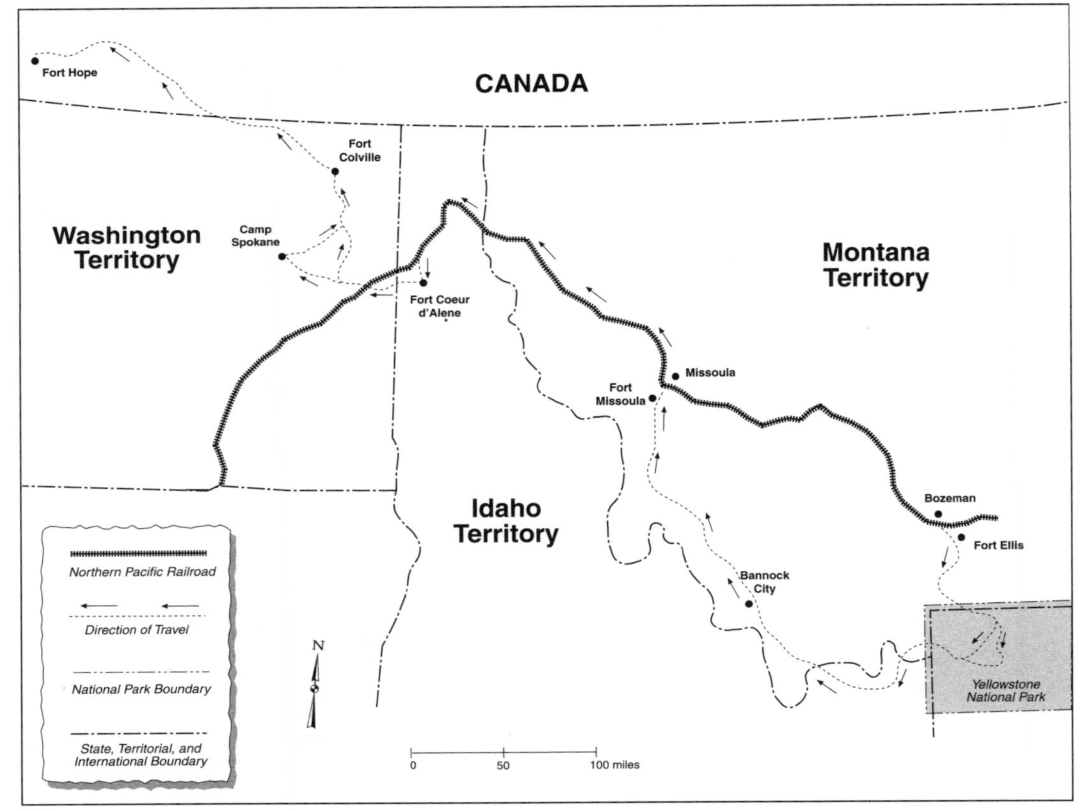

Route from Fort Ellis, Montana Territory, to Fort Hope, British Columbia, July 5–August 19, 1883

the bank of Frazers River, on the main street of the village. Got supper at Hotel - & a good one.[141] Paid up all servants & got all ready to take boat tomorro morning -

August 20, 1883. Steamer Western Slope

Up early, struck camp, & soon after 5 a.m. got on board steamer, where I found all our party.[142] Steamer stopped an hour to take on 97 head of cattle. River very swift. Stropped quite frequently - at one place took on 1 1/2 tons of cheese. Stopped for an hour at a Salmon cannery owned by a man named Adair. Inspected establishment - very interesting.[143] New Westminster was passed about 5 pm, beautiful little place At about 10 pm stopped for a landing 10 miles from Victoria to unload our Cattle. Took two hours, so I went to bed.

August 21, 1883. Port Townshend, Revenue Cutter Walcott

Was waked up about 1 am by Baldwin of Miles Staff. We were in Victoria & we were just forced to get up & go to a Hotel.

141. Sherman described Fort Hope as "a Hudson Bay Company Post still maintained, and a group of some forty houses with hotels stores &c" (WTS to Robert T. Lincoln, August 30, 1883—HQA LS).

142. Passing upstream, the *Western Slope* had reached Yale at midnight the night before. General Sherman and his party boarded it then and went to bed at once. Returning to Fort Hope, the ship took on Dodge, the personal baggage, and some horses and equipment from Vancouver Barracks.

From Fort Hope, Captain Jackson with his men returned overland to Fort Coeur d'Alene. Sherman, describing the country Jackson would pass through as he returned to the United States, predicted that it "never can amount to much." That judgment helped crystallize his assessment of future military needs in the region:

> I therefore conclude that now or in the near future we need no military Post between Colville and Bellingham Bay; that with the bridge and ferry, I have named in connection with Fort Spokane, the two Posts, Couer d'Alene and Spokane, will fulfil the problem; yet as developments may demonstrate a practicable steam boat line from the Little Dalles of the Columbia River, twenty seven miles north of Fort Colville, it may be well for us to retain the Site of Colville with the present buildings, some of which are in fair condition; and it may be well to reconnoiter the west bank of the Columbia River above the "Little Dalles," in the Colville Reservation, for the site of the only Post needed in Northern Washington Territory. (WTS to Robert T. Lincoln, August 30, 1883—HQA LS).

143. Tidball noted that numerous salmon canneries operated along the Fraser River. "The salmon are taken by Indians with gill-nets; Chinamen do the labor of canning" ("Report," p. 241).

Went to bed at once. Up at 8 am. Baldwin had been sent by Miles to send off his baggage, & as ours was piled with it, all has been sent to Tacoma by regular steamer except our hand bags. Got a chk cashed, & bought a lot of things

At 1 am the Genl visited the Governor.[144] At 12 m, we all went aboard the Rev. Cutter Wolcott - Capt Moore - & steamed for Squimault, the great Brittish Pacific Naval Station.[145] There we went aboard the great Iron Clad the Swiftsure. There were three other large men of war in the Harbor - all under Comd of Admiral Lyons, a cousin of Lord Lyons.[146] We were handsomely entertained shown through the vessel & had an exhibition drill.

At 4 pm we returned to our vessel, steamed for Port Townshend, where we arrived about 10 pm, went ashore & soon to bed -[147]

August 22, 1883. Tacoma, On Board the Revenue Cutter Wolcott

On board early, & sailed through the fog for Ft Townsend, which we inspected. Chambers in Comd - pretty post - 2 Cos.[148] Very quiet.

144. The party had taken rooms at the Driard House in Victoria. Early this morning they were waited on by the U.S. consul, Allen Francis, who joined them in a courtesy call on C. F. Cornwall, lieutenant governor of the province, at his home in the suburbs.

145. The U.S. revenue cutter *Oliver Wolcott*, commanded by First Lieutenant James B. Moore, had arrived at Victoria with orders to carry the Sherman party wherever they chose. However, thick smoke from forest fires led them to forego a full tour of Puget Sound. After a visit to their hotel by a group of dignitaries, they boarded the *Wolcott* and steamed a few miles down the Sound to the deep water bay of Esquimault.

146. The *Swift-sure*, of five thousand tons, was the admiral's flagship. Near it were anchored the *Sappho*, *Mutine*, and *Heroine*, a formidable assemblage of British naval might. The Lord Lyons mentioned by Dodge was Richard B. Lyons (1817-1887), British minister at Washington, D.C., 1858-1865.

147. Port Townsend, on the western shore of Puget Sound at its entrance, served the party for sleeping space since it was thought the *Wolcott* could not properly accommodate the whole group. However, see the journal entry for August 22.

148. According to Sherman, the fog was so thick that the *Wolcott* could reach Fort Townsend only by sounding its whistle and listening for the echo from across the water. Located on the western headland at the entrance to Puget Sound, the fort was commanded by Lieutenant Colonel Alexander Chambers, Twenty-first Infantry, whose hospitality Dodge had enjoyed in 1875 at Camp Sheridan, Dakota Territory. See *BHJ*, pp. 226-45 *passim*. Fort Townsend had been established in 1856 by Captain Granville O. Haller, Fourth Infantry, Dodge's regimental commander more than two decades afterward.

Then steamed away for Seattle, where we arrived 2 pm & found the whole town & country turned up to meet us.[149] The G.A.R. took us to their Hall, where there was speech making & hand shaking. Fog so thick could not see much of the town, which is having a great Boom[150] About 4.30 pm returned to the Walcott, & steamed for Tacoma, arriving about 8 pm There was not a bed to be had for love or money, so we retd. to the Walcott, where the Capt had made beds on the floor of his cabin. We went to bed & were very comfortable.

August 23. Fort Vancouver

Got breakfast at Hotel - bade good by to our hospitable entertainers on the Walcott & took cars for Kalama, & then <we> took boat for Vancouver where we arrived 4 pm.[151] Were met on the dock by General Miles, Morrow, Green & all hands.[152] Went with Green to his house - & soon after had a good dinner. At night we all went up to Miles house to call on Genl. After that went to Club, & waxed Green at Billiards, to his great chagrin. Went home & sat with Green until 11 1/2, gassing & drinking whiskey.

149. The *Seattle Post Intelligencer* concluded an article on General Sherman's expected arrival with the injunction that "We should all be rivals in giving him a warm welcome and due honor" (August 19, 1883, p. 2).

150. General Sherman was unenthusiastic about attending the formal reception at Seattle ("A crowd was on the wharf, and we had to go through the usual process of a speech and hand shaking"), but he was optimistic about the future development of the place: "Seattle is beyond question the most energetic prosperous city on Pugets Sound. I first visited it in 1877, again in 1880, and the rapidity of its development recalls to me San Francisco in 1849-50" (WTS to Robert T. Lincoln, August 30, 1883—HQA LS). For an earlier description of Seattle, see *ANJ*, April 12, 1871, p. 831.

151. At Kalama, on the Columbia River, the Oregon Navigation Company had placed the steamer *Lurline* at the disposal of General Sherman and his party. The group's arrival at Vancouver Barracks initiated another round of receptions, celebrations, and speeches. Located 124 miles inland from the mouth of the Columbia River, opposite Portland, Oregon, this post was surrounded by scenic views. A contemporary appreciation of its beauties, by "Vera," is in *ANJ*, April 8, 1882, p. 808.

152. Colonel Henry A. Morrow, Twenty-first Infantry, was post commander at Vancouver Barracks. Five companies of his regiment were stationed there, with one battery of light artillery. Lieutenant Colonel Oliver D. Greene, Second Artillery, was assistant adjutant general for the Department of the Columbia. Dodge and he were fellow West Point graduates in the class of 1848. Dodge had apparently written him from Fort Coeur d'Alene; see *ANJ*, August 18, 1883, p. 44.

August 24. Fort Vancouver

My trunk expressed from Spokane Falls not to be found. Went up to Dept Hd Qrs. Saw all the folks, & arranged to go to Portland with Kimball, Qr Mr.[153] Rode in ambulance miserable road. Bought quite a lot of things & found my trunk. Came back on the run to catch boat (Ferry) Genl S. dined with Green & we had the native terrapin cooked by Lt Wood 21st Infy.[154] All pronounced it a marked success, & to me it was just as good as the Maryland article – Miles gave a grand reception at night & all had to attend. It was a complete success.[155] Met Mrs Clarke 23d Infy.[156] Did not feel very well & did not dare to dance with one, as I would have had to dance with several. Tried to make myself agreeable, but gave it up as a bad job

153. Captain Amos S. Kimball, stationed at Portland, was acting chief quartermaster for the Department of the Columbia. On July 14 he had left Vancouver Barracks for Fort Spokane in order to make preliminary arrangements for transportation of General Sherman and his traveling companions when they were in that vicinity.

154. This was First Lieutenant Charles E. S. Wood, a West Point graduate (1870).

155. The *Army and Navy Journal* described the evening's entertainment at length, noting that it was attended by some guests who had traveled a great distance.

> The house was handsomely decorated, the general arrangements being on charge of Lt. O. F. Long, A.D.C. At 8:30 P.M. the presentation of guests commenced, the honors being done by Mrs. Morrow, wife of Gen. H. A. Morrow, in the absence of Mrs. Miles in the East. After the reception, dancing, to music by the 21st Infantry, began. At 11 P.M. came refreshments, and then dancing was resumed until 1 A.M., when one of the most enjoyable affairs ever held at Vancouver Barracks terminated. Amongst the military guests and their families present were Gen. O. D. Greene and Miss Greene; Lieut O. D. Long, aide-de-camp; Captain Frank D. Baldwin; Mrs. Baldwin and Miss Baldwin; Major W. A. Elderkin; Major John Moore; Captain Cullen Bryant; Capt. G. C. Smith; Dr. F. L. Town; Capt. J. H. Bartholf; Mrs. T. E. Willcox and Miss Willcox; Gen. H. A. Morrow and Mrs. Morrow; Lieut. D. Cornman; Capt. G. M. Downey; Lieut. E. B. Rheem; Lieut. C. A. Williams and Mrs. Williams; Lieut. C. H. Bonesteel and Mrs. Bonesteel; Lieut. F. J. Kernan; Capt. Geo. W. Evans; Lieut. F. E. Eltonhead; Capt. J. A. Haughey; Lieut. J. W. Duncan and Mrs. Duncan; Lieut. John S. Parke, Jr.; Miss Lee Boyle; Capt. F. E. Taylor; Lieut. R. H. Patterson; Lieut. John Pope; Major A. S. Kimball and Mrs. Kimball; Capt. C. F. Powell and Mrs. Powell; Capt. Geo. D. Hill (retired) and Mrs. Hill, of Seattle; Lieut C. E. S. Wood, 21st Infantry, and Lieut E. H. Brooke, 21st Infantry. (September 15, 1883, p. 133)

156. The wife of First Lieutenant William L. Clarke, of Dodge's former regiment.

& went home about 11.30 with Greene, leaving the female family to return with the son-in-law - Bonesteel.[157]

August 25. Portland, Oregon

Went up to Hd Qrs. Dep., & Post. Found Morrow & a large party at Breakfast. Called on Mrs Baldwin, found no one at home. Spent an hour & more with the Morrow family very delightfully.

Arranged all matters of baggage &c. Dined early at Greens & then bade farewell to this model Army family.

At 6 pm we took boat for Portland. Genl S., & Judge Grey went as guests with Senator Dolph.[158] Tidball & I went to the St. Charles Hotel. Genl S. had a grand reception by the G.A.R. spoke to & shook hands with about 5000 people. Tidball & I cut the whole thing. After it was over Miles, Morrow, ^Greene & a lot of the other Offs came to the Hotel after us, & taking us to Eppinger's saloon,[159] came near wiping us out with quantities of lush.

Fortunately they had to leave to catch 12 pm boat, & we got to bed the worse for wear but not helpless.

Sunday, August 26. Portland, Oregon, On Board Steamer Oregon

Up late, with a big head & disordered stomach Got a good breakfast then went to Steamer Oregon to see about our State Rooms &c. About 12 m tried to take a nap, but could not sleep, so sallied out to see the town. Fog & smoke so thick that only a little could be seen at a time. Took a bath & dressed myself for a dinner party at Senator Dolph's. T & I went up at 6.45, to find the dinner hour 7.30 tho we were not the first to arrive. Had a very pleasant party of 16 - all the senators of Oregon (ex- & otherwise) & a few others. Dinner

157. The marriage of Mary Greene, eldest daughter of Lieutenant Colonel Oliver D. Greene, to First Lieutenant Charles H. Bonesteel, Twenty-first Infantry, in June 1882 had been a brilliant social event, the ceremony taking place at the residence of General Miles (*ANJ*, July 3, 1882, p. 1135).

158. Joseph N. Dolph (1835–1897) was vice president of the Northern Pacific Railroad when in 1882 he was elected a U.S. senator from Oregon.

159. Louis Eppinger was proprietor of the Bureau Saloon, between First and Front Streets, Portland.

nothing extra, & wines not to my taste, being all native - Got away at 10.30, went to Hotel packed, paid bills & with all our baggage took refuge on Steamer Oregon,[160] which is to sail as soon as she can see her way. Genl & Judge came on about 11.30. To bed 12 m.

August 27, 1883. Steamer Oregon

Was waked up by a heavy surge & scrape to find ourselves aground. It was only 5 am, & I went to sleep again. When we got up to breakfast the ship was still aground, but we were only 3 miles from Portland & the Capt had gone for assistance. Our ship had her nose buried 11 feet in the sand & mud of the bank and was aground amidships.

By 9 am there were three powerful boats tugging at us, & a little before 10 am we swung clear, except the atmosphere which is so thick that we cant see the shores. At 4 pm reached Astoria. Took on great quantity of freight. Got under weigh at 6 pm but the fog was so thick that the captain was afraid to cross the bar so we dropped down to the anchorage just opposite Fort Stevenson & anchored.[161]

Good steamer - excellent food, good clean state rooms & beds. Mrs Capt McGregor 1st Cavy on board.[162]

Man left at Astoria family on board.

Good chance for sea sickness tomorrow.

August 28, 1883. Steamer Oregon

When I waked this am, the steamer was already under weigh, & as it was a bright beautiful morning I got up, to see the famed Bar - at mouth of Columbia Water smooth as glass, & we passed the ordeal as pleasantly as if sailing on a millpond. The Capt says he never saw the bar so smooth. After we got to sea, the ordinary rolling of the

160. The *State of Oregon*, a commercial vessel which would sail the party to San Francisco.

161. At Point Adams, nine miles west of Astoria and near the forbidding sand bar at the mouth of the Columbia River, Fort Stevens guarded the route inland. Its garrison was withdrawn in 1883.

162. This lady's husband, Captain Thomas McGregor, was being transferred with his company from the regimental headquarters at Fort Walla Walla, Washington Territory, to Fort Bidwell, in northern California.

vessel affected me unpleasantly, & I began to feel white about the gills Took a little drink, then a light breakfast, then a little smoke, then laid down for an hour, then got up & took a square drink - The sickness passed off without coming to any thing more than qualmishness[163] & I took a good square lunch - slept two hours - an excellent dinner & went to bed all right.

August 29, 1883. Steamer Oregon

Woke up at 7.30 ravenous Eat more breakfast than I have in a year before. Smoked & read & bathed until lunch - not omitting a couple of good drinks. Eat most heartily then went to bed & slept for two hours, then talked & smoked & read until 5 pm, when I finished off with a huge dinner. Seafaring is most excellent for eating & sleeping - three square meals since daylight & at least 14 hours of sweet sleep since yesterday.

So far have had a most delightful voyage. The Engineer has just told me that he hopes to sight the Punta Arenas light in half an hour, & if so we will sleep tonight in Frisco. I write this 8.30 pm.[164]

163. Queasiness.

164. Page [60R], which follows, is blank. On p. [60V] Dodge wrote three short calculations with the notebook in reversed position.

Journal Two August 30– September 28, 1883

August 30, 1883. San Francisco[1]

When I went to bed last night we had already passed the Lighthouse on which depended our entrance into the Golden Gate, but the fog was so thick & we poked along so slowly that all went to bed with full assurance that we would not get into dock until late this a.m - I was therefore rather surprised at 1 <am> this morning, on being awakened by the anchor going down, to find on looking out that the gas lights of the city were blazing full upon us. It was a pretty sight - no houses, sea or shipping - only long rows of gaslights ————

Turned in again very content. About 5 am the Genl rousted us up, very much against our will - & we went ashore.[2] Were met by a Qr Mr Agt,[3] who took charge of checks & furnished carriage & baggage

1. This manuscript journal is identical in style and dimensions to the notebook in which Dodge wrote Journal One except that it includes fifty-five pages, not sixty. On the front cover he wrote in black ink the following identification: "No 2 [/] Trip with [/] Genl Sherman [/] [*flourish*]." The remainder of the text is in pencil. Pages [1V], [24]-[47], [49R], [50V], [51R], and [52R] are blank. Pages [1R], [11R], [48], [49V], [50R], [51V], [52V], and [53]-[55] are written with the notebook in reversed position; pages [4V], [6V], [9V], and [10V] include some text written with the notebook reversed. The text on page [1R] includes two notations: "halladay" and "614." The first dated entry begins on page [2V].

2. The *San Francisco Chronicle* began its coverage of the visit by observing that "the arrival of California's veteran general has been the sole item of army and navy news attracting the general attention" in recent days (September 4, 1883, p. 8). As Dodge's journal only partially indicates, a crowded schedule of official and unofficial duties and appearances awaited General Sherman in San Francisco.

3. Quartermaster's agent, a civilian employee.

wagon. Reached Palace Hotel by 6, to find that we had been given almost a floor, each of us having a suite of four rooms.[4] Broke up that arrangement at once - & got into one suite - with a room over for Judge Grey. Breakfasted at 7 - then all seperated. Went to Bank with Genl. who gave me $200 - Schofield called & brought our letters[5] One from Worthington with a check for $988.20 June payment on my Book.[6] 30,149 copies sold all together which is very comforting - nothing but good news all around.

Took a turn about City with Mendenhall.[7] Visited all the markets. Subsequently I went to see the old plaza of Yerba Buena[8] - & by accident fell into China - where I spent at least an hour examining a thousand curious things. Boy with baby strapped on his back - Vegetables - nice looking Chinese Ladies - Queer shoes & costumes.

Dinner at 5. At 8 pm went to look for Gus. Bibby Found her & was really touched by the demonstration of affection of himself & Mamie.[9]

4. The Palace, which covered a city block and boasted twelve hundred rooms, was owned by William Sharon, who played host to the Sherman party at his own home on September 1. On August 24 Sherman had telegraphed General Schofield, commander of the Division of the Pacific, asking him to reserve four rooms at the Palace (HQA LS).

5. Actually, a check made out to Dodge by Sherman on August 30, and endorsed by Dodge, was in the amount of $250, not $200 (Jim Hayes, antiquarian, James Island, SC. List 183, February-March 2000). General Schofield's headquarters, near the Presidio, was on the south side of the entrance to San Francisco Bay.

6. This check from Dodge's publisher was dated August 1, 1883. Between January and June Dodge had earned royalty payments on sales of 10,490 copies of *Our Wild Indians* at ten cents each, less 127 copies "donated to promote the sales," or 10,363. A deduction of $48.10 for merchandise purchased from Worthington in January yielded a net amount of $988.20 (Statement of Account, A. D. Worthington & Co. with RID, August 1, 1883—Dodge Papers, Graff).

7. Dodge's guide was Major John Mendenhall, First Artillery, an 1851 graduate of West Point who was stationed at the Presidio.

8. Dodge wrote "plaxe." A village established in 1835 on a small cove near the present site of Telegraph Hill, Yerba Buena was formally renamed San Francisco in 1847. By 1851 the cove had been largely filled in.

9. Dodge's seeking out Gus Bibby on the day of his arrival in San Francisco suggests that she was a valued old friend. He referred to her in a journal entry for April 13, 1879, as "a dear old girl, and has a hard life of it. They have failed to realize the bright future they hoped was in store for them" (*ITJ*, p. 304). Probably Gus Bibby was the widow of Alfred Bibby, who lived at 418 Post Street and ran a store dealing in kid gloves for ladies and gentlemen (*Langley's San Francisco Directory* for 1881, pp. 107, 151).

They quite "set me up" - I have not had so much kissing in many a day. To bed at 11 pm -

August 31, 1883. San Francisco[10]

Up & breakfast 8 a.m. Took a walk - then went after Paymaster. Drew pay for July & August, & transpn up to this point amtg to $181 - & some cents. About noon commenced on my letters, & continued with very little intermission until 11 pm - Though I got tired about 5 pm & took a turn around the City. It is a very compact city & dont take much time to go over.

September 1, 1883. San Francisco

Went out about 11 am, after posting my letters. Gus Bibby came down to see me & spent an hour. Met Burt & did the town in his compy.[11] Bought a new watch. Met Royal T. Frank & lots of officers -[12]

At 4 pm Judge Grey, Tidball & myself started on train for Menlo Park guests of Ex Senator Sharon[13] 23 miles by rail, very curious country, dry parched - an arid desert but giving evidence of the most splendid crops. Sharon's home - Belmont wonderful place[14] - beautiful room for 50 guests. True hospitality - every one does as he pleases. Excellent dinner - fine wines & liquors ad lib. Noble live oaks - Ivy killing them - beautiful country

10. Dodge mistakenly dated this entry August 30.

11. Major Andrew S. Burt, Eighth Infantry, commanded the small army post at Angel Island in San Francisco Bay. He had been a member of Dodge's command on the Black Hills Expedition and had seen him socially in the years since. See *BHJ*, *passim*; *ITJ*, p. 302.

12. Major Frank, First Artillery, was post commander at Alcatraz Island, then the site of a military prison.

13. At this point, at the bottom of p. [4V], Dodge wrote and cancelled two items in an expense account: "Mr Justice Grey share box cigars 1.25" and "29 Dinner 75."

14. This property, in the Cañada del Raimundo in San Mateo County, was built by William Sharon's late business partner William C. Ralston (1826-1875), who had entertained there in magnificent style. Formerly a U.S. senator from Nevada, Sharon (1821-1885) was much interested in the financial affairs of the Pacific Slope. He had played host to General Sherman at Belmont in 1877.

places. No water. The desert blossoms as the rose[15] - Power of money.

To bed 1 am of 2d.

September 2, 1883. San Francisco

Big head & late breakfast. About 11 we all started for a ride to Menlo Park - Floods Palace - Regal state - wonders of cash.[16] House, grounds, statuary, stables horses. Kindly entertained by the Flood family Other elegant places. Retd 3 pm gorged with splendor. Fine dinner missed train. Tried again - made it & got to Hotel 8 pm - all right, but dazed with splendor.

September 3, 1883. San Francisco

Tidball & I took breakfast out this am at a common restaurant where they dont charge a dozen prices. Genl arrived about 9.30 - then the others began to drop in. At 10.15 we took carriages then boat. Visited Alcatraz first. Frank in comd everything lovely. Horrible place - all up & down - a lonely rock prison -

Then we steamed for Angels Island, & found a lovely little post in a cañon.[17] Spent an hour very pleasantly. Burt in comd.

15. A rough quotation from Isaiah 35:1.

16. James Clair Flood (1826–1889), a gold mining magnate, had once kept a saloon in San Francisco but now enthusiastically displayed his newfound wealth. The *New York World* accompanied its notice of his death by an illustration showing his palatial residence (October 12, 1888, p. 7). Estates such as Flood's helped confirm the region's reputation for extravagance. According to a contemporary observer, "The dwellings, furniture, tables, and dress of the people, indicate very liberal expenditure. San Francisco has the reputation of buying the most costly wines, cigars and silks. A saying, not deserving to be dignified as a proverb, declares that 'New York dresses better than Paris, and San Francisco better than New York.' The magnificent hotels and the palaces of a dozen millionaires are unsurpassed, if equaled by anything short of royalty in the luxury of their appointments" (Hittell, *A History of the City of San Francisco*, p. 457).

17. During his stay in San Francisco, Sherman inspected all the army posts around the bay. He judged the one on Angel Island "of no particular use" and agreed with General Schofield that the troops stationed there should be moved to the Presidio. The latter post, enlarged in recent years, he thought "admirably and beautifully located" and capable of housing a full regiment of infantry, a mounted battery of artillery, and a squadron of cavalry (WTS to Robert T. Lincoln, October 1, 1883—HQA LS).

Lunches & drinks all around - Then steam for Black Point Schofields Hd Qrs for more drinks & another lunch.[18] Took carriages for the Presidio where we reviewed five Cos Arty, & had a good show. Andrews in Comd, Mendenhall & Randal Majors.[19] After about two hours we again took Carriage & returned to Black Point to dine with Schofield. Nice dinner. At 9 pm we returned to City & to bed - rather the worse for wear.[20]

September 4. San Francisco

Went out with Gus Bibby to see the houses of the big bugs -[21] Loafed around city Could'nt find anybody. Stayed away until Genl & Tidball went off to the G A R reunion[22] then went to bed.

September 5. San Francisco

Started at 11 am for Alameda to visit Pollock & family.[23] Arrived about 1 pm - Nice family. After lunch took a long ride. Beautiful places in the foot Hills. Got back home about 10.30 pm & went to bed.

Genl & Tidball back about 12. Rousted me up & blew me up for not going to the M.O.L.L.U.S. reception.[24] Glad to get out of it.

18. The post at Black Point, at the entrance to San Francisco Bay, was known as Fort Point until 1882, when it was redesignated Fort Winfield Scott after the late major general. Its garrison consisted of a single company, a guard to the headquarters and the residence of General Schofield.

19. These officers were Lieutenant Colonel George P. Andrews, Third Artillery; Major John Mendenhall, First Artillery; and Major Alanson M. Randol, First Artillery.

20. At this point, at the bottom of p. [6V], Dodge wrote and canceled the following memorandum: "June 29 Chf Justice Waite Dinner 75."

21. People of consequence (Thornton, *An American Glossary*, 1:60). See also the journal entry for September 6.

22. At the George H. Thomas post of the Grand Army of the Republic, General Sherman met, as usual at such observances, many Civil War veterans who had served under him (*San Francisco Chronicle*, September 11, 1883, p. 3).

23. Captain Otis W. Pollock, Twenty-third Infantry, was currently on leave. An able officer, a witty correspondent, and a thoughtful man, during the 1870s he had participated in several of Dodge's campaigns and had won his regard. See *BHJ*, *passim*; *ITJ*, pp. 16-19, 378, and *passim*.

24. For an account of the Military Order of the Loyal Legion of the United States, a veteran's organization founded in 1865, see Davies, *Patriotism on Parade*. Dodge was not at this time a member of MOLLUS, but eventually he did become one (Aubin, *Register*, p. 73).

Must recollect Mrs. Thompson & her daughter Mrs. King - the latter an exceptionally pleasant woman - sister of Mrs Pollock. The little Pollock very sweet & friendly - a pleasant day -

September 6, 1883. San Francisco

Had one of my old time Whiskey Belly aches today & was utterly miserable until about 3 pm. Laid in bed most of morning. In evening went to dine with Genl Keyes.[25] Met Governor Stonman[26] and twenty of the biggest bugs - & had a pleasant party. Came back and went to bed about 12 pm.

September 7, 1883. San Francisco

Went with Mendenhall to Presidio - then to Fort Point. Met old Eakin,[27] & took some drinks with him.

Then to Cliff House nice lunch - seals - Park - Cemetery. At 3.30 pm went to bid good by to Gus Bibby Home at 4 pm & went to packing. <Got> Genl & I dined together at 5.[28] Tidball & Judge Grey absent. After dinner packed all my things - then at 8.30 pm started with Mendenhall to see Chinatown. Hired a policeman. Saw all sorts of sights & went to Theater. Got through all about midnight & returned home to write up four days of this diary & then to bed.

September 8. On Train

Left S. F. at 9, to take 9.30 train for Los Angeles[29] Have a beautiful car - that of the president of the road, & travel in style. The servants

25. Dodge's host was Erasmus Darwin Keyes, a graduate of West Point (1832) and an army officer until his resignation in 1864. Keyes, a major general of volunteers during the Civil War, was breveted a brigadier general in the regular army for his conduct in the battle of Fair Oaks, Virginia.

26. Another well-known soldier, George Stoneman (1822–1894) won brevets through the rank of major general during the Civil War and at the end of the conflict was made colonel of the Twenty-first Infantry. Owing to disability he retired in 1871 and established himself on a magnificent estate, Los Robles, near Los Angeles. In 1883 Stoneman was elected governor of California by a large majority.

27. This was Captain Chandler P. Eakin, First Artillery.

28. At this point in the manuscript, at the bottom of p. [6V], Dodge wrote and cancelled the following memoranda: "Col Tidball share box cigs 1.25" and "29. dinner 75."

29. The party took the ferry across the bay from San Francisco to Oakland, where they boarded a car provided them by A. M. Stevenson, president of the Central Pacific

are excellent & we are served sumptuously. Very hot & dusty in the San Joaquin Valley - Miles of wheat. Big Ferry boat.

Genl & Judge went to bed early. I sat till 11 pm talking with a Mr Bridger a civil engineer & ex-officer of Vols.

September 9, 1883. Sierra Madre Villa

Woke up just in time to be too late to see the desert, as the train was just entering the [*blank*] Canon.[30] Fine engineering. Arrived Los Angeles before 8 am, & at San Gabriel at 840 Left our car on
s[id]e
∧ track to wait for us - & took carriage for Sierra Madre Villa,[31] which we reached by 10. am Lovely place - Orange Groves, figs, pomegranates English walnuts, limes & lemons, everything of Tropical growth.

Took an excellent lunch at 12 m - & then went to bed tired out with heat & activity —

Railroad. The journey south through the San Joaquin Valley took them over the Tehachapi grade at the southern end, then across a stretch of the Mohave desert to the Soledad and San Fernando Passes and finally to Los Angeles.

30. Soledad Canyon. See Bowman, *Los Angeles*, p. 214.

31. Sherman was partial to this resort, a five-mile carriage ride toward the coastal range of mountains from the railroad terminal at San Gabriel. He had stayed here twice before, and in 1882 he recommended it to the Marquis of Lorne during his tour of the United States. During the present visit he expressed the view that Sierra Madre Villa was "the most attractive spot for having a quiet, good time, of any place on the American continent" (*Los Angeles Herald*, September 12, 1883, p. 3).

Tidball, who was seeing the villa for the first time, expatiated on its attractions:

> This place is elevated some 500 feet above the valley of the San Gabriel, which stretches out below some 20 miles to the Pacific. In clear weather Santa Catalina and other islands can be seen breaking the horizon to the westward. Over this entire region nature smiling has bestowed her richest gifts—a tropical climate, tempered by ocean breezes, to perennial spring, and a soil securing the broadest and highest agricultural and horticultural possibilities. As far as the eye can see, the plain below is a vast field of vineyards and orange groves, interspersed with lemons, pomegranates, limes, and other trees of semi-tropical growth. The fertile soil of this region is quickened into life by streams flowing from the water-bearing strata of the Bernardino Range. Every drop of this water is utilized for irrigating purposes, and tunnels have been driven into the mountain to tap a deeper supply. American enterprise has struck the rock, and copious fountains flow to invigorate the fruitful vine. ("Report," p. 242)

Good dinner at 6 pm & to bed by 10 -
Dolce far niente.

September 10, 1883. Sierra Madre Villa

After breakfast we took carriage & started for a survey of the show places of this valley. First to Baldwin's, the man called Lucky Baldwin for his uniform luck in stock operations -[32] A magnificent place a small insignificant house - no room for guests Place worth half a million, house not more than three thousand. Then to Rose the great manufacturer of wine on this Coast.[33] Has 800 acres in grapes, 300 in fruits - 7 or 800 in grain. Saw all the process of wine making. Shall stick to Whiskey henceforth. Then to Shorb, Wilson & Stoneman[34] wonderful vineyards - more wonderful orchards apples, peaches, pears, oranges lemons, limes, nectarines pomegranates, olives, figs Black & English walnuts almonds. Everything in the temperate & tropic zones. Returned 3 p.m. tired out - Nap - Dinner & to bed again 10.30 pm.

September 11, 1883. Mohave Station, On Special Car

Took an early breakfast then carriage to depot. Hitched our car on to the 9.05 train & arrived at Los Angeles 10 am where we were met by General Boughton & wife, & a Mr. Lynch editor of a paper in carriages, into which we were taken & driven about the city until 1 pm, then taken to the Pico House & entertained with a handsome

32. In 1875 E. J. Baldwin, formerly the keeper of a livery stable, bought Santa Anita Rancho for two hundred thousand dollars. He had then just sold for over $5 million his large interest in the Ophir Mine of the Comstock Lode. Santa Anita, which the Sherman party saw, was the first of many properties acquired by Baldwin in the vicinity of Los Angeles (McGroarty, *History of Los Angeles County*, 1:231).

33. Sunny Slope, the princely estate of L. J. Rose, was a center not only of wine and brandy production but of extensive fruit orchards. Rose was additionally a well-known breeder of trotting horses. A description of the Rose property is in Salvator, *Los Angeles in the Sunny Seventies*, pp. 153–54.

34. Dodge refers in passing to agricultural properties in the San Gabriel valley owned by James de B. Shorb, B. D. Wilson, and George Stoneman, the latter his recent companion at San Francisco.

lunch.[35] Mr Lynch presented us with half a dozen bottles of fine old whiskey & we were then driven to our car. Soon after 5 pm we were hitched on to the regular pass[enge]r. train - taken to Mojave station where we are side tracked to wait for the eastern train tomorro.[36]

Los Angeles very beautiful growing rapidly.[37] Oranges Lemons, limes, grapes, in endless variety. Visited a Banana plantation in bearing. Beautiful ornamental garden - finest I have seen - belongs to a man named Dillenback[38]

35. At the outbreak of the Civil War, Horace Boughton (d. 1891) enlisted in a New York volunteer regiment; for his later services he was breveted brigadier general of volunteers. J. D. Lynch was editor and publisher of the *Los Angeles Herald*. The Pico House, built in 1869 by Pio Pico, the last Mexican govenor of Alta California, was a three-story stone structure, considered the finest of its kind in southern California. Its large interior patio was beautified by plants, fountains, and singing birds. A photograph of the building is in Bowman, *Los Angeles*, p. 193.

The *Los Angeles Herald* described the "superb lunch, tendered by General Bouton, and served up in mine host Dunham's best style": "The company consisted of Gen. Sherman, Gen. and Mrs. Bouton, Miss Stella Binford, Gen. Tidball, Col. Dodge, Judge Gray, Dr. J. S. Griffin, and Mr. Joseph D. Lynch, of the Herald. A noted feature of the repast was a watermelon which weighed 104 pounds. Gen. Sherman and Dr. Griffin, who were compañeros in the old days in California, were specially happy as *raconteurs*. The hero of the 'March to the Sea' was as gay as a boy, and expressed not only resignation but delight at his approaching retirement from the army" (September 12, 1883, p. 3).

36. Mojave was the junction point for the Central Pacific Railroad's north-south route and another line that extended 240 miles east across the Mojave Desert to Needles, on the Colorado River.

37. Tidball shared Dodge's admiration of the climate and crops of Los Angeles but had mixed impressions of the town itself, noting that the "old Mexican town remains intact in its squalor, surrounded by a new, neat, and thrifty city of 20,000 inhabitants" ("Report," p. 243). Sherman contrasted "the small adobe town" he had seen in 1847 with the present city, and its "street cars, electric lights and all the modern improvements" (WTS to Robert T. Lincoln, October 1, 1883—HQA LS).

38. Dodge confused the name of Captain John W. Dillenback, First Artillery, whom he had met in San Francisco, with J. E. Hollanbeck, an old friend of Sherman whose elegant homestead near Los Angeles the touring party had visited. "The parterres and terraces of the Hollenbeck grounds were duly inspected and admired, the whole party descending to inspect the banana grove, which is a unique feature of Mr. Hollanbeck's charming home. . . . They next took the liberty of invading Mr. Hollanbeck's terraced vineyard, and helping themselves to the choice grapes which abound there" (*Los Angeles Herald*, September 12, 1883, p. 3).

September 12, 1883. On Train

Terrible wind storm during night, tho' the natives say it was unusually mild.

A special engine took us in tow about 7 am & we went into the desert. Arrived at The Needles about 5 pm - & at once transferred our baggage into a special car of the A. & P. R. R.[39] After waiting about an hour we went on. Crossed Colorado on a temporary bridge. Kept awake until two oclk to see then went to bed. Yucca Sand - Movahave River - Silver Milles.

September 13, 1883. Fort Wingate

Found ourselves this am well up on the San Francisco Mountain. Cool & pretty - pine woods - open glades - good grass - Saw Mills - good engineering - Sunset crossing - Abominable place & country - Lithodendron creek - Big trees in stone. Arrived Wingate Station 5 p.m. Met Bradley & a lot of his officers & took ambulance for post 3 miles.[40] Dined with Bradley, who had a reception at night. Went home with the Reg[imenta]l Q[uarte]rm[aster] Lt Mumfort[41] & spent the night. Met a lot of pleasant people Fine manual of arms. Post fair to middling[42] - poor band.

September 14, 1883. Albuquerque, N.M.

Left post 10 a.m. - & arrived in Albuquerque about 4.30. Met by a deputation with carriages who took us over all the new & old towns.

39. Here the party boarded a car placed at its service by Charles R. Williams, general passenger agent for the Atlantic and Pacific Railroad, whose just completed line extended from the bridge over the Colorado River to Albuquerque, New Mexico.

40. Fort Wingate, New Mexico, was then garrisoned by four companies of the Thirteenth Infantry and two of the Fourth Cavalry. The post commander, Colonel Luther P. Bradley, Thirteenth Infantry, had been a gracious host to Dodge at Fort Laramie in 1875. See *BHJ*, pp. 38–44, 244–46.

41. First Lieutenant Thomas Staniford Mumford, Thirteenth Infantry.

42. Both Sherman and Tidball were more liberal in their estimates. Sherman described Fort Wingate as "a well built adobe fort with shingle roofs . . . well located in every respect, and . . . all sufficient for that country" (WTS to Robert T. Lincoln, October 1, 1883—HQA LS). Tidball drew attention to the comfortable men's quarters, constructed of grayish-blue clay, "very neat and pleasing to the eye" ("Report," p. 245).

Then at 7.30 a dinner at the Armijo House - then adjourned to Aztec Club for speeches & wine.[43] Then at 12 pm to car & bed.

September 15, 1883. Santa Fe, N.M.

Was kept awake by people & did not get over an hours sleep all night. Just getting a comfortable send-off that way when porter roused me - 4 am Got up of course but the train due at 5 did'nt arrive until 7. am Heavy frost last night & very[44] hail storm here yesterday doing great damage -

Breakfast at Wallace Arrived Santa Fe 12.30 pm. Mackenzie & staff[45] Nap at Palace Hotel. Dined with Mackenzie & did not get away until about 10 pm - Mail - Letters from Joe & Laura & other parties. Tidball inflicted me, & I did not get to bed until 12 - pm

September 16, 1883. Santa Fe

Breakfast at 8. am Stroll after for an hour. Wrote letters & took nap. At 1.30 was roused by a Servt who said that the Genl wanted me at dinner. Went down & dined - then to my room & to bed again Greatly oppressed by the altitude. In afternoon strolled again. At 7 pm Tidball & I went the rounds, visiting all the Ladies. Visited the fairgrounds in morning.[46] Had a very pleasant evening - part of it spent at a gambling house where however there was no play - only drinks & conversation.[47] Met a pleasant lot of people today &

43. Sherman shared in some measure the optimism of the Albuquerque city fathers, now that the town was the sole point in New Mexico where several railroads converged. In his view, Albuquerque was destined to replace Santa Fe as a commercial center. "The old town on the river bank remains but little changed, whilst the new town about a mile back shows all the activity, and go-aheaditiveness of Modern America, and its leading citizens expect it soon to rival Chicago" (WTS to Robert T. Lincoln, October 1, 1883—HQA LS).

44. Dodge omitted a word here.

45. Brigadier General Ranald S. Mackenzie, Dodge's former cohort in the Powder River Expedition of 1876 and his commander in the Ute Expedition of 1880, now commanded the military district of New Mexico. See *PREJ*, index; *ITJ*, pp. 366-81. A few weeks after this meeting he assumed command of the Department of Texas.

46. This was the site of a recent exhibition commemorating the 350th anniversary of the founding of Santa Fe.

47. September 16 was a Sunday.

tonight & had a very good time. Dickey of 22d our pilot.[48] To bed at 11 pm

September 17, 1883. On Cars

Up at 5 a.m. At 6, took ambulance & had a very delightful ride of 28 miles to Espanola,[49] arriving at 11 am. Found train waiting for us - Presidents car & kitchen car.[50] Pulled out as soon as we got our baggage on board.

valley
Rio Grande ∧ well cultivated Fine canon & good engineering. Arrived Antonito <1>3 pm Took main line west. Toltec Canon - fine scenery.[51] To bed 10 p.m. after a day of very varied pleasure. Good food

48. The single company then stationed at Santa Fe was commanded by Captain Charles J. Dickey, Twenty-second Infantry.

49. As the result of an agreement between the Atchison, Topeka and Santa Fe Railroad and the Denver and Rio Grande Railroad that neither line should pass within twenty miles of the other, a gap in the rail line north of Santa Fe forced the Sherman party to ride in ambulances to the southern terminus of the latter road, at Espanola. On his return to Washington, D.C., Sherman registered his astonishment at this awkward arrangement. Noting the greatly lessened military usefulness of that railroad route as a consequence of the gap, he urged speedy construction to close it, by private or by public means (WTS to Robert T. Lincoln, October 30, 1883—HQA LS).

50. William J. Palmer, president of the Denver and Rio Grande, provided red-carpet treatment to the Sherman party from Espanola until their arrival at Denver, Colorado, ten days later. A Mr. Andrews, secretary to the general manager, David C. Dodge, had charge of the train, which carried the visitors first west to Durango, then east to Pueblo, Colorado, then further west on a more northerly route to Salt Lake City, Utah, and finally back east on the same route to Pueblo before making the run north to Denver. Tidball calculated the distance traveled by the party on the Denver and Rio Grande Railroad at 2088 miles.

51. The party was now traveling over a narrow-gauge (three feet wide) railway, adopted by the Denver and Rio Grande for its superior adaptability to broken country. At Antonito, just north of the New Mexico–Colorado boundary, the southernmost east-west route of the railroad passed slightly north of west toward Durango, near the southwest corner of Colorado. Tidball recorded his impressions of the recently constructed rail route through mountainous country: "This was our first experience with narrow-gauge railroads, and greatly were we astonished at beholding their capabilities for climbing mountains, passing cañons and gorges, clinging to the edges of precipices and overcoming steep grades" ("Report," p. 246).

September 18, 1883. On Car

About 1 am we arrived at Durango & switched off on side track. All up by 6 am The town much better than I expected - 2500 inhabitants & good stores of specialties.[52] Expected ambulances to meet us, but <g>found none. By accident a post ambu[lan]ce came in with paymaster[53] We gobbled it & arrived at Fort Lewis 11 am. Hall in Comd.[54] Had recd. no telegram, & did'nt know we were coming - Arm of a corp[ora]l blown off in firing salute.

Dont fancy post badly located - badly built.[55] The 22d a dandy horse-riding Regt, but a very pleasant set of officers.[56] Spent a dull day - while the Genl & Tidball went around. Elevation 8000 ft - & oppressive. Dined with Hall & staff. At 8.45 p.m. took ambulance for Durango. Bright moonlight night a lovely ride but a little risky as the driver was full. 13 miles in 1 hour & 35 m To bed on car

September 19. On Car

Slept peacefully on side track until 6 am, then got up, as the train commenced moving towards Silverton. Splendid ride.[57] Arrived

52. Tidball described Durango as "a thrifty town of about 3,000 inhabitants, and the business center of the San Juan mining district" ("Report," p. 246). During the summer of 1880 Dodge had been stationed approximately one hundred miles from Durango, then little developed.

53. Major William F. Tucker, the paymaster, had just paid the troops at Fort Lewis, twelve miles west.

54. Fort Lewis, established in July 1880 adjacent to the Southern Ute agency, afforded protection to the Indians against further encroachment on their lands, deterred the Indians from violence against settlers and railroad crews, and helped ensure order at the agency. The post commander in 1883 was Major Robert H. Hall, Twenty-second Infantry.

55. Sherman found "nothing striking" about the location of Fort Lewis, in the narrow upper valley of the La Plata River, and like Dodge, he was not pleased with the construction of the post. It "seems to have been built according to the varied tastes of its several Commanders, the Barracks and quarters being of various patterns, some fronting the parade, and others presenting their gables" (WTS to Robert T. Lincoln, October 1, 1883—HQA LS).

56. Fort Lewis was headquarters of the Twenty-second Infantry, under command of Colonel David S. Stanley, whom the Sherman party had met on its railroad journey across Arizona. He was then on an excursion to see the Grand Canyon.

57. The forty-five mile excursion to Silverton, a mining town at an elevation of ninety-five hundred feet, excited Tidball's wonder at the passage of the railroad through the canyon of the Las Animas River:

Silverton 10 am - walked & rode around until after 12 - then took car & returning over our route had a good view of the route <ton and> to & on the San Juan river. Night overtook us before we arrived at Toltec gorge - so did not see it again. Went to bed 10 pm.

September 20. Pueblo

Waked up by hearing some one say we were at Veta, which is on east side of the mountains. Got up soon after. About 9 am we were at Pueblo.[58] <Got lunch & then> Took carriages to visit the steel works - very interesting. Retd & got lunch - then at 3 pm carriages again to visit the silver smelters - not greatly impressed.[59] Rode about city. It is improved out of my knowledge.[60] Some very handsome buildings. Bids fair to be a fine city. Met Bancroft - Supdt. R. R - who I used to know when at Fort Dodge.[61]

It is a gorge with a stream rushing through it over rocks and bowlders. The sides are rough walls of rocks, almost perpendicular, and of vast height. Through this defile the railroad winds its way, a marvel of engineering skill. For a considerable distance the track, cut from the solid face of the cliff, is several hundred feet from the torrent below. In places the roadway is supported by a wall, over the edge of which we look from the car to the chasm below. One involuntarily shrinks back and clings to the railing of the platform. There being no footing in which to plant telegraph poles, the wires are sustained by iron bars, set, like brackets, in the rocky faces of the cañon" ("Report," p. 247).

General Sherman had thought of continuing north from Silverton to the town of Ouray, but on learning that the route there was over a little-used mountain trail that would require a pack train and horses, he gave up the idea.

58. The party had retraced its route to Antonito, then turned north to Garland and east through the La Veta Pass to Pueblo, Colorado.

59. The party witnessed first the production of steel railroad track, at the Bessemer Steel Works of the Colorado Coal and Iron Company, then the processes that yielded silver bullion at the Pueblo Smelting and Refining Works.

60. Between 1869 and 1871, prior to the rapid growth of Pueblo, Dodge was post commander at Fort Lyon, a few miles east.

61. W. H. Bancroft was superintendent of the Utah Division of the Denver and Rio Grande Railroad. When Dodge was post commander at Fort Dodge, Kansas, in 1872 and 1873, Bancroft was an employee of the Atchison, Topeka and Santa Fe Railroad. On p. [55R] of his journal, Dodge wrote an address: "Mrs. Bancroft [/] 478 California St [/] Denver."

Strolled about city after dinner - pretty rough place. Met several people whom I have known before

Returned to Car at 9 pm, & went to bed soon after - very tired

September 21. On Cars

At 6 am an engine took us in hand, & away we went. Got up early to see canon of Arkansas - Splendid.[62]

About noon we left Arkansas, & entered the Marshall Pass - not so fine, as to scenery, but engineering magnificent. Pass 10,500 feet above sea level - highest <in U.S.> R. R. pass in U.S.[63] From top one can see tank on west side apparently under our feet. Got up & down all safe Gunnison a growing town - fine hotel. Black Canon of Gunnison River - very fine - passed old fishing ground of mine on Cimarron, where I fell in creek 3 years ago. Passed in cars over my old road.[64] Could'nt see post of Uncompaghre & could recognize scarcely anything. Ran down river to mouth - all settled up - towns & farms.

62. Tidball tasked his descriptive powers in an effort to convey the experience of passing through the canyon of the Arkansas River: "The Grand Cañon is 30 miles long, the first 8 of which is a gorge only 20 to 30 yards wide, with perpendicular sides of rock 3,000 feet high. The Arkansas is generally a broad river, but through this cañon is so contracted that a cat could jump across it, and rushes through its rocky trough with turbulent rapidity. In some places the jagged granite so overhangs the chasm as to make the sky, seen from below, appear as only a blue streak. The cañon is barely wide enough for the contracted river and the track of the road. In many places the latter has been blasted from the solid rock, and in one place there is not room enough for even this, and the track is suspended above the river from iron rafters that have footing in the rocky sides" ("Report," p. 248). The railway journey from Pueblo to Salt Lake City, Utah, was 615 miles in length.

63. Sherman considered the railroad through the Marshall Pass "one of the boldest and most successful pieces of Engineering I have ever seen. The grades are about 4 feet rise to every hundred feet of distance or 211 feet per mile, and though one is made almost dizzy by looking back on the road travelled, I believe the bed is firm and secure, there being little more risk to the safety of the train than on the ordinary level" (WTS to Robert T. Lincoln, October 1, 1883—HQA LS).

64. Dodge was recalling his service in the summer of 1880 at a supply camp, later named Cantonment on the Uncompahgre River, and still later Fort Crawford. At that time the railroad had not yet reached the vicinity of his duty station. See *ITJ*, pp. 372-79.

Went to bed just after the train passed the Grand River - Ovation of Citizens[65]

September 22, 1883. Salt Lake City

Beautiful landscape & colors -[66] Arrived at Salt Lake City about 1 pm.[67] General & Judge went to the Fort with McCook[68] [-] Tidball

65. At the crossing of Grand River, in western Colorado, a group of citizens clamored with drum and fife for a sight of General Sherman by light of their lanterns. Upon his appearance, they informed him that they wished a military establishment in the vicinity to protect them from Indians. According to Tidball, Sherman "ridiculed the idea of such a lot of stalwart fellows wanting protection from a few miserable Indians. The ludicrousness of the idea struck them, and amid their shouts and laughter we steamed away" ("Report," p. 249).

66. Tidball wrote: "The Wasatch range, where the railroad crosses it, is made up of rounded mountains, the sloping sides of which were covered with a dense growth of dwarf aspens, maple, and scrub oak. These having been touched by frost gave out colors of the greatest brilliancy, harmony, and beauty. With one voice we pronounced it the most beautiful picture we had ever seen" ("Report," p. 250).

67. The *Deseret News* of Salt Lake City announced the expected arrival of General Sherman in friendly fashion, noting that he had visited the city several times before: "He has a warm place in the hearts of the community, concerning whom he, like a true and honest man, has said some kindly things, at the risk of being abused by bitterly prejudiced partizans. The general, however, possesses both classes of courage—moral and physical. While religiously differing as widely as the poles with the 'Mormons,' he recognizes the fact that they have rights that are entitled to respect" (September 22, 1883, p. 5).

68. Located on a height of land east of Salt Lake City, Fort Douglas was headquarters of the Sixth Infantry. Both post and regiment were under command of Colonel McCook, the boon companion of party members earlier in the summer. Sherman's inspection of the fort yielded a recommendation that additional funds be authorized for construction of army posts after a pattern exemplified by some portions of it:

> Fort Douglas is a well built Post of Stone . . . is garrisoned by six Companies of the 6th Infantry, in perfect order and in good discipline, and I was sorry to see that to enable him to receive and quarter the other four Companies of his Regiment, Col. McCook was forced by economy to construct two new barracks of wood. This is bad economy, because the chances are that Fort Douglas will be a permanent Post, and should be wholly built of stone or brick. The difference between the first cost of stone and frame should not exceed 30 per cent, whereas the duration of stone over frame must be four or five years to one. It is too late now to amend this, and I only allude to it to illustrate the principle. (WTS to Robert T. Lincoln, October 1, 1883—HQA LS)

& I to the Walker House - Erb proprietor - Very good house.[69] After dinner Erb drove me up to the Fort to a Ball - Very pleasant met all the people. Danced once Talked & drank and had a good time. To bed 2 am

September 23, 1883. Salt Lake City

I spent yesterday afternoon *doing* the city, the churches &c - & it was fortunate for I had little time today. Devoted morning to writing letters. Genl & party came down to Hotel to lunch with Erb. All lunched together then went to the tabernacle. I stood the nonsensical gabble for an hour & left.[70] Went down to Lake - pleasant ride beautiful colors of water at sunset. Tame gulls. Back to city 7 p.m.[71] Loafed round, wrote letters, packed then went to bed 10 pm

September 24, 1883. On Cars

Erb would not let Tidball or I pay any bill at Hotel. Went to car at 8.30 & were soon joined by Genl. Got off at 9.30 am Quiet day. Reached crossing of Green River at dark, & went to bed 9 pm.[72]

69. Located on Main Street, the Walker House boasted a "Passenger Elevator and all other modern improvements" in addition to the "Largest Billiard Hall in the City" (*Salt Lake City Directory for 1879-80*, p. ii). G. S. Erb owned two hotels in Salt Lake City, the Walker House and the smaller, two-story Continental.

70. The Tabernacle service for Sunday, September 23, began with a hymn sung by the choir, an opening prayer by Bishop H. B. Clawson, and a choral response, after which the sacrament was administered by the Priesthood of the Tenth Ward. This was followed by two speakers, Elder P. F. Goss, who gave an account of his recent mission in Europe, and Elder C. W. Penrose, who dealt with popular misconceptions of Mormon doctrine. Elder Penrose set in a true light "the nature, authority, and duties of the Priesthood" and explained how "the character and organization of the Church [were] the same in form and spirit as described in the Bible." Dodge appears to have left the service during Penrose's exposition of doctrine. The service concluded with another anthem by the choir and a benediction by Elder Bliss Morris (*Deseret News*, September 24, 1883, p. 3).

71. The Utah and Nevada Railway Company ran two Sunday "bathing trains" to and from the Great Salt Lake. Dodge left the city on the 4:15 p.m. train, which was scheduled to return at 7:10 p.m. (*Deseret News*, September 4, 1883, p. 4).

72. The party was returning to Pueblo, Colorado, along the same route they had followed to Salt Lake City. However, Sherman had arranged to pass over by daylight the section of the railroad he had failed to see owing to darkness on the trip west.

September 25, 1883. On Cars

When I woke up the train was stationary at Gunnison - soon moved. At Salida took road for Leadville,[73] where we arrived 3 pm. Were met by the G. A. R. a big turn out. Took carriages for the mines Did not go down.[74] Nice supper at Continental Hotel. <Genl hy> Genl held informal reception after. I took a turn around town. Regular mining town - rough.

Left at 10 p.m. very well pleased.

Altitude 10,300 ft.

September 26. Denver

Woke up with cars stationary at Cañon City - 2 bridges burned last night ahead of us. About 11 am got off. Crossed bridges safely, arrived Pueblo 1.30 pm & Denver 5.30 pm Met by the G. A. R. & a rousing crowd. Went to Windsor Hotel - very good. Genl & Tidball went to G A R. at night. I cut it. Met Hatch, of Fort Lyon memory[75] - went to bed 11 pm tired.

September 27. Denver, Colorado

Met Hatch early am & we did the town together City Hall - Fire Dept &c G A R. took possession of Genl & Tidball & kept them going all day. At night we all went to Theater to see Langrich in the serious family - only tolerable.[76] Went to bed 11 1/2 pm tired out, &

73. The visit to Leadville involved a sixty-mile excursion north from a junction with the main railroad line at Salida. Leadville, a busy mining town of twenty thousand inhabitants, reminded General Sherman of Stockton, San Francisco, and Sacramento, California, in 1849, "but the comparison favors Leadville, because the Churches, Schools, and dwellings and orderly streets show that the miners and business men of Leadville had their families with them, and consequently were not likely to commit the excesses which marked the early days of California" (WTS to Robert T. Lincoln, October 1, 1883—HQA LS).

74. Sherman and Tidball toured the famed Chrysolite mine.

75. This was Colonel John P. Hatch, Second Cavalry. The nature of his connection in Dodge's memory with Fort Lyon, Colorado, is unknown.

76. Jack Langrishe (1829-1895), actor and theater manager, and his wife Jeannette were celebrated entertainers on the Colorado mining frontier. At the grand opening of the handsome Tabor Opera House in Leadville, in November 1879, Langrishe starred in George Colman the Elder's *The Serious Family*, already a fixture of his repertory. Shortly afterward he left Leadville and built a theater in Sixteenth

Route from San Francisco, California, to Denver, Colorado, September 8–26, 1883

glad the day was over. Denver a large, & prosperous City growing rapidly

September 28, 1883. On Cars[77]

[*Items in the lists of provisions that follow, on pp. [54V]-[52V], are accompanied by a variety of check marks, asterisks, "x" marks, and other symbols not included here.*]

Stove & fixtures[78]
Closed grid-iron -
Saucepans &c -
Plates, dishes
Cups, knives & forks
Spoons, table & tea
<Table cloths - napkins>
<Wash basins>
<Candlesticks - Lamps>
<Blacking & brush>
<Matches ->
Salt cellars - & peppers
<Change - 10 cts.>
<pickles>
Dish Towels
Tin lunch box

From Comy.
Fresh Beef
Flour

Street, Denver, where he continued to perform. See Cochran, "Jack Langrishe and the Theater of the Mining Frontier," pp. 329–34.

77. This headnote, at top of p. [23V], is the only notation on the page. Pages [24]-[47] are blank; the text that follows is written from the back forward with the notebook reversed, beginning on p. [55V]. That page includes only a few calculations and a fragmentary map without identifying names or marks; p. [55R] contains an address.

78. This list and the one "From Comy" that follows it represent Dodge's initial thought and effort to obtain supplies and foodstuffs he would need as general camp outfitter and person in charge of mess arrangements. See the journal entries for June 25 and 27.

Baked Beans
Rice
Coffee
Tea
Vinegar
Candles - Ad. & Lanthern
Soap, Kitchen
<Lan> Soap - washing & Toilet
Salt
Pepper - Blk
Yeast powder
Blacking & brush
Whisk broom - small
Can opener
<Chili - Cayenne pepper>
Needle book (?)
Thread
Chili pepper
<Pickles>
Prunes
Sardines
Worcester Sauce
Sugar - cut
Sugar - gran[ulate]d
<Molasses>
<Tobacco —Durham>
Tomattoes

Towels	For Judge
Soaps	& Genl.

3 Shirts[79]
1 Vest

79. This list of clothing items, on p. [53R], enumerates Dodge's purchases for his own use at St. Paul, Minnesota, on June 27; see the journal entry for that date. A sum of four amounts totaling $202.62 also appears on this page of the manuscript journal.

1 Under Shirt
7 Collars
1 pr. Cuffs
1 pr. Drawers
1 Towel
5 Handks
1 pr Socks

———

21

<Stove——4 holes>
<4-joints pipe>
<Gridiron>
<Mending-handle>

Compass	3.00[80]
Buck gloves	2.50
Small funnel	
Locks	.90
Cartridges	3.00
Marketing	2.70
Butter-plates	.30
Stove - &c -	22.90
Gridiron	1.50
<Butter-pl>	
Meat	2.70
Chickens	1.50

———[81]

Ralegh Lamme 70	7.45
Lamme &c	23.55

80. The list that follows, on p. [52V], records items purchased and prices paid at Bozeman, Montana Territory, for camping equipment, food, and drink on July 2; see the journal entry for that date.

81. Page [52R], which follows, is blank. The text resumes on p. [51V].

Candlesticks	3.00
Twine	20

[82]

Fort Ellis[83]	July 4th
Missoula	July 26th
Ft Cour de Laine	July 31st
Ft Spokane	Aug 7th
Colville	Aug 9
Fraziers River	Aug 17
Victoria	Aug 20
Seattle	Aug 22
Portland	
Ft. Vancouver	Aug 25
Dalles	Aug 28
San Francisco	Aug 31
Monterey	Sep. 3d
Los Angeles	Sepr 10
Santa Fe	Sepr 17
Fort Lewis	Sepr 20
Denver	Sepr 25[84]

20 lbs flour[85]
Hams
Breakfast Bacon
12 Soups -
6 Corned beef

82. Pages [51R] and [50V], which follow, are blank. The text resumes on p. [50R].

83. The list of destinations and dates that follows corresponds roughly to the itinerary and schedule of the 1883 summer tour. However, it includes the names of two places (The Dalles, Oregon, and Monterey, California) that General Sherman and his party did not visit. Probably Dodge copied this list from an estimate of the tour's likely course given him by Tidball near its outset.

84. Page [49R], which follows, is blank.

85. The list that follows describes the supplies purchased by Dodge from the commissary of subsistence at Fort Ellis, Montana Territory; see the journal entries for July 2 and 3.

6 Tongue –
6 Tomatoes
Peaches
Corn
Butter
Crackers
2 Lard
2 Chow-chow
2 doz. Sardines
<Dried-Apples>
Ex Lemon
3 Yeast powders
12 Milk
Worcestershire –
Salt
Pepper
Oat Meal *none*
6 Baked Beans
50 Potatoes
Corn meal
Rice
Vinegar
Soap
3 Cakes Toilet soap
Cracked Wheat
Maple syrup
Chili con carne

Kitchen towelling

Afterword
Careers' End

THE INSPECTION TOUR BROKE UP AT ST. LOUIS, MISSOURI, where Dodge left the party to return to his post, via Chicago, and the other members continued east toward Washington. For Dodge, the return to regular duty brought with it re-initiation to the exacting requirements of army office procedures. At St. Louis he had written out for the general's signature two copies of an order directing him to proceed thence to his duty station, Fort Sully. One of these he would carry with him, and the other the general would place on file in the Office of the Adjutant General. However, shortly after his arrival at the post, Dodge discovered that the order lacked one formula declaration—"This travel is necessary for the public service"—that was required by law in order to permit remuneration of his travel expenses. In view of the light duty he had performed during the summer, this inadvertent omission was perhaps ironic, but Dodge could ill afford the expense out of his own pocket. Accordingly, he wrote the adjutant general in Washington, explaining the situation. He requested that the order left there by Sherman be amended to include the missing statement and that he be authorized to correct his own copy.[1]

This seemed a reasonable solution to the problem, but for administrative purposes it proved not satisfactory. On November 6, five days after Sherman had relinquished command of the army, General Drum informed Dodge that the order in question, issued by the former

1. RID to AG, October 21, 1883 (RID ACP File, AGO). The original order, dated October 2, 1883, also forms part of the file.

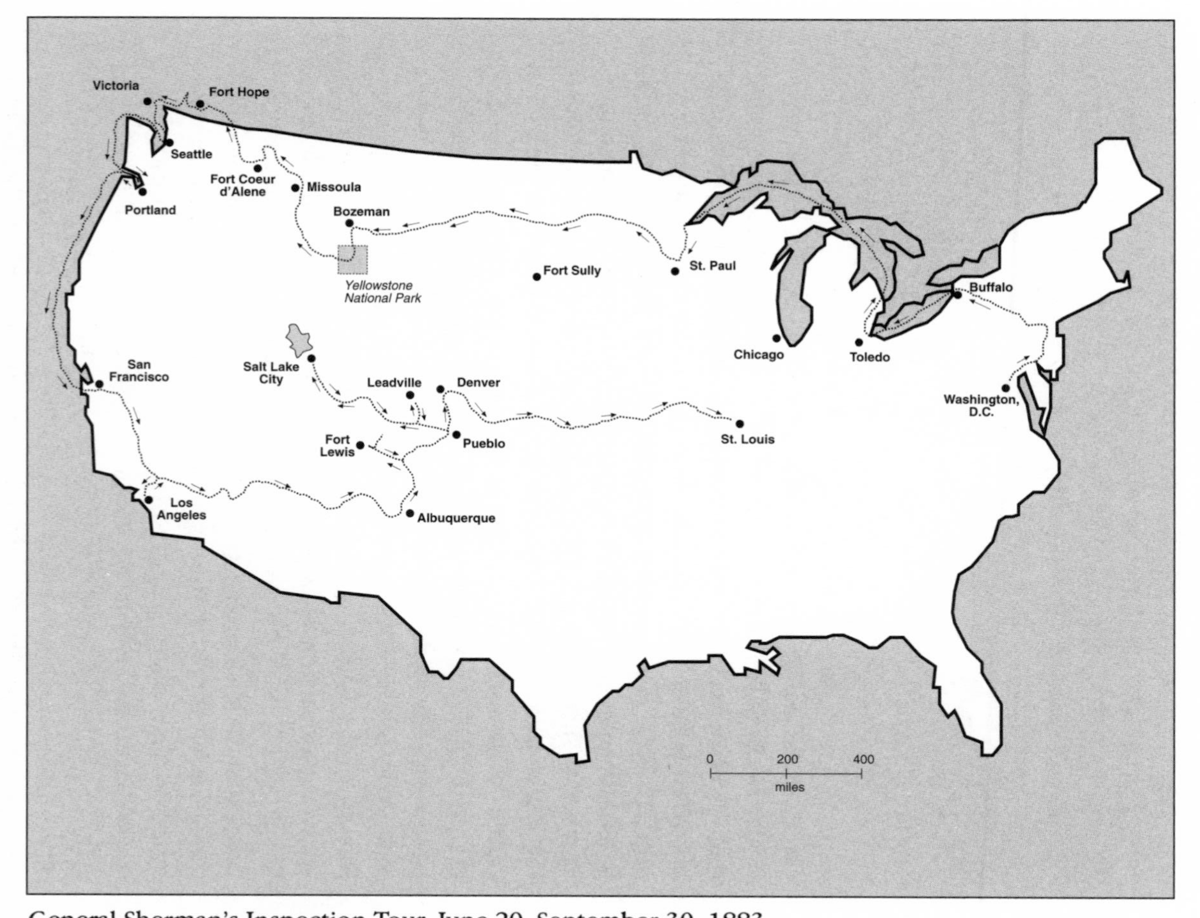

General Sherman's Inspection Tour, June 20–September 30, 1883

commanding general in St. Louis, could not be amended by that office in Washington. Only General Sherman himself could do so, and by that time he had left the city.[2] Dodge therefore addressed a note to Sherman at his new residence in St. Louis, explaining the difficulty once more and enclosing for his signature two corrected copies of the original order.[3] All was now in due form. The revised orders were signed, the travel expenses authorized, and after two months' delay, repaid.[4] Clearly, the summer idyll of freedom from bureaucratic usages was over.

Perhaps emboldened by his friendly relations with Sherman, and also bearing in mind the fact that Sherman had set aside his role as commanding general, in the draft of his November 13 letter Dodge included a familiar salutation, "Dear General," and a short personal sentiment in closing. But he thought better of both.[5] After all, he was addressing a senior in rank, and on official business. He knew well the stiff formulae of accepted army usage, and he also knew that not to continue observing them might seem disrespectful. Now and afterward, the contacts between the two officers were friendly, familiar, and evinced mutual regard, but on Dodge's part they never lost the tone of respectful deference.

Prior to vacating his office in favor of General Sheridan, Sherman had busied himself preparing his annual report, arranging new assignments for his aides, and retrieving his own maps and books from the little reference library at headquarters for transfer to his new home. These last weeks moved ahead smoothly, and at a reunion of the Army of the Tennessee in Cleveland, Ohio, Sherman was reported "brisk and

2. R. C. Drum to RID, November 6, 1883 (RID ACP File, AGO). A slip dated November 3, 1883, and summarizing the facts of the case as correspondence continued also forms part of this file.

3. RID to WTS, November 13, 1883 (Dodge Papers, Graff).

4. The amended order bearing Sherman's signature was received at the Adjutant General's Office on November 22 (RID ACP File, AGO).

5. He deleted "Dear" and the following statement: "With best wishes for your health & happiness in your new sphere of life." Other revisions exhibit a similar intention to maintain a tone not personal but official. For example, Dodge began the penultimate statement with the phrases, "Will you please do me the favor to sign these . . ." but revised them to "You will please sign these . . . ." (RID to WTS [draft], November 13, 1883—Dodge Papers, Graff).

happy as a lark."[6] His career in the national capital ended with an outpouring of testimonial praise. A flattering historical coincidence was noticed, that Generals Washington and Sherman had issued their farewell orders to the army on November 1, 1783 and 1883 respectively, exactly one century apart.[7] *Harper's Weekly*, the nation's most popular magazine, printed on the cover page of its November 3 issue an engraved bust portrait of the general, suitable for display.[8] Evidently a folk hero was still in the making.

Following his departure from Washington, Sherman passed a few days in New York City before returning to St. Louis, where until the date of his retirement he would be attended by two aides, Colonels Bacon and Tourtelotte. In November, at a meeting of the Grand Army of the Republic's post in St. Louis, he and his daughter Lizzie received a rousing welcome. He concluded his remarks that night with the assurance that he had come to St. Louis to stay. Henceforward, he said, he intended to live a modest, quiet life as a plain citizen.[9]

As Sherman attempted, with indifferent success, to settle into the new mode of life he had envisioned, his former aide Colonel Dodge resumed the active service that would terminate in his own retirement eight years later, in 1891. Though somewhat out of the way, Fort Sully was proving not without its satisfactions. A telegraph line had reached the fort three years before, and the railhead at Pierre afforded an easy avenue to the east. Hunting for small game in the vicinity continued good,[10] and his men seemed well disposed. Assisted by Joe and Laura, on Christmas Eve he hosted a gala supper party and dance for the officers and ladies of Forts Sully and Bennett.[11]

6. *ANJ*, October 20, 1883, p. 224.

7. *ANJ*, November 10, 1883, p. 284.

8. *Harper's Weekly*, No. 1402 (November 3, 1883), p. 693.

9. *ANJ*, December 1, 1883, p. 347.

10. RID to Frederick Paulding Dodge, December 4, 1884 (Dodge Papers, Yale); *ANJ*, March 6, 1886, p. 649.

11. RID to Julia Rhinelander Paulding Dodge, December 20, 1883 (Dodge Papers, Yale). The Fort Sully correspondent of the *Army and Navy Journal* reported that the "grand ball and supper" Dodge gave "his many friends on Christmas eve . . . was simply 'immense,' the objects of particular mention being the many wreaths and mottoes of evergreens, made interesting by their beautiful design. Our spacious library, adjoining the entertainment hall, was used as the banquet department" (*ANJ*, January 5, 1884, p. 455).

Garrison life moved forward on a steady course until the night of February 12, 1884, when calamity struck. A fire broke out, destroying much government property and several buildings. Other buildings were seriously damaged, and in the absence of sufficient barrack space, one company was ordered to Fort Bennett for temporary housing until something better could be provided.[12] This emergency in the dead of winter precipitated official tensions that cast a shadow over Dodge's service in the Department of Dakota for several years to come.

A "boom in economy," as Dodge had paradoxically termed it the previous summer,[13] still prevailed in the department. General Terry was attempting to stretch a small allotment of quartermaster's funds so as to accomplish both the expansion of Fort Snelling, site of his headquarters, and also construction at the other posts likely to be designated permanent in the army's program of consolidation. Fort Sully, whose location gave it strategic value only so long as the Sioux reservation remained forbidden for settlement by non-Indians, did not rank high on Terry's priority list for expenditures.[14]

Dodge's urgent need to replace quartermaster's sheds, barracks, and other essential buildings exacerbated an already strained fiscal situation. Nevertheless, assisted by First Lieutenant Ralph W. Hoyt, his able post and regimental quartermaster, Dodge pressed the claims of his post forcefully[15]—so forcefully as to give offense to members of Terry's staff. He refused to accept as definitive the discouragements he received from two of the general's trusted subordinates, his own inferiors in

12. John M. Schofield to AG, February 15, 1884, forwarding a report by RID dated February 13 (AGO LR). A consolidated file of correspondence relating to the fire at Fort Sully, 688 AGO 1884, is available in NARA microfilm publication M689, Roll 260. An account of the fire appeared in *ANJ*, February 28, 1884, p. 603.

13. See Journal One, June 26, 1883.

14. However, Sherman had listed Fort Sully among the posts in the interior of the nation that should be regarded as permanent; see *ANJ*, November 25, 1882, p. 373. Terry's priorities had long favored the larger posts in his department and some of those along the Northern Pacific Railroad: Forts Assiniboine, Buford, Custer, Keogh, Meade, Missoula, Snelling, and Yates. See *ANJ*, May 11, 1878, p. 650; *Report of the Secretary of War* (1884), p. 108; Bailey, *Pacifying the Plains*, pp. 196–98.

15. In addition to documents in the consolidated AGO file concerning the fire at Fort Sully, see letters from RID forwarded by Schofield to the adjutant general on March 25, May 6, June 26, and August 30, 1884 (AGO Reg LR).

rank, Major James M. Moore, the department's quartermaster general, and Captain Robert P. Hughes, Third Infantry, its acting inspector general. Hughes, a brother-in-law, aide-de-camp, and longtime friend of Terry, appears to have taken particular offense at Dodge's persistence.[16] Meanwhile Dodge made known his urgent needs directly to Terry.[17] His determined advocacy bordered on insubordination, some thought, but he was not a man to back away from an official quarrel if he thought himself in the right.[18] "The 'Powers' would be very glad to try me by Court Martial," he informed his son Fred in October, "& I am very willing to be tried."[19]

By "the Powers" he of course meant Terry, who considered the recent correspondence as an affront to his authority. In fact, Dodge had ruffled the department commander by his efforts to correct two problems that fell within his own sphere of responsibility. First, as post commander Dodge had appealed repeatedly in the matter of rebuilding Fort Sully. Second, as commander of the Eleventh Infantry he pointed out the impracticably wide dispersion of his regiment. After two years in the Department of Dakota he had not yet had opportunity even to see five of its ten companies—a situation that clearly required correction.[20] Given no satisfaction on either point, he at last made his case to Terry's immediate superior, Major General Schofield, who had assumed command of the Division of the Missouri, and was

16. In January 1884 Captain Hughes had inspected Fort Sully and four other posts—two of which, Forts Buford and Missoula, were of particular interest to Terry (Inspector General to AG, January 26, 1884—AGO Reg LR). For Terry's close relationship with Hughes, see Bailey, *Pacifying the Plains*, p. 135. Dodge later commented to Sherman that Terry, a bachelor, "is as tender of his staff as he would be of his wife's honor—if he had one" (RID to WTS, November 8, 1884—Sherman Papers, LC).

17. RID to WTS, December 10, 1884 (Sherman Papers, LC).

18. "A good fight," Dodge wrote in the midst of an official quarrel in 1879, "is a splendid sharpener of the intellect, & keeps man from rusting out" (*ITJ*, p. 202).

19. RID to Frederick Paulding Dodge, October 12, 1884 (Dodge Papers, Yale).

20. In May 1884 the companies of the Eleventh Infantry were posted as follows: A, D, E, and K at Fort Sully; B and F at Camp Poplar River, Montana Territory; C and H at Fort Buford, Dakota Territory; G at Fort Leavenworth, Kansas; I at Fort Bennett (Eleventh Infantry Regimental Return). Dodge had seen only the companies at Forts Sully and Bennett.

promptly sustained.[21] As a result, construction and repairs went on swimmingly at Fort Sully during the summer of 1884, and the Eleventh Regiment could anticipate a change of station that would eventually bring its units within closer mutual reach. However, Terry was not a commander to be crossed lightly. Dodge had alienated himself from the general's good will, and the likelihood of hearty support from departmental headquarters for any future initiative was remote.

In the midst of these official difficulties, Dodge received from General Sherman a request for information and assistance concerning topics that recalled their association in preparing *Our Wild Indians*. Sherman had agreed to preside at a convention of cattlemen that was to meet for the first time at St. Louis in November, and he wished to acquaint himself beforehand with facts surrounding some of the issues that might concern that body. As part of his course of study he intended to re-read two of Dodge's books, *The Plains of North America and Their Inhabitants* and *Our Wild Indians*, but he had lent his copy of the latter to a friend and so had lost it. Stipulating that he wished to pay for a replacement, he asked Dodge to order one sent him.

In the remainder of his letter Sherman set down some thoughts about the great historical forces that were determining the fates of the buffalo and the Indians, two topics on which Dodge was a published authority. He discerned the operation of these same forces in another development that now interested him, the increasing numbers of cattle and cowboys on lands that were once the preserve of the native inhabitants. The near-extinction of the buffalo seemed to him "almost a decree of the Almighty" in which, by Darwinian law, "the fittest survived." Moreover, the reputed inability of most breeding cattle to survive the birth of an offspring sired by a buffalo bull he took as evidence

21. RID to WTS, December 10, 1884 (Sherman Papers, LC). On August 30, 1884, Schofield forwarded to the adjutant general, with his approval, a communication from Terry reporting that he had reconsidered his earlier recommendation against the rebuilding of Fort Sully. Terry now believed that the garrison at the fort should be maintained at its present strength. In addition, he asked authority and funds to construct a barracks at the fort in addition to the structures already authorized (AGO Reg LR). The originals of these documents have not been located, but the summary of their contents in the adjutant general's register strongly suggests a capitulation by Terry.

that the two species were distinct and could not intermingle. The sterility of buffalo-cattle hybrids confirmed this view.[22]

Sherman now extended his speculation to encompass the approaching fate of the Indians, formerly dependent for survival on the buffalo and other wild game, as to be determined by the nature of their interaction with the new possessors of their ancestral lands. Just as the doomed buffalo could not survive except through intermixture with neat cattle, so the Indian's doubtful future was "in the course of natural selection." Native Americans must alter their customs and be absorbed into the successor population, or else they must die out. He was convinced that it was "as idle to resist the Conclusion as it was for old Canute to command the tide to cease reaching his feet." What part the powerful cattle interests might play in the grand scheme of history Sherman did not address in his letter, but he was evidently attempting to relate developments on the western plains in recent decades to some large pattern of development. "You and I have seen mighty things on this continent," he wrote Dodge, "and if there be useful lessons let us teach them to the rising generation."[23]

Sherman's letter initiated a lively exchange of views in the months that followed, at first centered on topics the general had begun to explore but later branching out to include army gossip and other subjects, including a professional visit to St. Louis by Frederick Paulding, Dodge's son. With his response to the initial letter Dodge forwarded a handsomely bound copy of *Our Wild Indians*, from the twentieth thousand printed. He had just received a still more lavishly bound copy from the thirty-seventh thousand, he explained, and could readily spare the one he sent. Lest the general refuse to accept the volume, he noted also that the copy that had been lent and lost was one of two—one for Dodge, one for Sherman—sent free of charge by the publisher.

Dodge then set forth in considerable detail the results of his inquiries as to the history and total population of the Indians of North America, the practicality or otherwise of breeding buffalo with cattle, and other

22. WTS to RID, September 16, 1884 (Sherman Papers, LC).
23. Ibid.

topics. In this and subsequent letters he expressed hostility to the powerful cattle interests, whose monopolistic practices he considered a threat to Indians and settlers alike. He knew from experience that, unless secured by military force, the boundaries of Indian reservations were routinely ignored by cattle drivers moving their herds toward the railroads for transportation to market.[24] Nor were the cowboys' capitalist employers any more respectful of property occupied by homesteaders. Cattle interests that effectively denied farmers access to desirable lands were interfering with a powerful force, he told Sherman, the tide of immigration. "When this happens, bloodshed is inevitable. A cattle-man with fifty or a hundred cow-boys at his back may easily over-awe and drive away a few would-be settlers, but that tide cannot be stopped & in a little while it will cut down those fences & kill those cattle men." He held that in a country like the United States no single interest, no matter how powerful, could ignore the rights of the others. "But this is a question of Statesmanship, and in the absence of statesmen will probably finally eventuate as you said of the buffalo question, 'by the decree of the Almighty.'"[25] Thus these veteran officers discussed the continuing impact of historical forces their own military service had helped set in motion.

The cattleman's convention met in the Exposition Hall at St. Louis between November 17 and 22, but Sherman's part in it proved less substantial than he had anticipated. He was called upon only to speak a few words of welcome to the twenty-five hundred attendees on opening day, a task he accomplished with playful grace and to much applause. At the close of his speech the band broke into "The Star-Spangled Banner," then "Yankee Doodle." A business meeting began

24. See *ITJ*, pp. 414–15. In May 1884 Running Buffalo, a Cheyenne Indian with whom Dodge become friends during his tour of duty in Indian Territory, was slain by a cattle herder near Fort Supply. Running Buffalo was attempting to resist a herd's being driven across land he considered his own.

25. RID to WTS, September 30, 1884. Dodge returned to this general theme in subsequent letters to Sherman dated October 14, October 21, and November 8, 1884 (Sherman Papers, LC). For a survey of the cattle industry's impact on the Great Plains in the 1870s and 1880s, see Paul, *The Far West and the Great Plains in Transition,* pp. 193–206.

next, moderated by the temporary chairman, C. C. Rainwater, and from that point Sherman performed no further function.[26]

However, another military man did play a major role in the days that followed. This was Major James S. Brisbin, Seventh Cavalry, then on leave from Fort Keogh, Montana Territory. In recent years Brisbin had pursued business interests in the region of his post with energy and success. He had purchased a cattle ranch, obtained permission to operate a steamboat on Yellowstone Lake, and published a book, *The Beef Bonanza*; or, *How to Get Rich on the Plains* (1881), among other enterprises.[27] By acclamation, Brisbin was elected vice president of the newly organized National Association of Cattlemen. However, even with the leadership of visionaries like him and the president, Colonel R. D. Hunter of St. Louis, the organization managed only two tangible accomplishments at its inaugural convention: first, formation of a committee to recommend a national trail, specifically for cattle herds, extending from the Red River in Texas to the Canadian border and possibly beyond; and second, agreement to meet again in one year.[28]

26. "The Round-Up," *St. Louis Post-Dispatch,* November 17, 1884, p. 2. Sherman's remarks were purportedly given in full in this article. A partial version, including some variants from the corresponding portion of the speech as reported in the *Post-Dispatch*, appeared in the *Army and Navy Journal,* November 22, 1884, p. 317. The latter version is reproduced here, as representing with equal likelihood Sherman's exact words and more clearly reflecting his recent correspondence with Dodge: "I used to regret to see the buffalo, elk and antelope disappearing from the plains, and to see in their stead a race of scrawny, long horn Texas cattle. I can now see, however, it was a decree of nature, and that you gentlemen have reared a race of twenty millions of fine breeding cattle which supply the world with meat."

27. *ANJ*, November 20, 1880, p. 311; February 21, 1882, p. 609; April 22, 1882, p. 867; September 30, 1882, p. 199; January 13, 1883, p. 524; June 27, 1883, p. 581; September 22, 1883, p. 152. Beginning in 1881 Brisbin, a prolific writer, contributed a series of letters to the *New York Herald* in which he described the scenic beauties and investment opportunities to be found in Montana Territory. On receiving a copy of *Our Wild Indians,* he wrote A. D. Worthington praising the handsome appearance of the book and proposing that the publisher also bring out a volume he had in mind, to be entitled *The Trees*. However, Worthington declined (A. D. Worthington to RID, December 30, 1882—Dodge Papers, Graff). Several years afterward, Brisbin's *Trees and Tree-planting* was issued by Harper & Brothers of New York; see *ANJ*, January 2, 1889, p. 453.

28. *St. Louis Post-Dispatch,* November 18, 1884, pp. 2, 4; November 19, 1884, p. 2; November 20, 1884, p. 2; November 21, 1884, p. 2; November 22, 1884, p. 2.

From his reading of St. Louis newspapers, Dodge informed Sherman that he judged the cattle convention "rather a fizzle," none of the various business interests represented there seeming to know just what it wanted.[29] Of greater interest to him, and probably also to the general, was the appearance of Frederick Paulding in the city on the days immediately after the close of the meeting. Between November 24 and 28 Fred would perform at the Olympic Theater as leading man to a popular young actress, Margaret Mather. The earlier seasons of travel with his own company had won him some reputation as a promising actor, and the contract with the Mather troupe, under the managership of J. M. Hill, was a step forward professionally.[30]

For a time Dodge had hoped to obtain a leave of absence that would enable him to join Fred at Kansas City, Missouri, and travel with the company as far as St. Louis. He informed Sherman of this possibility, and the prompt result was an invitation for father and son to be guests at the general's home.[31] However, the sour relations between Dodge and General Terry made it imprudent to request the time away from Fort Sully that would be required. Only Fred would be able to accept the hospitality of the Sherman family, none of whose members he had ever met. Dodge assured his son that Lizzie Sherman was "a great friend of mine" and that he would be made welcome. "Don't fail to be very polite to them all," he counseled, "but don't offer any boxes, as the old man might decline, & if published make you ridiculous. Cultivate them *socially* all you can."[32]

29. RID to WTS, December 10, 1884 (Sherman Papers, LC).

30. Details of Frederick Paulding's activities in New York City beginning in 1879 are given by Odell in *Annals of the New York Stage,* volumes 10–15. Reports of his engagements and performances while on tour are scattered through issues of a trade magazine, the *Dramatic Mirror* of New York. A broader but less detailed treatment than either is by Bordman, *American Theatre,* pp. 132, 229, 317, 576, 639–40.

31. RID to WTS, November 8, 1884 (Sherman Papers, LC).

32. RID to Frederick Paulding Dodge, October 12, 1884 (Dodge Papers, Yale). The caution not to offer box seats to the Shermans may have been prompted by a ripple of public criticism that followed Fred's offering a similar courtesy to Brigadier General Oliver O. Howard, commander of the Department of the Platte, at Omaha, Nebraska in November 1883. See *Omaha Republican,* November 24, 1883, p. 4; November 25, 1883, p. 5; *ANJ*, December 1, 1883, p. 347; January 5, 1884, p. 348.

The Mather company performed four plays while in St. Louis, all standard fare: *Romeo and Juliet,* with Fred in the male lead; *Macbeth; The Hunchback,* a comedy by Sheridan Knowles; and *The Honeymoon*, another comedy, by John Tobin. Owing in large part to the exertions of J. M. Hill, a publicist no less energetic than A. D. Worthington, Margaret Mather received the lion's share of attention in newspaper coverage. For example, one lengthy article was derived entirely from a pre-performance interview in which Hill explained why Mather's youth and small stature did not detract from her representation of Lady Macbeth, which he said was based on an original interpretation of the character.[33] The role of Juliet was more congenial to the actress, and here she gave popular satisfaction, even though her demeanor onstage was at times extravagant.[34] She and Frederick Paulding won praise from the *St. Louis Post-Dispatch* for their work together in *Romeo and Juliet,* Fred's Romeo being judged "excellent . . . in some parts really fine," and also in *The Honeymoon*.[35]

Whether the Shermans attended any of the performances cannot be stated with certainty, but Fred was gratified by the kindnesses he received as their house guest. Not long afterward Dodge wrote the general expressing his own gratitude. Fred "is a very affectionate boy,

33. "Lady Macbeth," *St. Louis Post-Dispatch*, November 27, 1884, p. 8. In a promotional pamphlet issued late in 1883, *Miss Margaret Mather under the Management of J. M. Hill,* the manager recounted the fourteen-month history of his business relationship with the actress, quoting from reviews of her performances by newspaper critics in Chicago, St. Louis, Cleveland, Boston, and Cincinnati. Hill declared Mather "the greatest Juliet the world has ever seen" (p. 9).

34. The reviewer for the *St. Louis Post-Dispatch* thought Mather better adapted to characters displaying "tender sentiment and the milder emotions of the average woman" than to the higher tragic roles. "If heaving of the bosom be distress; if shrugging of the shoulders be scorn and contempt; if fierce and vigorous action be passion; if short, hard breathing and moans be despair, or shrieking or ha-ha-haing be madness, then Miss Mather is all of these." In the potion scene of *Romeo and Juliet,* Mather fell to the stage with "about as graceful and skillful an exhibition of tragic gymnastics as can be seen any where. 'A whirlwind tumble' comes nearer to being the proper name for the act than anything else. She starts in one direction, changes her mind, and, catching herself, starts in another; then she hesitates a few moments, and, starting in all directions at once, the natural consequences are several quick turns, which wrap her draperies all about her and bring her to the floor with a murderous thud. It must be seen to be appreciated" (November 25, 1884, p. 8).

35. *St. Louis Post-Dispatch,* November 25, 1884, p. 8; November 26, 1884, p. 3.

Margaret Mather and Frederick Paulding Dodge, from sketches in the *St. Louis Post-Dispatch,* November 25, 1884

& these things touch him very deeply," he wrote. With his letter he sent "a small token of my appreciation of your friendship & many kindnesses, more substantial than words"—namely, a box of grouse he had shot and had frozen. These, he explained, were "not the half-civilized 'pinnated' grouse (prairie chicken) but the wilder denizens of the northern wilds, the 'sharp-tailed' or willow grouse. You have been everywhere & eaten almost everything (with, I fear, *an almost equal relish*) but if you have not before hit upon these birds, I can assure you of a new sensation."[36]

36. Sherman was not a finicky eater, but probably Dodge also intended a playful reference to the varied fare which, as chief caterer, he had served up during the inspection tour.

By now Dodge felt no constraint in writing to Sherman of his own recent service and hopes for future duty. He described with satisfaction the recent construction at Fort Sully, declaring that he had done wonders with the funds made available to him. He also explained the circumstances that had led to Terry's ill-will toward him. Should he be "fired out of the department" by Terry, so much the better, he wrote, dismissing the matter with a hopeful exclamation: "O! for Coeur d'Alene, or the Pacific."[37]

Dodge and Sherman also exchanged gossip concerning two mutual acquaintances, one an army officer still in service, the other retired. Colonel McCook, whom the party had chanced to meet in Yellowstone National Park, had been left desolate at the death of his wife in the summer of 1881. However, he later became acquainted with another woman, Miss Annie Colt of Milwaukee, Wisconsin, whom he was now engaged to marry.[38] Sherman was a guest at the couple's society wedding in Milwaukee on October 8, and he wrote Dodge an account of the day which the latter thought charming. "I can see every line of [McCook's] old face," he wrote, "every swagger of his fat body, all denoting most perfect satisfaction & self confidence." He had himself written McCook a congratulatory letter, Dodge added, but found difficulty in wording it since he had known the first wife.[39]

One month later Dodge confided to Sherman his thoughts about another wedding which, next to McCook's, had "excited more talk & speculation & *fun* than any other occurrence of late." This was the marriage at St. Louis, on November 12, of the eighty-four-year-old General William S. Harney, long since retired, to the sister of his deceased wife. "The old Gentleman was always celebrated for his sexual power & appetite," Dodge wrote; "but, that at 84, they should still so burn as

37. RID to WTS, December 10, 1884 (Sherman Papers, LC). Unable to resist a quotation from Shakespeare, in this letter Dodge declared his possible expulsion from the Department of Dakota "a consummation devoutly to be wished"—yoking his own troubles with the "outrageous fortune" that beset Prince Hamlet; see *Hamlet* III.i.63-64.

38. *ANJ*, August 6, 1881, p. 12; August 30, 1884, p. 78; October 11, 1884, p. 200; October 18, 1884, p. 228.

39. RID to WTS, October 21, 1884 (Sherman Papers, LC).

to force him to a marriage is rather a stumper."[40] He judged, correctly, that the union was simply an arrangement by which Harney could ensure compliance with his wishes for the distribution of his considerable property when he died.

During the winter of 1885–1886 Sherman destroyed the greater part of his correspondence of the previous thirty years, retaining only that which, he said, was of historical value.[41] If he continued to correspond with Dodge after December 1884, their letters have not survived. Nevertheless, in the years that followed the two men remained aware of each other's activities and were often reminded by events of their earlier association. Their large circles of friends included many mutual acquaintances, such as William C. Church, editor and co-owner of the *Army and Navy Journal,* with whom they both corresponded and at whose office they both called when in New York City. As an interested observer of current developments in the army, Sherman often learned of innovations by Dodge in directions he supported.[42] In the revised edition of his *Memoirs* he expressed his regard for Dodge,

40. RID to WTS, December 10, 1884 (Sherman Papers, LC). See also *ANJ*, August 26, 1882, p. 71; November 15, 1884, p. 299; September 11, 1886, p. 127.

41. On December 6, 1885, Sherman wrote from St. Louis to William C. Church: "I have overhauled all my letters received since 1853, arranging them in books, selecting only such as have historic value—rejecting 9-10—and am impressed with the fact that our judgments are formed by private correspondence and conversation far more than by official reports" (*ANJ*, February 21, 1891, p. 446).

42. For example, on receiving the resignations of his regimental quartermaster, First Lieutenant Ralph W. Hoyt, and regimental adjutant, First Lieutenant George G. Lott, in May 1886 Dodge announced a change of policy within his regiment for service in these two positions. "Under the present accepted system," he wrote, "the tenure of office of a competent and agreeable regimental staff officer is terminated only by his promotion." However, he believed that in times of peace the good of the army would be better served by affording each first lieutenant the opportunity "to make himself thoroughly proficient not only in line but in staff duties." Hence he intended to appoint officers to staff positions for a maximum period of three years (Regimental Order, May 1, 1886, reprinted in *ANJ*, May 15, 1886, p. 852). The potential for cozy continuance in office to be enjoyed by a colonel's favorites had been criticized before, but Dodge's unilateral change of policy attracted respectful attention. See *ANJ*, April 18, 1885, p. 765; February 12, 1887, p. 575; *New York Times,* February 7, 1887, p. 2. In February 1887 a General Order was issued from army headquarters limiting regimental staff appointments to a maximum of four years, with the result that in the two months that followed, twenty-three regiments reported changes in their staff details (*ANJ,* February 26, 1887, p. 607; May 7, 1887, p. 815).

McCook, and other aides-de-camp "who were faithful, intelligent, and patriotic—not only an official respect, but a personal affection for their qualities as men, in the full belief that they were model soldiers and gentlemen, such as should ever characterize the headquarters of the army of the United States."[43]

During the winter of 1886–1887 Sherman returned with his family to New York City, where he took rooms at the Fifth Avenue Hotel for two years before moving to a residence of his own further uptown. St. Louis had proved deficient in the activity and stir that he now found suited him, especially since the appeals that he enter politics had grown less frequent. In July 1887 he informed a reporter that he planned to remain in New York City until all his children were provided for. Then, he said, he hoped to locate on Lake Coeur d'Alene, which he had picked out as among the loveliest places in the world.[44] Appropriately enough, three months before that interview Fort Coeur d'Alene had been officially redesignated as Fort Sherman, "in honor of General William Tecumseh Sherman, U.S. Army (retired), by whom the site was selected."[45] For the present, when in the city Sherman fell into a comfortable routine that included attending to correspondence at his office in the army building, conversation and newspaper reading at his club, and travel around town by streetcar to one event or another, often accompanied by Lizzie. In the evenings he indulged his taste for the drama even more frequently than before.

Frederick Paulding performed regularly in New York City during these years, first opposite Margaret Mather and then in other roles, including one as a supporting actor in a company co-owned by Sherman's friend, the veteran comedian Joseph Jefferson.[46] In all probability the general witnessed several productions that included Fred,

43. Sherman, *Memoirs,* 2:460.

44. *ANJ,* July 23, 1887, p. 1030. The interview is acknowledged as from the *Washington Critic.*

45. G.O. 30, HQA, April 12, 1887, reprinted in *ANJ*, April 16, 1887, p. 754.

46. RID to Frederick Paulding Dodge, May 27, 1887, and December 23, 1888 (Dodge Papers, Yale); Odell, *Annals of the New York Stage,* 13:25–26, 44, 50, 159, 587; 14:29, 153, 166, 259, 511, 519; *New York World,* May 18, 1888, p. 2; August 26, 1888, p. 13; *ANJ,* November 17, 1883, p. 306; April 25, 1891, p. 591.

but recollections of the young man's stay in St. Louis were inevitable for him when, in 1888, a dispute between the temperamental Mather and her manager developed into a much publicized lawsuit. Fred was not a contender in this affair, though his mother gave testimony that weighed against the claims of the aggrieved actress.[47] Prior to the lawsuit, Fred had borne the brunt of Mather's determination to have him displaced from performing as Romeo, some said in favor of her husband, Emil Haberkorn. According to the *New York Sun*, night after night she placed pins in her Juliet costume so that Fred would scratch his hands when he embraced her, leaning her head against his chest so as to impede his efforts to speak. Knowing, too, that he suffered from corns, as he declaimed his most passionate lines she would plant the heels of her slippers on his toes. Reports of these malicious acts appeared in the *Army and Navy Journal*, where Fred received special attention.[48]

At Fort Sully, Dodge busied himself with several army programs that had been set in motion during Sherman's tenure as commander and also with initiatives that took shape afterward. His interest in target firing led to the fort's being designated one of ten posts where samples of the three rifles recommended by the Magazine Gun Board for possible adoption were subjected to thorough testing.[49] The Eleventh Infantry continued to rank well in the annual competitions, even as the army's emphasis shifted toward the skirmish firing Dodge considered of greater practical value. After the regiment was transferred to the Department of the East, in July 1887, its officers played major roles in conducting the rifle competitions of the Division of the Atlantic at Fort Niagara, New York, one of the posts it garrisoned.[50]

47. *New York World,* June 3, 1888, p. 6; June 23, 1888, p. 1; June 27, 1888, p. 3; June 28, 1888, p. 5.

48. *ANJ,* June 9, 1888, p. 910; the article is acknowledged as from the *New York Sun.*

49. The Magazine Gun Board had recommended the Lee, the Chaffee-Reece, and the Hotchkiss guns for testing, which was performed during 1885. The consolidated file that includes correspondence relating to tests of the three models is 4943 AGO 1884, available in NARA microfilm publication M689, Roll 77.

50. For example, see *ANJ,* August 27, 1887, p. 82; July 28, 1888, p. 1055; September 21, 1889, p. 63.

Dodge's efforts to develop the Eleventh into an active, efficient unit were conspicuously successful. By November 1888, of thirty-three officers listed on the regimental roster, only one was on sick leave or assigned to other than regular duty.[51] The regiment's excellent band, under the direction of Achille La Guardia, a recent immigrant from Italy, did much to bolster morale. On January 13, 1886, the band had played a benefit concert for La Guardia to a packed house at the Fort Sully Music Hall. The performances that evening began with a composition by the band director, the Eleventh Regiment March, "dedicated to Col. R. I. Dodge, U.S.A."[52]

Dodge's reputation as a progressive regimental commander grew steadily. In 1886 his essay "The Enlisted Soldier" won honorable mention in a contest sponsored by the Military Service Institution and was published in the *Journal* of the organization.[53] In this discussion he addressed the conditions that discouraged many able men from entering army service—low pay and social status, a five-year term of enlistment, poor living conditions, dreary labor—and offered proposals to ameliorate the situation. He encouraged an atmosphere of mutual respect between commissioned and noncommissioned officers despite the social gulf that separated them. In fact, his later avowal that he had sat down with noncommissioned officers and private soldiers at

51. The Regimental Return of the Eleventh Infantry for October 1888 confirms these facts, reported by the *Army and Navy Journal* on the basis of a roster printed on the regimental press. The editors judged the roster "a model of typographical excellence" (November 17, 1888, p. 227).

52. *ANJ*, January 23, 1886, p. 516. A photograph showing the Eleventh Infantry band in 1885 is reprinted in Schuler, *Fort Sully*, p. 88. Chief Musician Achille La Guardia was the father of Fiorello La Guardia, later the mayor of New York City. In July 1890 the elder La Guardia, then on duty at Madison Barracks, was granted an unusual privilege, a six-month leave of absence with permission to go beyond seas (*ANJ*, August 2, 1890, p. 909).

53. *JMSI* 8 (May 1887): 259–318. The essay was also printed as pamphlet on the regimental press (Fort Sully, 1886). The winning entry, also entitled "The Enlisted Soldier," was by a staff officer, Surgeon Alfred A. Woodhull; see *JMSI* 8 (March 1887): 18–70; *ANJ*, April 2, 1887, p. 718. On reading Dodge's discussion, Surgeon Woodhull wrote him a gracious note expressing pleasure that they agreed on so many points. He was gratified, he wrote, "that as a staff officer my views on a subject in which I have always had deep concern have received such effective reinforcement from an officer of the line" (Woodhull to RID, September 27, 1887—Dodge Papers, Graff).

his own dinner table excited comment, especially from those who believed he was thereby undermining essential distinctions.[54] At his new regimental headquarters, Madison Barracks, New York, Dodge also supported the experiment of establishing "canteens," later known as post exchanges, run by enlisted men themselves. The canteen at Madison Barracks was one of the first in the army and proved a great success, providing a recreation facility for men off duty and serving food, beer, and wines at moderate prices.[55] Within a few months of its establishment, three "grog shops" in the nearby village of Sackett's Harbor were closed for business, their military patrons having taken their business elsewhere.[56]

In the later years of the decade, General Sheridan's wish to maintain a combat-ready standing army led to a program of "practice marches" during summertime. The movements were intended to ensure some awareness among officers and men of the conditions actually encoun-

54. See *ANJ*, January 11, 1890, p. 389; February 15, 1890, p. 471.

55. G.O. 10, HQA, establishing rules and regulations for the conduct of post canteens, was issued on February 10, 1889, and in that year an official test of canteens then in operation was conducted at ten posts, one of which was Madison Barracks. The favorable reports from these posts were summarized in *ANJ*, August 31, 1889, p. 10. Correspondence relating to the testing program forms a consolidated file, 6114 AGO 1889, available in NARA microfilm publication M689, Roll 732. A list of the canteens established in 1889 appeared in *ANJ*, January 4, 1890, p. 369.

56. *ANJ*, October 12, 1889, p. 123; the information was attributed to a correspondent of the *New York Times*. Elsewhere Dodge was quoted at some length on the positive effects produced by the canteen at his post:

> As a moral influence in the interest of discipline and good order the canteen has achieved a remarkable and generally unexpected success. Though within the limits of a village abounding in barrooms and other temptations, this post is more free from drunks, disorders, unauthorized absences and neglects of duty than any I have ever commanded (more than twenty). . . . In my opinion no step has been taken for the improvement of the moral, social, and intellectual condition of the enlisted man more efficacious than the establishment of the canteen. With pride I am able to say that in discipline and general good conduct I have a command superior to any I have ever seen in the Army. As my general rules and mode of command have not changed . . . I can attribute the very marked improvement only to the very wonderful influence of the canteen. (*ANJ*, September 14, 1889, p. 40)

Portions of this statement were incorporated in the Army Appropriations report to the House of Representatives for 1890, p. 81. That report, G.O. 10, and other documents relating to the establishment of canteens form parts of a consolidated file, 364 AGO 1889, which is available in NARA microfilm publication M689, Roll 666.

tered by an army in the field. Units of the Eleventh Infantry undertook these marches, in 1888 to Burlington, Vermont, where they encamped with the militia of that state, and in 1889 southward to Mount Gretna, Pennsylvania.[57] A related program, involving cooperation between state and federal authorities, was to ensure that the militia of the several states achieved a level of military knowledge and discipline that would enable them to cooperate with regular army troops in case of need.[58] Dodge was among the senior army officers who were assigned to inspect and provide instruction to state militia at their summer encampments. Though far from convinced that brief meetings of this sort would yield the greatly increased efficiency of the states' volunteer units that seemed to be hoped for, he performed this duty on two occasions, for the Iowa state troops in 1886 and for those of his home state of North Carolina in 1889.[59]

Varied services like these marked Dodge as a veteran officer of reliable judgment, willingness to innovate, and devotion to the army. In the spring of 1889 General Schofield, who had assumed command of the army on the death of Sheridan the summer before, appointed him to membership on two highly publicized courts-martial in Washington, both touching on the morale and reputation of the service. In the first case the accused officer was Major Garrett J. Lydecker, of the Engineers, who was alleged to have been derelict in his duty as supervisor of civilian labor on an underground aqueduct to provide fresh water to the national capital. Lydecker, the son of a former deputy

57. *ANJ*, August 18, 1888, p. 1114; August 24, 1889, p. 1064; August 31, 1889, p. 6. According to the *Watertown (New York) Times*, during the 1889 march "The available fences in the vicinity of the camps were lined with vehicles of all sorts which had brought people from miles around to see the soldiers in their picturesque camp, their outdoor life, their morning roll call and inspection, the evening guard mount, and to hear the beautifully rendered music of the regimental band" (quoted in *ANJ*, September 7, 1889, p. 23).

58. See Cooper, *The Rise of the National Guard*, pp. 75–86.

59. See *ANJ*, July 17, 1886, p. 1042; August 21, 1886, p. 79; May 18, 1889, p. 783; July 13, 1889, pp. 938, 951; *Des Moines Iowa State Register*, July 31, 1886, p. 6; August 4, 1886, p. 2; August 7, 1886, p. 2; August 17, 1886, p. 6; August 19, 1886, p. 2; *Wilmington (North Carolina) Morning Star*, July 8 through 18, 1889, *passim*. A copy of Dodge's report on his inspection of the Iowa National Guard forms part of the Dodge Papers (Graff). Official correspondence relating to that inspection is in a consolidated file, 3344 AGO 1886, available in NARA microfilm publication M689, Roll 465.

collector of customs in New York City and himself a commissioner of the District of Columbia, had been a fixture in Washington's social circle for years. Moreover, his competence and diligence had not previously been impugned.[60] The case therefore attracted considerable attention, both within and outside the army.

In March and early April the court, under the presidency of Major General George Crook, heard several days of testimony, none of which seriously discredited Lydecker. Inspections had been made on sections of the aqueduct tunnel that had later proved defective in construction, but the lighting was so poor, and the contractors so deft in concealing their derelictions, that responsibility for the failure of the project could not rest solely upon the accused officer. Nevertheless, since Lydecker had assumed full charge over construction but had not himself regularly conducted examinations of its progress, the court found him guilty of neglect of duty. It recommended a light sentence—one which, when confirmed by the president, pleased almost no one.[61] Lydecker resented his transfer soon afterward to Vancouver Barracks, a reaction that must have seemed ironic to Dodge, for whom Vancouver was an almost ideal posting. To Lydecker, exile on the Pacific Coast amounted to further punishment for performance of duty that had warranted none in the first place.[62]

Dodge's membership on the Lydecker court led to his appointment as president of a second court only a few days afterward. Unlike Lydecker, who enjoyed general respect within the army both before and after his trial, the defendant in this case, Captain George A. Armes,

60. *ANJ*, May 13, 1882, p. 942; May 20, 1882, p. 956; November 3, 1883, p. 273; March 9, 1889, p. 557. The proceedings of a court of inquiry into Lydecker's performance of duty during construction of the Washington Aqueduct Tunnel, with the charges and specifications subsequently drawn up for his trial by court martial, together with other related material, comprise a consolidated file, 4845 AGO 1888, available in NARA microfilm publication M689, Roll 647.

61. *ANJ*, March 9, 1889, p. 552; March 30, 1889, p. 615; April 6, 1889, pp. 643–44; May 11, 1889, p. 765. The findings of the court were published in GCMO 21, HQA, May 2, 1889. Lydecker was sentenced to forfeit $100 of his pay for nine months and to be reprimanded in orders (p. 9). The findings were reprinted in *ANJ*, May 11, 1889, p. 760.

62. *ANJ*, July 13, 1889, p. 939. For a more balanced analysis of the proceedings, see the issue for June 8, 1889, p. 848.

had for years been a byword among his fellow officers for emotional instability and self-destructive impertinence. Armes had won attention for bravery and pluck as a combat officer during the Civil War and on the western plains for a few years afterward, but by the time of his forced retirement for incapacity in 1883 he had been court-martialed six times, with a separate inquiry conducted as to his mental state.[63] General Sherman had twice approved sentences of dismissal from the service, both mitigated by the president. Though fortunate not to have been dismissed earlier, Armes considered himself an aggrieved party when a Retiring Board recommended his removal from active service just when, after seventeen years at the rank of captain, he was about to be promoted to major.[64] In the years following that action he resided in Washington, where he conducted a real estate business, but he held fast to his self-image as a soldier.

In the court proceedings presided over by Dodge, Armes pled not guilty to charges of conduct unbecoming an officer and a gentleman. These related to his behavior, first in the inaugural parade on March 4 for the newly elected president, Benjamin Harrison, and also in related incidents in the weeks that followed. Wearing the dress uniform of a captain of cavalry and mounted on a fine bay horse, Armes rode in the parade as an aide to the grand marshal, Governor James Adams Beaver of Pennsylvania, taking a position only a short distance from the presidential carriage. However, once Beaver discovered his presence in the line, he ordered him removed by two regular officers, Colonel Horatio G. Gibson, Third Artillery, and Captain John G. Bourke, Third Cavalry, which was forcibly done. Outraged, Armes had Gibson and Bourke arrested for assault and addressed a heated letter to the adju-

63. *ANJ*, June 12, 1880, p. 916; January 15, 1881, p. 475; July 9, 1881, pp. 1022, 1025; *New York Times*, June 9, 1889.

64. *ANJ*, August 18, 1883, p. 43; September 8, 1883, p. 105; September 22, 1883, pp. 144, 147; November 10, 1883, p. 291; November 24, 1883, p. 331. Actually, the length of Armes's service at the rank of captain was far less than seventeen years. He was promoted to that rank on July 28, 1866, but on June 7, 1870, he was honorably discharged from the army. Eight years later, on May 11, 1878, he returned to active duty at the rank of captain and was placed on the seniority list as receiving his commission on July 28, 1866 (Heitman, *Historical Register*, 1:169). Armes later recounted his career in a volume aptly entitled *Ups and Downs of an Army Officer* (1900).

tant general, subsequently published in the *Washington Critic,* in which he accused them of drunkenness and unsoldierly conduct. On March 27, at the Riggs House in Washington, Armes confronted Governor Beaver and demanded an apology for the part he had played in the incident at the parade. The governor refused, and as he turned away Armes was alleged to have pulled his nose, an act that delighted Beaver's political enemies but was characterized in the charges against Armes as "a cowardly and disgraceful violent public assault upon his excellency."[65] Earlier in the month Captain Bourke had responded to Armes's initial complaint with a countersuit, but this seemed unlikely to be acted upon by the War Department until the confrontation with the governor occurred. An order detailing a court to hear charges against Armes was issued from army headquarters on April 3.[66]

Understandably, the ten days of testimony before the Armes court, which met between April 11 and 24, included moments of angry confrontation and also tense levity. Notwithstanding the accused officer's brash behavior, testimony elicited from him and other witnesses brought to light some mitigating circumstances. Weeks before the inauguration, Armes had applied to Governor Beaver to serve as a mounted aide, and in due course, though under a misapprehension of his identity, a member of the governor's staff had sent him an appointment. Moreover, he had declined a second appointment before being informed without further explanation that the one from Beaver was withdrawn.

65. GCMO 31, HQA, June 7, 1889, pp. 1–3; the quotation is from p. 3. See also *ANJ,* March 16, 1889, p. 574; June 15, 1889, p. 863; *New York Times,* April 9, 1889, p. 2; April 13, 1889, p. 3; April 24, 1889, p. 3. Armes included in *Ups and Downs of an Army Officer* an illustration of "a beautiful gold medal" that was sent him by one hundred subscribers in Pittsburgh, Pennsylvania, "in approval of his pulling Gov. Beaver's nose" (p. 593).

66. S.O., HQA, April 8, 1889; *ANJ,* April 13, 1889, p. 659. Members of the court were Dodge; Colonel Edwin F. Townsend, Twelfth Infantry; Colonel John Mendenhall, Second Artillery; Captain John G. Turnbull, Third Artillery; Captain Sanford C. Kellogg, Fifth Cavalry; Captain John R. Myrick, Third Artillery; Captain Greenlief E. Goodale, Twenty-third Infantry; Captain Lewis Smith and Captain Frank W. Hess, Third Artillery; Captain George S. Anderson, Sixth Cavalry; Captain James Parker, Fourth Cavalry; Captain James O'Hara, Third Artillery; Captain Thomas T. Knox, First Cavalry; and Major George B. Davis, Judge Advocate. The court was an unusually large one, reflecting the gravity of the matters under review.

George A. Armes (Massachusetts Commandery, Military Order of the Loyal Legion; U.S. Army Military History Institute)

Furthermore, testimony given in closed session established that he had participated in the inaugural parade under separate, secret orders, as one of ten picked men who comprised a special body guard to the president. In view of facts like these, Major George B. Davis, the judge advocate, declined in his summary of the case even to argue its legal merits. Instead, he urged court members to give the accused officer the benefit of every doubt and every piece of extenuating testimony.[67] But to Dodge and his fellow court members it remained clear that, in three of the four specifications of the charge against him, Armes was guilty of conduct unbecoming an officer, and that by his extravagant behavior he had sullied the service. It sentenced him to dismissal.[68]

Dodge had now been absent from Madison Barracks for more than a month, but as a mark of regard General Schofield selected him to perform one more task before the return to his regular duty station. More prominently than he had ever done before, Dodge would represent the United States Army in a great civic parade. A celebration was forthcoming in New York City on April 30, the centennial of George Washington's inauguration there as the nation's first president. The day's observances would include thanksgiving services, concerts, fireworks, a parade of warships, and a banquet, but the chief event would be a five-mile parade up Broadway and Fifth Avenue, from the Battery to 57th Street. Comprised of army and navy units, militia brigades representing twenty-four states, veteran's organizations, and various high officers including state governors, Supreme Court justices, and members of Congress, the procession would include fifty thousand participants. Larger by far than the body that had marched at the inauguration

67. *ANJ,* April 20, 1889, pp. 684, 694; April 27, 1889, p. 706; Armes, *Ups and Downs of an Army Officer,* pp. 590–93.

68. Armes was convinced that the court's members had been "specially picked out" to return a sentence of dismissal (*Ups and Downs of an Army Officer,* p. 591). However, after several weeks' delay in reviewing the proceedings of the court, President Harrison commuted his sentence to confinement within such limits as the secretary of war might designate and deprivation of the right to wear the army uniform and insignia of rank for a period of five years. Armes, the father of a large family, would lose none of his retirement pay. The secretary of war later prescribed the place of confinement as to be within a radius of fifty miles of the District of Columbia (GCMO 31, HQA, June 7, 1889, pp. 3–4). A portion of the court-martial order was reprinted in *ANJ,* June 15, 1889, p. 863.

of President Garfield, it would be the most extensive quasi-military demonstration in the United States since the Grand Review in Washington at the close of the Civil War. As the grand marshal, Schofield would lead the procession, accompanied by his aides and an escort. Next after him would come a body of regular army troops, with Dodge at their head, and then the rest of the parade. At Twenty-third Street, near Madison Square, President Harrison would occupy a reviewing stand with other dignitaries and would receive the tributes of all the passing units.

Preparations in the city were elaborate, and on the morning of April 30 the relief was general when a rainbow appeared, an auspicious promise of good weather. Along the parade route portraits of George Washington were hung out by the thousand, in festoons of national flags. The housetops were packed with spectators, while wreaths, banners, mottoes, shields, and more flags diversified the scene below. As those who would march in the parade searched out their designated assembly points, the streets filled with more than 1 million spectators. After some delay, shortly before noon the presidential party reached the reviewing stand. The crowd nearby, packed to suffocation on the sidewalks and in rows of bleachers, greeted individual members of the distinguished group as they came into view and were recognized. The shout that went up for General Sherman was one of the heartiest.

Now was heard the roar of voices drowning out the martial music as the body of the parade came into distant view. According to a reporter for the *New York Times,* the sight from the reviewing stand down Fifth Avenue was memorable. "The effect produced by the compact mass of waving plumes of the helmetted troops was that of a moving bed of flowers. First there was a strip of bright yellow, next a strip of white, then one [of] red, and away beyond could faintly be discerned successive repetitions of those streaks of color."[69] The approaching body of colors gradually assumed human form, and in a few more minutes General Schofield, an expert horseman, moved past the review-

69. *New York Times,* April 29, 1889, p. 1; April 30, 1889, p. 1; May 1, 1889, pp. 1-2. The quotation is from "The Great Procession. The Military Parade As Seen By The President And Those With Him," May 1, p. 11.

ing stand with graceful dignity. He saluted the president, and in response the latter removed his hat and bowed, to great applause. Schofield proceeded forward, leaving behind him a free space, and then came Dodge, leading 265 West Point cadets and three brigades of regulars—cavalry, artillery, and infantry. President Harrison and former President Cleveland exchanged remarks on the fine marching and soldierly bearing of the West Pointers, and the *Times* reporter noted that Dodge "looked as if he was proud of them."[70] The companies selected to represent the infantry arm in the parade were of Dodge's regiment, the Eleventh.

After all these, up the avenue came units of the Marine Corps, with its famous band, followed by the various bodies of state troops extending for more than a mile. Instructions circulated by Schofield several days before the parade had specified that the leaders of various military contingents should acknowledge the commander-in-chief all in the same fashion, by a salute with drawn sabre.[71] Dodge was thus the second officer to recognize the chief executive in this manner. As his mount reached the reviewing stand, he drew his sword, turned his head to the right, lifted his gaze, and raised the sword in salute to the president.

Possibly in that long moment Dodge also caught sight of General Sherman among the official party. Whether he did so or not, thoughts of his former commander must have entered his mind as he led the army troops through the streets of New York on that day. In one sense, the honorable position he occupied near the head of the parade marked the high point of his career as an army officer. But it invited comparison to other, perhaps even more valued distinctions he had enjoyed not many years earlier: Sherman's selection of him as an aide-de-camp,

70. *New York Times,* May 1, 1889, p. 11.

71. The full text of Schofield's circular containing an elaborate set of directions for parade participants was reprinted in the *New York Times,* April 25, 1889, p. 9. The instructions for saluting the president were as follows: "While passing in review all officers in uniform should carry drawn swords. Commanding officers of divisions, brigades, battalions, and batteries salute with the sabre when passing the Commander in Chief. All other officers carry the sword on the shoulder as on inspection. Chiefs of the Loyal Legion and of Grand Army divisions not in uniform will salute by removing the hat. The staffs will not salute. All colors dip to the Commander in Chief."

Sherman's public support of *Our Wild Indians,* and the opportunity Sherman had given him to participate in the valedictory inspection tour of 1883. What Sherman had written of Dodge in the *Memoirs* was true in reverse: his regard for the general had become not only professional but personal. However, whether the two veteran officers met and conversed during that event-filled day of patriotic celebration cannot be stated with certainty. So far as is known, the centennial parade was the last occasion in which they appeared together in public.

Observers pointed to Schofield's success in gathering, housing, and coordinating the movement up Broadway of twenty-seven brigades of regular and volunteer troops as proof of the nation's capacity to respond promptly to a military emergency by calling upon its citizen soldiery. Of course, in 1889 there was no prospect of such a call, any more than when General Sherman had conducted his final inspection tour six years before. To younger Americans, bodies of regular troops were now to be seen only at civic observances such as this one, not in the field, and those who marched across country once a year did so only for practice. During his last years of active duty Sherman had asserted tirelessly the need to maintain the regular army in a high state of preparedness, since by their very nature national crises often arose unexpectedly. He pointed to the Civil War as an unforgettable instance, but even at that time his warnings were little heeded, for to many persons the protracted trauma of the war already seemed remote.[72] By the time of the centennial parade in New York City it had become yet more so. In 1891 the *Army and Navy Journal* pointed out that July

72. For example, in a speech before the Society of the Army of the Potomac, in 1881, Sherman spoke of the need to "preserve the results of an experience which may be of inestimable value in the *next* war."

> I remember well the public apathy which immediately preceded the Mexican War and the Civil War. . . . [E]ven as late as March, 1861, if any one spoke openly of civil war he was laughed at for his folly or upbraided for being stampeded, and when war actually did come, no people were less prepared for it than those of the United States. Only twenty years have passed since that dread epoch and I sometimes fear our people are again becoming so engrossed in their pursuit of wealth that they are liable to forget the lessons of that war (*ANJ,* June 11, 1881, p. 945).

For earlier statements by Sherman on the need to maintain military preparedness, see *ANJ,* October 24, 1874, p. 167; August 4, 1877, p. 832.

21 of that year marked the thirtieth anniversary of First Bull Run, the initial major battle of the War between the States, "a fact remembered by some, but forgotten by many."[73]

Sherman and Dodge had surely not forgotten, for both had taken the field at First Bull Run, the former winning his military fame in the almost four years of bloody conflict that followed. Beginning in 1867, when Dodge was assigned to duty protecting Union Pacific employees against assault by Indians, he devoted his own mature energies to the military support of another prolonged campaign, the national movement west. And in 1869, after four intervening years in the Military Division of the Missouri, the war-hardened Sherman assumed command of the peacetime army of which Dodge was a field officer. In the years that followed, both men questioned the wisdom and humanity of some federal policies they were called upon to help enforce, but both played out their appointed parts, confident that they were serving the forces of progress. In the scheme of historical development Sherman traced out at the close of his career, the army of postwar settlers had moved westward for peaceful purposes with fateful inevitability, manifesting a force no less irresistible than the fighting men under his command had unleashed in their March to the Sea. And the steady extension of railroad lines across the continent after the war was a confident, patterned procession, as of a great parade.[74]

Like other generals, in the years after his retirement Sherman was no longer at the center of public consciousness, but he retained a lasting hold on the affections of many Americans. His well-earned reputation as a stern warrior, his erect bearing and angular features, his humor and still tart tongue, his modest republican dignity—these combined to form a distinctively American personality, one that his fellow citizens delighted to honor. His death early in 1891 occasioned

73. *ANJ*, July 25, 1891, p. 821.

74. Earlier in his lifetime, Sherman had likened the inevitable spread westward of modern American civilization to the operation of natural processes. In 1872, responding to a toast at the annual dinner of the New England Society, he described the "little army, a handful of men, [as] over on the frontier, moving like the waves of the sea" further west (*ANJ*, December 28, p. 308). In 1874 he observed in testimony before a congressional committee that new settlements "are creeping along the line of railroad just as leaves follow the limb of a tree" (*ANJ*, February 7, p. 407).

widespread demonstrations of regret, and it marked the end of an era. On February 19 of that year a funeral cortege accompanied his remains from New York City to Jersey City, New Jersey, where they were to be transported to St. Louis for burial. The procession, numbering thirteen thousand persons, included many of the same officials and marching units that had formed part of the centennial parade two years earlier. Crowds again lined the streets and covered the rooftops, but now church bells tolled along the route of march as the sound of muffled drums alternated with a dirge.

Dodge was on regular duty at Madison Barracks that day, exactly three months from his mandated retirement from active service upon reaching the age of sixty-four. The end of his career would come close upon the end of the general's lifetime.[75] On February 23, the day of the funeral, seventeen-gun salutes to the memory of General Sherman were fired at Madison Barracks every half hour, beginning at 8:00 A.M. Together with all other officers of the United States Army, Dodge wore on his uniform a badge of mourning.[76]

75. Dodge died at his home in Sackett's Harbor, New York, on June 16, 1895. After observances at Madison Barracks, his remains were transported to Washington, D.C., for burial with military honors at Arlington National Cemetery, Virginia (RID ACP File, AGO; *ANJ,* June 22, 1895, p. 711).

76. The General Orders announcing the death of General Sherman and prescribing the observances in his memory in New York and at all military posts were reprinted in *ANJ,* February 21, 1891, p. 445. Shortly after the funeral, Colonel Poe described to another former aide-de-camp, Colonel Tidball, the "loving respect" army veterans had shown as the funeral train made its way toward St. Louis: "There were hundreds of men standing out at midnight, bareheaded, to raise their hands in salute." (Poe to Tidball, February 26, 1891; quoted in Tidball, "General Sherman's Last March," p. 29).

Bibliography

MANUSCRIPT MATERIALS

Dodge, Richard Irving. Papers, 1865–1949. Everett D. Graff Collection of Western Americana. Newberry Library, Chicago.

———. Papers, 1867–1895. Yale Collection of Western Americana. Beinecke Library, Yale University, New Haven, Connecticut.

Office of the Secretary of War. Letters Sent, 1881–1883. National Archives and Records Administration, Washington, D.C. Record Group 107. Microcopy M6, Rolls 82–85.

Sherman, William T. Microfilm Edition of the William Tecumseh Sherman Family Papers, 1808–1891. University of Notre Dame Archives, 1967, Notre Dame, Indiana.

———. Papers. Manuscript Division, Library of Congress, Washington, D.C.

Tidball, John C. Papers. Special Collections, U.S. Military Academy Library, West Point, New York.

Trade Catalogs. Special Collections, University of Delaware Library, Newark, Delaware.

United States Army. Eleventh Infantry Regimental Returns, 1880–1891. National Archives and Records Administration. Record Group 94. Microcopy M665, Rolls 126, 127.

———. Headquarters. Letters Received, 1883–1884. National Archives and Records Administration. Record Group 108. Microcopy M1635, Roll 121.

———. Letters Sent, 1873–1883. National Archives and Records Administration. Record Group 108. Microcopy M857, Rolls 8, 9.

———. Madison Barracks Post Returns, 1887–1891. National Archives and Records Administration. Record Group 94. Microcopy M617, Roll 724.

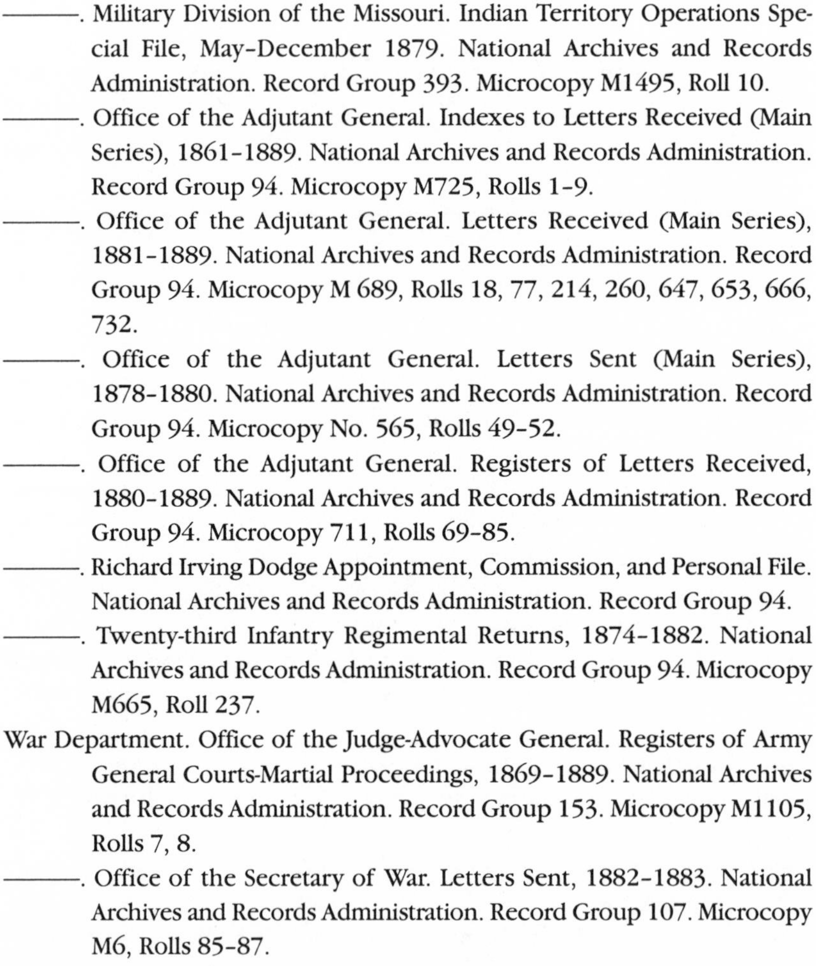

———. Military Division of the Missouri. Indian Territory Operations Special File, May–December 1879. National Archives and Records Administration. Record Group 393. Microcopy M1495, Roll 10.

———. Office of the Adjutant General. Indexes to Letters Received (Main Series), 1861–1889. National Archives and Records Administration. Record Group 94. Microcopy M725, Rolls 1–9.

———. Office of the Adjutant General. Letters Received (Main Series), 1881–1889. National Archives and Records Administration. Record Group 94. Microcopy M 689, Rolls 18, 77, 214, 260, 647, 653, 666, 732.

———. Office of the Adjutant General. Letters Sent (Main Series), 1878–1880. National Archives and Records Administration. Record Group 94. Microcopy No. 565, Rolls 49–52.

———. Office of the Adjutant General. Registers of Letters Received, 1880–1889. National Archives and Records Administration. Record Group 94. Microcopy 711, Rolls 69–85.

———. Richard Irving Dodge Appointment, Commission, and Personal File. National Archives and Records Administration. Record Group 94.

———. Twenty-third Infantry Regimental Returns, 1874–1882. National Archives and Records Administration. Record Group 94. Microcopy M665, Roll 237.

War Department. Office of the Judge-Advocate General. Registers of Army General Courts-Martial Proceedings, 1869–1889. National Archives and Records Administration. Record Group 153. Microcopy M1105, Rolls 7, 8.

———. Office of the Secretary of War. Letters Sent, 1882–1883. National Archives and Records Administration. Record Group 107. Microcopy M6, Rolls 85–87.

GOVERNMENT PUBLICATIONS

Annual Report of the Board of Regents of the Smithsonian Institution . . . for the Year 1881. Washington, D.C.: Government Printing Office, 1883.

Annual Report of the Board of Regents of the Smithsonian Institution . . . for the Year 1882. Washington, D.C.: Government Printing Office, 1884.

First Annual Report of the Bureau of Ethnology to the Secretary of the Smithsonian Institution 1879–'80. Washington, D.C.: Government Printing Office, 1881.

Official Army Register. Washington, D.C.: Government Printing Office, 1873, 1880–1889.

Report of an Examination of the Upper Columbia River and the Territory in its Vicinity in September and October, 1881, to Determine its Navigability, and Adaptability to Steamboat Transportation . . . by Lieut. Thomas W. Symons, Chief Engineer of the Dept. of the Columbia. Washington, D.C.: Government Printing Office, 1882.

Report of an Exploration of Parts of Wyoming, Idaho, and Montana, in August and September, 1882, Made by Lieut. Gen. P. H. Sheridan. Washington, D.C.: Government Printing Office, 1882.

Report of Lieut. General P. H. Sheridan, Dated September 20, 1881, of His Expedition Through the Big Horn Mountains, Yellowstone National Park, etc. Washington, D.C.: Government Printing Office, 1882.

Reports of Inspection Made in the Summer of 1877 by Generals P. H. Sheridan and W. T. Sherman of Country North of the Union Pacific Railroad. Washington, D.C.: Government Printing Office, 1878.

Seventeenth Annual Report of the Bureau of American Ethnology to the Secretary of the Smithsonian Institution 1895–96. Washington, D.C.: Government Printing Office, 1898.

U.S. Army. *Regulations of the Army of the United States and General Orders in Force on the 17th of February 1881.* Washington, D.C.: Government Printing Office, 1881.

———. Department of Dakota. *Roster of Troops Serving in the Department of Dakota, July 20th, 1882.* Fort Snelling, Minn.: The Department [of Dakota], 1882.

———. Office of the Adjutant General. *General Orders, Circulars, and General Court-Martial Orders,* Washington, D.C.: Office of the Adjutant General, 1879–1889.

U.S. Congress. House. *Army Appropriations* (1890). Report No. 529, 51st Congress, 1st Session. Serial 2808.

———. House. *Report of the Secretary of War* (1877). Executive Documents No. 1, Part 2, 45th Congress, 1st Session. Serial 1794.

———. House. *Report of the Secretary of War* (1880). Executive Documents No. 1, Part 2, 46th Congress, 3rd Session. Serial 1952.

———. House. *Report of the Secretary of War* (1881). Executive Documents No. 1, Part 2, 47th Congress, 1st Session. Serial 2010.

———. House. *Report of the Secretary of War* (1882). Executive Documents No. 1, Part 2, 47th Congress, 2nd Session. Serial 2091.

———. House. *Report of the Secretary of War* (1883). Executive Documents, No. 1, Part 2, 48th Congress, 1st Session. Serial 2182.

———. House. *Report of the Secretary of War* (1884). Executive Documents No. 1, Part 2, 48th Congress, 2nd Session. Serial 2277.

———. House. *Revised Army Regulations.* Report No. 85, 42nd Congress, 3rd Session (1873). Serial 1576.

NEWSPAPERS AND PERIODICALS

Army and Navy Journal, 1872–1891, 1895.

Chicago Inter-Ocean, 1883.

Chicago Tribune, 1875.

Cincinnati Gazette, 1867.

Harper's Weekly, 1881, 1883, 1889.

Iowa State Register (Des Moines), 1886.

Journal of the Military Service Institution of the United States, 1881, 1882, 1886, 1887, 1889.

Los Angeles Herald, 1883.

New York Dramatic Mirror, 1879–1889.

New York Times, 1867, 1880–1891.

New York World, 1887–1889.

Omaha Herald, 1883.

Omaha Republican, 1883.

Publisher's Weekly, 1881–1883.

Salt Lake City Deseret News, 1883.

San Francisco Chronicle, 1883.

St. Louis Post-Dispatch, 1884.

Seattle Post Intelligencer, 1883.

Washington (D.C.) Herald (Army and Navy Edition), 1881.

Wilmington (North Carolina) Morning Star, 1889

ARTICLES

Cochran, Alice. "Jack Langrishe and the Theater of the Mining Frontier." *Colorado Magazine* 46 (Fall 1969): 324–37.

Dodge, Richard Irving. "The Desertion Question." *Journal of the Military Service Institution of the United States* 11 (1889): 163–65.

———. "The Enlisted Soldier." *Journal of the Military Service Institution of the United States* 8 (May 1886): 259–318.

Hoeckman, Steven. "The History of Fort Sully." *South Dakota Historical Collections* 26 (1952): 222–77.

Irvine, R. J. "11th Infantry Regiment." *Journal of the Military Service Institution of the United States* 12 (1891): 379–81.

Kime, Wayne R. "'Not Coarse . . . But Not Delicate': Richard Irving Dodge's Portrayal of Plains Indians in *The Plains of the Great West and Their Inhabitants*." *Platte Valley Review* 17, no. 1 (Winter 1989): 69–83.

Mooney, James. "Calendar History of the Kiowa Indians." In *Seventeenth Annual Report of the Bureau of American Ethnology to the Secretary of the Smithsonian Institution 1895–96*. Washington, D.C.: Government Printing Office, 1898: 131–468.

Parker, Dangerfield. "The Regular Infantry in the First Bull Run Campaign." *United Service* 12 (1885): 521–31.

Reade, Philip. "Chronicles of the Twenty-third Regiment of Infantry." *Journal of the Military Service Institution of the United States* 35 (1904): 422–27.

Tidball, Eugene C. "General Sherman's Last March." *Colorado History* 46, no. 1 (1997): 1–29.

Woodhull, Alfred A. "The Enlisted Soldier." *Journal of the Military Service Institution of the United States* 8 (March 1887): 18–70.

BOOKS AND PAMPHLETS

Adams, Henry. *The Education of Henry Adams: An Autobiography*. Boston: Houghton Mifflin, 1918.

Aderman, Alice R. *A Genealogy of the Irvings of New York: Washington Irving, His Brothers and Sisters, and Their Dependents*. N.p.: privately printed, 1981.

A. D. Worthington and Company. *Illustrated Descriptive Catalog of Popular and Standard Books*. Hartford, Conn.: Worthington, 1877.

Allen, Joel Asaph. *History of the American Bison, Bison Americanus*. Washington, D.C.: Government Printing Office, 1877.

Armes, George A. *Ups and Downs of an Army Officer*. Washington, D.C.: n.p., 1900.

Athearn, Robert G. *Rebel of the Rockies: A History of the Denver and Rio Grande Western Railroad*. New Haven: Yale University Press, 1962.

———. *William Tecumseh Sherman and the Settlement of the West.* Foreword by William M. Ferraro and J. Thomas Murphy. Norman: University of Oklahoma Press, 1995.

Aubin, J. Harris. *Register of the Military Order of the Loyal Legion of the United States.* Boston: Commandery of the State of Massachusetts, 1906.

Bailey, John W. *Pacifying the Plains: General Alfred Terry and the Decline of the Sioux, 1866–1890.* Westport, Conn.: Greenwood Press, 1979.

Beal, Merrill D. *"I Will Fight No More Forever": Chief Joseph and the Nez Perce War.* Seattle: University of Washington Press, 1963.

Belden, George P. *Belden, The White Chief: or, Twelve Years Among the Wild Indians of the Plains.* Edited by Gen. James S. Brisbin, U.S.A. Cincinnati, Ohio: C. F. Vent, 1870.

Berthrong, Donald J. *The Cheyenne and Arapaho Ordeal: Reservation and Agency Life in the Indian Territory, 1875–1907.* Norman: University of Oklahoma Press, 1976.

Bigelow, Donald N. *William Conant Church and The Army and Navy Journal.* New York: Columbia University Press, 1930.

Bordman, Gerald. *American Theatre: A Chronicle of Comedy and Drama, 1869–1914.* New York: Oxford University Press, 1994.

Bourke, John G. *The Snake-Dance of the Moquis of Arizona; Being a Narrative of a Journey from Santa Fé, New Mexico to the Villages of the Moqui Indians of Arizona, with a Description of the Manners and Customs of This Peculiar People, and Especially of the Revolting Religious Rite, the Snake-Dance, to Which is Added a Brief Dissertation upon Serpent-Worship in General, with an Account of the Tablet Dance of the Pueblo of Santo Domingo, etc.* New York: Charles Scribner's Sons, 1884.

Bowman, Lynn. *Los Angeles: Epic of a City.* Berkeley, Calif.: Howell-North Books, 1974.

Boyd, William H., comp. *Boyd's Directory of the District of Columbia.* Washington, D.C.: Boyd, 1882.

Brayer, Herbert O. *William Blackmore: A Case Study in the Economic Development of the West.* 2 vols. Denver: Bradford-Robinson, 1949.

Brisbin, James S. *The Beef Bonanza; or, How to Get Rich on the Plains. Being a Description of Cattle-grazing, Sheep-farming, Horse-raising, and Dairying in the West.* Philadelphia: J. B. Lippincott & Co., 1881.

———. *Trees and Tree-planting.* New York: Harper & Brothers, 1888.

Bryant, Keith L., Jr. *History of the Atchison, Topeka, and Santa Fe Railway.* Lincoln: University of Nebraska Press, 1974.

The Centennial of the United States Military Academy at West Point, New York, 1802–1902. 2 vols. Washington, D.C.: Government Printing Office, 1904.

Check List of Publications of the Smithsonian Institution. Smithsonian Miscellaneous Collections, No. 745. Washington, D.C.: Government Printing Office, 1890.

Chittenden, Hiram M. *The Yellowstone National Park.* Edited by Richard A. Bartlett. Norman: University of Oklahoma Press, 1964.

City Directories of the United States, 1860–1901: Guide to the Microfilm Collection. Woodbridge, Conn.: Research Publications, 1983.

Clark, William P. *The Indian Sign Language: With Brief Explanatory Notes of the Gestures Taught Deaf-Mutes in Our Institutions for Their Instruction, and a Description of Some of the Peculiar Laws, Customs, Myths, Superstitions, Ways of Living, Code of Peace and War and Signals of Our Aborigines.* Philadelphia: L. R. Hamersley and Co., 1885.

Cody, William F. *The Life and Times of Hon. William F. Cody, Known as Buffalo Bill, the Famous Hunter, Scout, and Guide: An Autobiography.* Hartford, Conn.: F. E. Bliss, 1879.

Coffman, Edward M. *The Old Army: A Portrait of the American Army in Peacetime, 1784–1898.* New York: Oxford University Press, 1986.

Cooper, Jerry. *The Rise of the National Guard: The Evolution of the American Militia, 1865–1920.* Lincoln: University of Nebraska Press, 1997.

Corbett and Ballenger's Denver City Directory for 1881. Denver: Rocky Mountain News Printing Co., 1881.

Crook, George. *General George Crook: His Autobiography.* Edited by Martin F. Schmitt. Norman: University of Oklahoma Press, 1960.

Cullum, George W. *Biographical Register of Officers and Graduates of the U.S. Military Academy at West Point, from its Establishment to the Army Re-organization of 1866–1867.* 2 vols. New York: D. Van Nostrand, 1868.

———. *Supplement to the Biographical Register.* New York: D. Van Nostrand, 1868.

Davies, Wallace Evan. *Patriotism on Parade: The Story of Veterans' and Hereditary Organizations in America, 1783–1900.* Cambridge: Harvard University Press, 1955.

Davis, William C. *Battle at Bull Run: A History of the First Major Campaign of the Civil War.* Baton Rouge: Louisiana State University Press, 1977.

DeMontravel, Peter R. *A Hero to His Fighting Men: Nelson A. Miles, 1839–1925.* Kent, Ohio: Kent State University Press, 1998.

Dodge, Richard Irving. *The Black Hills: A Minute Description of the Routes, Scenery, Soil, Climate, Timber, Gold, Geology, Zoölogy, etc. With an Accurate Map, Four Sectional Drawings, and Ten Plates from Photographs, Taken on the Spot.* New York: James Miller, 1875.

———. *The Black Hills Journals of Colonel Richard Irving Dodge.* Edited by Wayne R. Kime. Norman: University of Oklahoma Press, 1996.

———. *The Indian Territory Journals of Colonel Richard Irving Dodge.* Edited by Wayne R. Kime. Norman: University of Oklahoma Press, 2000.

———. *A Living Issue.* Washington, D.C.: F. B. Mohun, 1882.

———. *Our Wild Indians: Thirty-three Years' Personal Experience Among the Red Men of the Great West. A Popular Account of Their Social Life, Religion, Habits, Traits, Customs, Exploits, Etc. With Thrilling Adventures and Experiences on the Great Plains and in the Mountains of Our Wide Frontier.* Hartford, Conn.: A. D. Worthington & Co., 1882.

———. *The Plains of North America and Their Inhabitants.* Edited by Wayne R. Kime. Newark: University of Delaware Press, 1989.

———. *The Powder River Expedition Journals of Colonel Richard Irving Dodge.* Edited by Wayne R. Kime. Norman: University of Oklahoma Press, 1997.

Dunraven, Windham Thomas Wyndham-Quin, Fourth Earl of. *The Great Divide: Travels in the Upper Yellowstone in the Summer of 1874.* New York: Scribner, Welfrod, and Armstrong, 1876.

Durham, Nelson W. *History of the City of Spokane and Spokane Country, Washington. From Its Earliest Settlement to the Present Time.* 3 vols. Chicago: S. J. Clarke, 1912.

Eisenschiml, Otto. *The Celebrated Case of Fitz-John Porter: An American Dreyfus Affair.* Indianapolis: Bobbs-Merrill, 1950.

Farrow, Edward S. *Farrow's Military Encyclopedia: A Dictionary of Military Knowledge.* Second edition. 3 vols. New York: Military-Naval Publishing Co., 1895.

Fellman, Michael. *Citizen Sherman: A Life of William Tecumseh Sherman.* Lawrence: University Press of Kansas, 1997.

Fisher, John S. *A Builder of the West: The Life of William Jackson Palmer.* Caldwell, Idaho: Caxton Press, 1939.

Foner, Jack D. *The United States Soldier Between Two Wars: Army Life and Reforms, 1865–1898.* New York: Humanities Press, 1970.

Frazer, Robert W. *Forts of the West: Military Forts and Presidios and Posts Commonly Called Forts West of the Mississippi River to 1898.* Norman: University of Oklahoma Press, 1965.

Greene, Jerome A. *Battles and Skirmishes of the Great Sioux War, 1876–1877: The Military View.* Norman: University of Oklahoma Press, 1993.

———. *Yellowstone Command: Colonel Nelson A. Miles and the Great Sioux War, 1876–1877.* Lincoln: University of Nebraska Press, 1991.

Hamersley, L. R., comp. *Records of Living Officers of the United States Army.* Philadelphia: L. R. Hamersley and Co., 1884.

Hedges, James B. *Henry Villard and the Railways of the Northwest.* New Haven: Yale University Press, 1930.

Heitman, Francis B. *Historical Register and Dictionary of the United States Army.* 2 vols. Washington, D.C.: Government Printing Office, 1903.

Hibben, Paxton. *Henry Ward Beecher: An American Portrait.* New York: Readers Club, 1942.

[Hill, J. M.] *Miss Margaret Mather Under the Managership of J. M. Hill.* Buffalo: Courier Lithograph Co., [1883]. Available in the general collection of the New York Public Library.

Hirshson, Stanley P. *The White Tecumseh: A Biography of General William T. Sherman.* New York: John Wiley & Sons, 1997.

Hittell, John S. *A History of the City of San Francisco and Incidentally the State of California.* San Francisco: A. L. Bancroft and Co., 1878.

Hoig, Stan. *Fort Reno and the Indian Territory Frontier.* Fayetteville: University of Arkansas Press, 2000.

Hutton, Paul A. *Phil Sheridan and His Army.* Lincoln: University of Nebraska Press, 1985.

Hutton, Paul A., ed. *Soldiers West: Biographies from the Military Frontier.* Introduction by Robert M. Utley. Lincoln: University of Nebraska Press, 1987.

Jackson, Donald. *Custer's Gold: The United States Cavalry Expedition of 1874.* New Haven: Yale University Press, 1966.

Jackson, Helen Hunt. *A Century of Dishonor: A Sketch of the United States Government's Dealings with Some of the Indian Tribes.* Minneapolis: Ross & Haines, 1964.

Johnson, Virginia W. *The Unregimented General: A Biography of Nelson A. Miles*. Boston: Houghton Mifflin, 1962.

Kroeker, Marvin E. *Great Plains Command: William B. Hazen in the Frontier West*. Norman: University of Oklahoma Press, 1976.

Laidley T. T. S. *A Course of Instruction in Rifle Firing*. Philadelphia: J. B. Lippincott, 1879.

Langford, Nathaniel Pitt. *The Discovery of Yellowstone Park: Journal of the Washburn Expedition to the Yellowstone and Firehole Rivers in the Year 1870*. Foreword by Aubrey L. Haines. Lincoln: University of Nebraska Press, 1972.

Langley's San Francisco Directory for 1881. San Francisco: H. Langley, 1881.

Los Angeles City and County Directory for 1881–82. Los Angeles, Calif.: L. Whitworth, 1881.

Lyman, Horace S. *History of Oregon: The Growth of an American State*. 4 vols. New York: North Pacific Publishing Society, 1903.

McChristian, Douglas C. *An Army of Marksmen: The Development of United States Army Marksmanship in the Nineteenth Century*. Fort Collins, Colo.: Old Army Press, 1981.

McGroarty, John S. *History of Los Angeles County*. 3 vols. Chicago: American Historical Society, 1923.

Manypenny, George W. *Our Indian Wards*. Cincinnati: R. Clarke & Co., 1880.

Marcy, Randolph B. *Border Reminiscences*. New York: Harper & Brothers, 1872.

———. *Thirty Years of Army Life on the Border. Comprising Descriptions of the Indian Nomads of the Plains; Explorations of New Territory; A Trip Across the Rocky Mountains in the Winter; Descriptions of the Habits of Different Animals Found in the West, and the Methods of Hunting Them; With Incidents in the Life of Different Frontier Men, &c &c*. New York: Harper and Brothers, 1866.

Marszalek, John F. *Sherman: A Soldier's Passion for Order*. New York: Vintage Books, 1994.

Merritt, John I. *Baronets and Buffalo: The British Sportsman in the American West, 1833–1881*. Missoula, Mont.: Mountain Press Publishing Company, 1985.

Moore, E. C. *Los Angeles: A Guide Book*. Los Angeles, Calif.: Neuner, 1907.

Odell, George C. D. *Annals of the New York Stage*. 15 vols. New York: Columbia University Press, 1939-1953.

Our Famous Women. Comprising the Lives and Deeds of American Women Who Have Distinguished Themselves in Literature, Science, Art, Music, and the Drama, or Are Famous as Heroines, Patriots, Orators, Educators, Physicians, Philanthropists, etc., With Numerous Anecdotes, Incidents, Personal Reminiscences and Experiences in Their Careers. Hartford, Conn.: A. D. Worthington & Co., 1883.

Parker, Watson. *Gold in the Black Hills.* Norman: University of Oklahoma Press, 1966.

Paul, Rodman W. *The Far West and the Great Plains in Transition, 1859–1890.* Foreword by Martin Ridge. Norman: University of Oklahoma Press, 1998.

Poor, Henry V. *Manual of the Railroads of the United States for 1883.* New York: Green Printing Co., 1883.

Porter, Joseph C. *Paper Medicine Man: John Gregory Bourke and His American West.* Norman: University of Oklahoma Press, 1966.

Priest, Loring Benson. *Uncle Sam's Stepchildren: The Reformation of United States Indian Policy, 1865–1887.* New Brunswick, N.J.: Rutgers University Press, 1942.

Prucha, Francis P. *The Great Father: The United States Government and the American Indians.* 2 vols. Lincoln: University of Nebraska Press, 1984.

Rickey, Don, Jr. *Forty Miles a Day on Beans and Hay: The Enlisted Soldier Fighting the Indian Wars.* Norman: University of Oklahoma Press, 1963.

Roberts, Robert B. *Encyclopedia of Historic Forts: The Military, Pioneer, and Trading Posts of the United States.* New York: Macmillan, 1988.

Robinson, Charles M., III. *A Good Year to Die: The Story of the Great Sioux War.* New York: Random House, 1995.

Ruby, Robert H., and John A. Brown. *Half-Sun on the Columbia: A Biography of Chief Moses.* Norman: University of Oklahoma Press, 1965.

Rusling, James F. *Men and Things I Saw in Civil War Days.* New York: Eaton and Mains, 1899.

Salt Lake City Directory for 1879–80. Salt Lake City, Utah: G. Owen, 1879.

Salvator, Ludwig Louis. *Los Angeles in the Sunny Seventies: A Flower from the Golden Land.* Translated by Marguerite Eyre Wilbur. Los Angeles: Bruce McAllister, 1929.

Schofield, John M. *Forty-Six Years in the Army.* Foreword by William M. Ferraro. Norman: University of Oklahoma Press, 1998.

Schoolcraft, Henry R. *Information Respecting the History, Condition and Prospects of the Indian Tribes of the United States.* 6 vols. Philadelphia: Lippincott, Grambo, 1851–1857.

Schuler, Harold H. *Fort Sully: Guns at Sunset.* Vermillion: University of South Dakota Press, 1992.

Sherman, William T. *Memoirs of General William T. Sherman.* Second edition. 2 vols. New York: D. Appleton, 1886.

———. *Travel Accounts of General William T. Sherman to Spokan [sic] Falls, Washington Territory, in the Summers of 1877 and 1883.* Fairfield, Wash.: Ye Galleon Press, 1984.

Smith, Sherry L. S*agebrush Soldier: Private William Earl Smith's View of the Sioux War of 1876.* Norman: University of Oklahoma Press, 1989.

———. *The View from Officers' Row: Army Perceptions of Western Indians.* Tucson: University of Arizona Press, 1990.

Storm, Colton. *A Catalogue of the Everett D. Graff Collection of Western Americana.* University of Chicago Press for the Newberry Library, 1968.

Strahorn, Robert E. *The Resources of Montana Territory and Attractions of Yellowstone Park. Facts and Experiences on the Farming, Stock Raising, Lumbering, and Other Industries of Montana, and Notes on the Climate, Scenery, Game, Fish, and Mineral Springs, with Full and Reliable Data on Routes, Distances, Rates of Fare, Expenses of Living, Wages, School and Church Privileges, Society, Means of Acquiring Homes, and Other Valuable and Reliable Information Applicable to the Wants of the Capitalist, Homeseeker, or Tourist.* Helena: Montana Legislature, 1879.

Tate, Michael L. *The Frontier Army in the Settlement of the West.* Norman: University of Oklahoma Press, 1999.

Thornton, Richard H. *An American Glossary.* 3 vols. New York: Frederick Ungar, 1962.

Tibbles, T. H. *Hidden Power: A Secret History of the Indian Ring, Its Operations, Intrigues, and Machinations.* New York: G. W. Carleton & Co., 1881.

Tidball, John C. *Manual of Heavy Artillery Service.* Second edition. Washington, D.C.: J. J. Chapman, 1881.

Travel Accounts of General William T. Sherman to Spokan [sic] Falls, Washington Territory, in the Summers of 1877 and 1883. Fairfield, Wash.: Ye Galleon Press, 1984.

Turchen, Lesta V., and James D. McLaird. *The Black Hills Expedition of 1875.* Mitchell, S.D.: Dakota Wesleyan University Press, 1975.

U.S. Bureau of Indian Affairs. *Biographical and Historical Index of American Indians and Persons Involved in Indian Affairs.* 8 vols. Boston: G. K. Hall, 1966.

Utley, Robert M. Frontier *Regulars: The United States Army and the Indian, 1866–1891.* New York: Macmillan, 1973.

Wheeler, John H. *Reminiscences and Memoirs of North Carolina and Eminent North Carolinians.* Baltimore: Genealogical Publishing Co., 1966.

White, Richard. *"It's Your Misfortune and None of My Own": A New History of the American West.* Norman: University of Oklahoma Press, 1991.

Williams, Stanley T. *The Life of Washington Irving.* 2 vols. New York: Oxford University Press, 1935.

Willis, Bailey. *A Yanqui in Patagonia: A Bit of Autobiography.* Stanford, Calif.: Stanford University Press, 1947.

Wooster, Robert. *The Military and United States Indian Policy, 1865–1903.* New Haven: Yale University Press, 1988.

Index

The following abbreviations are used in the index:

A.T.	Arizona Territory
B.C.	British Columbia
D.T.	Dakota Territory
I.T.	Indian Territory
Id.T.	Idaho Territory
M.T.	Montana Territory
N.M.T.	New Mexico Territory
OWI	*Our Wild Indians*
RID	Richard Irving Dodge
Tour	General Sherman's Inspection Tour of 1883
W.T.	Washington Territory
WTS	William T. Sherman
Wy.T.	Wyoming Territory

References to illustrations are in **boldface** type

$34.95